Neil Mercer has been a print and television journalist for more than 45 years. He started his career as a cadet reporter on *The West Australian* and has also worked for *The Daily Telegraph*, *The Sunday Telegraph* and *The Sydney Morning Herald*. His first job in television was as a researcher/producer for *60 Minutes* before moving to ABC's *Four Corners* as an on-camera reporter. Neil was a presenter on the Channel 7 programs *11AM*, *Today Tonight*, *The Times* and *Face to Face*. From 2015 to 2017, he was the editor of ABC's national reporting team.

Neil is the winner of a Walkley Award and a NSW Law Society award for excellence in legal reporting. His first book, *Fate: Inside the Backpacker Murders Investigation*, told the story of how NSW Police caught serial killer Ivan Milat.

Ruby Jones is an award-winning investigative journalist and documentary host. Her stories have appeared on ABC TV's *7.30* and *Lateline* programs, and she has worked as part of the ABC's national reporting team and as the news host of Triple J's breakfast show. Ruby was the Marchbanks Young Journalist of the Year in 2015.

Neil and Ruby co-hosted the Walkley Award–nominated #1 podcast and a three-part documentary TV series *Barrenjoey Road.*

BARRENJOEY ROAD

Neil Mercer & Ruby Jones

All sexual assault victims in this book, female and male, have been given pseudonyms.

WARNING

Barrenjoey Road deals with issues of sexual abuse, murder and suicide, which some readers may find disturbing. If you find any of the content triggering, or need to talk to someone, confidential 24-hour support is available. Call:

Lifeline – 13 11 14

Kids Helpline – 1800 55 1800

HarperCollins*Publishers*
Australia • Brazil • Canada • France • Germany • Holland • Hungary
India • Italy • Japan • Mexico • New Zealand • Poland • Spain • Sweden
Switzerland • United Kingdom • United States of America

First published in Australia in 2021
by HarperCollins*Publishers* Australia Pty Limited
Level 13, 201 Elizabeth Street, Sydney NSW 2000, Australia
ABN 36 009 913 517
harpercollins.com.au

A catalogue record for this book is available from the National Library of Australia.

ISBN: 978 0 7333 4046 8 (paperback)
ISBN: 978 1 4607 1191 0 (ebook)

Cover design by George Saad, HarperCollins Design Studio
Front cover image by Eddie Pearson / stocksy.com/ 2010934
Back cover image of Trudie Adams © Steve Otton
Author photograph by Andy Baker / Copyright © 2018 WildBear Entertainment, all rights reserved
Photograph of Trudie Adams on dedication page © Steve Otton
Map produced by flatEARTHmapping.com.au, contains data © OpenStreetMap contributors 2020
Typeset in Bembo Std by Kirby Jones
Printed and bound in Australia by McPherson's Printing Group
The papers used by HarperCollins in the manufacture of this book are a natural, recyclable product made from wood grown in sustainable plantation forests. The fibre source and manufacturing processes meet recognised international environmental standards, and carry certification.

In memory of Trudie Adams

1959–1978

Contents

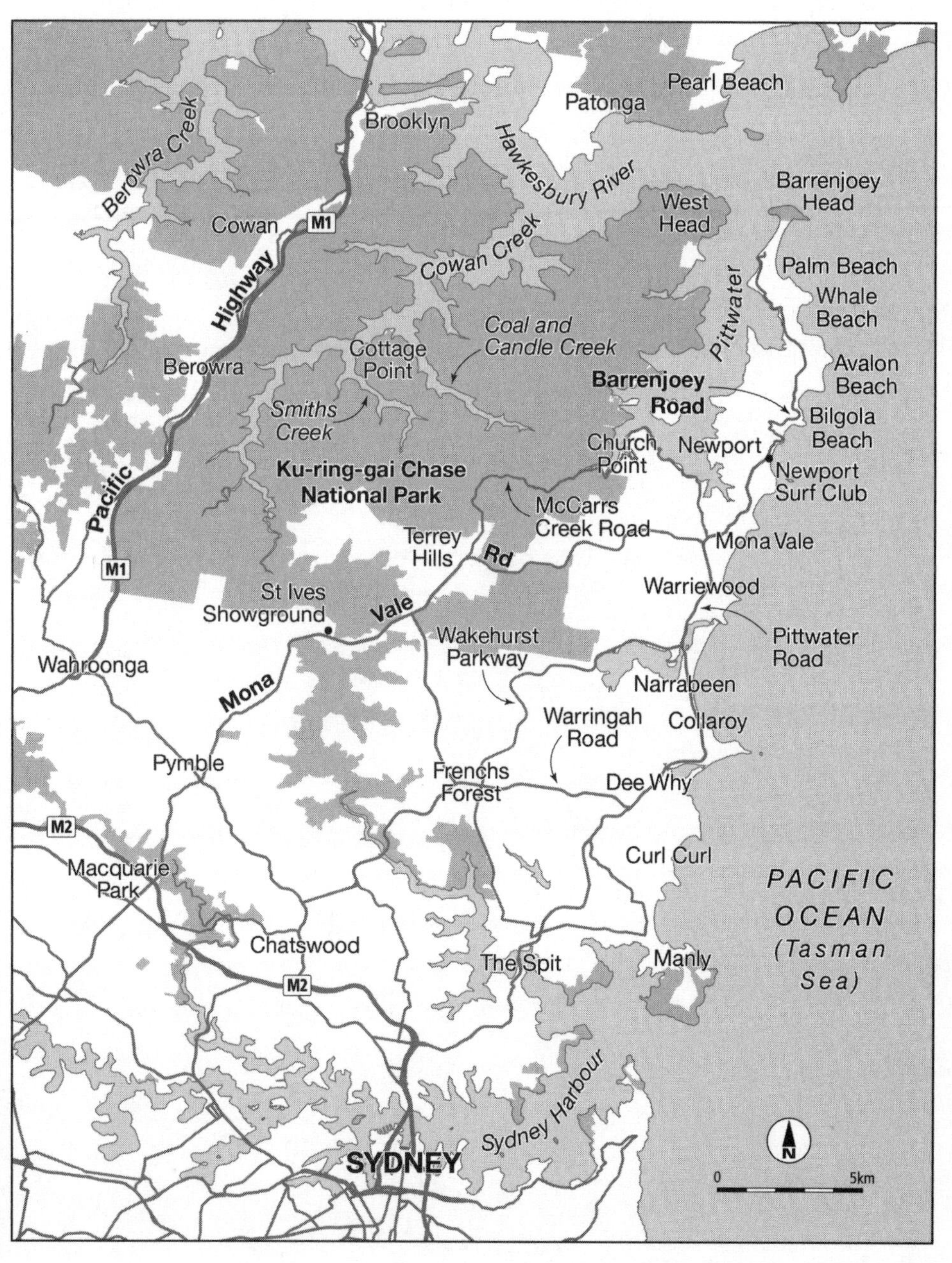
Pearl Beach
Patonga
Brooklyn
Berowra Creek
Hawkesbury River
Barrenjoey Head
West Head
Cowan
M1
Cowan Creek
Palm Beach
Whale Beach
Highway
Pittwater
Coal and Candle Creek
Cottage Point
Berowra
Avalon Beach
Barrenjoey Road
Smiths Creek
Bilgola Beach
Church Point
Newport
Ku-ring-gai Chase National Park
Newport Surf Club
Pacific
McCarrs Creek Road
Terrey Hills
Mona Vale
Rd
M1
Warriewood
St Ives Showground
Vale
Wakehurst Parkway
Pittwater Road
Wahroonga
Narrabeen
Mona
Warringah Road
Collaroy
Pymble
Frenchs Forest
Dee Why
M2
Curl Curl
Macquarie Park
PACIFIC OCEAN (Tasman Sea)
Chatswood
The Spit
Manly
M2
Sydney Harbour
SYDNEY
N
0
5km

Prologue

Two Days in March 1971

She sat in the near dark, feet on the concrete steps that curved down to Manly beach. It was two in the morning and she was alone. The soft glow of the streetlamps behind her, the sound of the ocean in front. The minutes passed. Eventually, she stood up. And, at three-thirty on the morning of 2 March 1971, Jane Hampshire walked the five minutes to Manly Police Station, an arched brick building on the north side of Sydney Harbour.

She told the officers on duty that she had been sexually assaulted. We know this much because the NSW Police Incident Report – reference No 023475 – detailing Jane's case has survived down through the decades. It's just two pages but, even now, 50 years later, it makes for confronting reading, on two counts. First, the brutality of the attack; second, the apparent indifference of the police working the graveyard shift that morning.

Two sentences from the official report sum up the attitude of the officers. 'At the time she was first interviewed by police at the Manly Police Station she appeared upset and had been crying, but there were no visible marks of any violence on her body and her clothing was not torn or dishevelled.'

The report concluded: 'Because of the doubtful nature of the report she was requested to return to her home.'

Which was what Jane did. She went back to her flat, which, it appears, was not far from the Manly beachfront and the police station itself.

Courageously, however, she returned to the police station about noon the same day. But the detectives on duty appear to have been as unsympathetic and unconcerned with their job as their night shift colleagues.

The incident report from that day makes it clear that Jane was 'very frightened', but then goes on to note that she had not screamed or called for help. And, as far as the police were concerned, there was some further scepticism because 'during the alleged acts committed on her she did not struggle to any degree, although, as she stated, the acts did cause her some pain'.

A policewoman who had 'viewed parts of her body' saw no signs of violence.

Perhaps not surprisingly, given the attitude of the police, Jane didn't want to make a formal statement, submit to a medical examination, or go to court 'in the event of suspects being charged'.

Detectives concluded: 'Under these circumstances the complaint could be considered one of a very doubtful nature.'

Which was how it was recorded on the incident report. Alongside the heading 'Complaint' there are two boxes: one for 'Rejected' and the other for 'Doubtful'. There is no box for 'Accepted' or 'To Be Investigated Further'.

Police dismissed 18-year-old Jane's report, with apparently zero investigation: no canvassing of residents, no interview with Jane's flatmate. None of the basics.

Little wonder that so few women ever went to the police.

***

Jane Hampshire was from Britain, and, like many before and since, she had no doubt been attracted to Manly's famously laidback lifestyle. Decades earlier, the ferry service had sought to tempt tourists and locals alike to make the short, scenic trip from the Sydney CBD across the harbour with the slogan: 'Seven miles from Sydney and a thousand miles from care.'

Manly is just the first of many beautiful beaches that stretch some 30 kilometres to the north. Dee Why, Collaroy, Mona Vale, Newport, Bilgola and Avalon, with the peninsula ending at Palm Beach. Collectively, they make up Sydney's Northern Beaches. Whether Jane stayed in the Manly area we simply don't know. It appears from the remaining records that police never spoke to her again, which, given what happened just a few days later, seems remarkable – and devastating.

Because, five nights afterwards, on Sunday, 7 March, a 14-year-old girl went with her parents to Collaroy Police Station, just a few kilometres to the north of Manly. Jackie Billings was interviewed by detectives and told them that the previous evening she and her 15-year-old friend Sarah Sharpe had been hitchhiking near Warringah Mall shopping centre when they were abducted and raped. Her description of the attack was very similar to Jane Hampshire's.

This time, the response was very different – possibly because, unlike Jane, Jackie had a relative in the NSW Police.

The teenager was taken to Mona Vale Hospital for examination by a doctor. Some weeks later, Jackie went to a police station and was shown some photographs in an attempt to identify the attackers. She also took part in a line-up but at which police station that took place is not known because the statement she made at the time was subsequently lost. In any event, she was unable to identify her attackers.

It's not clear whether her friend was shown any photographs. Years later, Jackie just couldn't remember. But she did recall something. 'I remember that the driver had snaky type of eyes.'

Exactly what inquiries or investigations were launched is now unclear. But this time at least, the police did something. With their approval, a television segment that focused on unsolved crimes aired a re-enactment of the abductions and appealed for help from the public. But, if information was forthcoming, it was not enough to bring the attackers to justice.

Jane Hampshire was abducted and raped on 1 March, Jackie and Sarah on 6 March. With three women attacked within a week, you would think that New South Wales would prepare for the possibility of more assaults. But there were none, or at least no more women came forward to say they had been sexually assaulted in similar circumstances.

As quickly as they'd started, the attacks appeared to stop.

But those two days in 1971 – 1 March and 6 March – mark the beginning of a 35-year saga involving at least two murders, possibly three, and 14 sexual assaults (unofficially, many more), all of which to this day remain unsolved.

And then there's the collateral damage: the grief, the addiction, the overdoses. Even some police would find themselves traumatised, in fear of their lives and disillusioned, quitting the job they loved.

When you put it all together, despite the best efforts of a handful of dedicated and determined detectives, it represents one of the greatest investigative failures in the history of the NSW Police.

How on earth could it possibly happen?

PART ONE

Chapter 1

The Day of the Dance

The twenty-fourth of June 1978 had been much like any other Saturday for 18-year-old Trudie Adams. That morning, she was walking down her street – Central Road, Avalon, in Sydney's Northern Beaches – when her friend Gillian Dollery happened to be driving past and picked her up.

Together, they headed to Palm Beach, a half-moon stretch of sand 5 kilometres north of Avalon, near the northernmost tip of the peninsula, where the Barrenjoey Lighthouse stands like a tall, white exclamation mark.

Today, Palm Beach is the backdrop for daily fables of heroism and heartbreak in Australia's most popular soap opera, *Home and Away*. But in the 1970s, it was locals only, and the families and teenagers of Sydney's Northern Beaches had free rein over their little slice of paradise. Every bay along the peninsula more pristine than the next, the coves hemmed in by the endless blue of the Pacific on one side, and the thick bushland of Ku-ring-gai Chase National Park on the other. The headland is called Barrenjoey Head, meaning 'little kangaroo'. Its other moniker is 'the Insular Peninsula' –

referring to the way everyone knows everyone else, and there's no reason to leave.

Sitting on the sand that day, with their frayed sun-bleached hair and winter tans, Gillian and Trudie looked like so many other young women on the Northern Beaches. This was their turf, and without them even being aware of it, the tides of the Pacific Ocean provided the calming rhythm of their days. That morning, they were discussing plans for their coming trip to the Indonesian island of Bali, just over a month away: what they'd take, where they'd go, who they'd see.

Trudie wanted adventure, and Bali was a good place to start. It had become a destination for a growing number of young Australians coming of age in the '70s, with its empty beaches and legendary surf. In some places, you might be the only person on the wave.

It was cheap, too, which suited Trudie, who had been broke since finishing high school the previous December. She'd been looking for part-time work while she studied at the local secretarial college. Luckily, her dad, Charles, better known as Edge, was a Qantas engineer – so Trudie's return flights to Bali would be virtually free. But she still needed cash for everything else.

In a letter Trudie wrote that afternoon to her friend Narelle, who was studying in Canberra, Trudie mentioned that she'd taken the day off from college to get her passport photos and injections for the Bali trip. The letter, written in a rounded, sloping hand, is peppered with exclamation marks and a mood of excitement:

> Don't worry, I'll make it – whoo! I can't wait. Can you imagine when I land in Bali, step off the plane, and see

> [friends like] Gillian [Gill] & Annette, peaced out Bali groovers, waving from the fence.

Friends like Narelle and Gillian were hugely important to Trudie. They were all part of a close-knit group of Northern Beaches girls who spent their days on the sand and their evenings at dances and parties.

Loyalties shifted, but Trudie always remained the leader, the 'glue' that held them together, and most of the girls would describe her as their best friend. If there was a minor argument, Trudie would sort it out, reminding them what it was they liked about each other. It was a role that suited her, and in photographs she's always smiling and usually in the centre of the picture.

Trudie was smart too – in her final year at Barrenjoey High School she'd finished in the top 25 per cent in the state, despite the fact that she and her friends regularly skipped classes to hang out at the beach.

It was difficult not to be tempted. Barrenjoey High was built close to Avalon beach and while you couldn't quite see the ocean from the classroom window, you could hear it calling. Science, maths or the sand? It was hardly a tough choice.

Once, when they were caught at the beach during school hours, a teacher had tried to humiliate them by forcing them to wait outside the principal's office, all still in their bikinis. It didn't work – the next week the girls were straight back down there, enjoying the sun, the water, the endless horizon.

On this Saturday night, like so many others, Trudie was planning to go to a dance with friends.

In a letter to her friend Narelle, she wrote:

> Tonight should be good. I'm going to Annette's for dinner and then going to a bop at Newport Surf Club (mind you) ... – and I think even the Bilgola Bop Band is playing – whooeee! I'm going to dance to every bracket. And it's Steve Bryant's 21st tomorrow, which should be a blaighton [sic] rage – hmmm.
>
> I could easily fill another sheet of paper with boring – crapping on – bullshit but I'll have mercy on you and stop. Drop a quick hello if you can so I know Canberra hasn't turned you into an iceblock.
>
> Good luck in your exams.
>
> Luv and kisses, Trudie

Trudie had arranged to meet up with her friends Debbie Jeffries and Annette Daly. The three girls had been friends for most of their lives. They'd grown up together, been to school together, had sleepovers at each other's houses, kept each other's secrets.

Sometime around 8pm that evening, the three girls arrived at the Newport Arms Hotel, a sprawling landmark pub on the peninsula. The joint was packed with locals, most in their teens and twenties but plenty of underage drinkers as well – it was a big pub so it was easy to get past security and sneak in.

But the Newport Arms was just the heart starter – the girls had bigger plans. So when it closed a bit after 10pm, Trudie, Debbie and Annette got a lift with their friend Tim Holland in his mum's Valiant sedan. They drove to the Newport Surf Club, a large, two-storey brick building on Newport Beach facing the Pacific Ocean, its car park ringed by Norfolk pines.

But, after pulling into the car park at about 10.30pm, the teenagers at first stayed inside the car. Trudie had been looking forward to the dance all day but when they actually arrived, she wasn't so sure. She'd thought the Bilgola Bop Band – one of her favourites – was going to be playing, but they weren't. Bummer.

It was Trudie who suggested that they do something else instead. Maybe they could drive into the city? She knew of a band playing in town that was much better than the one at the surf club. But that would be a one-hour drive, and another hour home again. In the end, they decided to stick with their original plan and pay the $2 to get into the Newport Surf Club.

Inside the club, the band was in full swing and the dance floor heaving with more than a hundred or so surfers and their girlfriends. Some were spilling out into the car park, bourbons and beers in hand. Trudie had a swig from a rum bottle that was being handed around before wandering off into the crowd.

As the dance continued, the place grew rowdier.

Trudie was mostly in a good mood, dancing and talking to friends. Occasionally, she took a sip from someone else's drink – as she complained several times to Debbie, she couldn't afford to buy her own.

She also told Debbie her arm was bothering her. It was still sore from the vaccinations she'd had to get for her upcoming trip to Bali, and it hurt when she got jostled by the crowd inside the club.

At about 11.30pm, she ran into her younger brother, Mark. 'Geez, this dance is slack,' she said, before teasing him about his new-found success with women. 'Don't go off with too many girls,' she joked before disappearing into the crowd.

Fifteen minutes later, Trudie saw Tim Holland, and they hung out together until he left about half an hour later.

Then, just after midnight, it seemed Trudie had had enough. But as she was about to leave the club, her boyfriend, Steve Norris, approached.

Trudie and Steve had met two years earlier. He was a few years older than Trudie and worked with his father as a painter, though he was never far from the surf. The pair had started going out a few months after they met, and to outsiders they made a golden couple – Steve with his shaggy blond mullet and surfboard, Trudie with her open smile and grey-green eyes.

They'd gone away for weekends together and had seemed to be in love, but since Steve's return home from a trip to Bali, things had begun to sour. Trudie wanted her independence and was now in the process of breaking up with her boyfriend.

Steve approached and asked Trudie for a dance, but she refused. He asked again, but she shook her head and set off down the stairs.

From a window upstairs, he saw Trudie make her way across the car park, towards Barrenjoey Road.

Steve wasn't sure why she'd refused to dance with him – they were supposed to be a couple. As far as he was concerned, she was still his girlfriend and he cared about her, so he decided to follow her home.

From the car park, he spotted Trudie about 100 metres away, standing alone near the intersection of Barrenjoey Road and Neptune Road. It was a well-known spot for hitchhikers heading north. From there, Trudie's home was just a six-minute drive.

In a matter of moments, a car pulled over. The vehicle obscured Steve's view of Trudie, but when it drove off, she was gone.

Trudie had hitched a ride. Most of the surf crowd on the Northern Beaches did it – buses were few and far between, especially at night. But more often than not, someone you knew would pull over, or a friend of a friend.

Steve decided he'd hitchhike to Trudie's house to make sure she was okay. He walked to where she'd been standing and waited. Soon, a yellow Lancer pulled over. The driver was Gregory Rowe, a local bloke he knew.

Minutes later Steve got out on the corner of Barrenjoey Road and Avalon Parade, and from there walked the backstreets to Trudie's house.

***

Connie Adams, Trudie's mum, was sitting in the lounge-room with a scotch and a cigarette in hand when the back door opened at about 1.15am and Steve Norris walked in.

'What do you want,' she asked.

'Is Trudie home?'

'No, she's not. I'm waiting for her.'

Steve sat down beside Connie on the lounge and asked for a cigarette.

They spoke briefly and after a few minutes Steve left the way he'd come in, via the back door.

Shortly after, Connie's eldest son, John, came wandering into the lounge before heading off to bed.

Her other son, Mark, appeared soon after, having hitchhiked home.

But there was no sign of Trudie.

Connie waited through the night, her anxiety building by the moment.

Chapter 2

Wireless Message 31

It wasn't like Trudie; it wasn't like her at all. She always called Connie if she was going to stay with a friend. Trudie's brothers, John and Mark, did the same. It was the way the family worked. They all knew Connie fretted.

So when Trudie still hadn't come home by Sunday morning, Connie woke her husband. She was ready to call the police, but while Charles was concerned, he thought they should ring around first. Maybe Trudie had stayed at Annette's, or perhaps one of her other friends would know where she was?

At about 9am, Trudie's friend Debbie Jeffries phoned and asked for her. 'She hasn't come home,' Connie replied. 'Didn't she stay at your place?' When Debbie said no, they both wondered whether she had gone to Annette's. But around noon, Annette also called looking for Trudie. Debbie called again too, as did Gillian Dollery.

Connie was making her own increasingly anxious and desperate calls. Where was her daughter? She and Trudie were close, and very much alike. Just the day before, they'd spent time together relaxing and chatting in the backyard, eating avocados and flicking through magazines.

Connie was a leader who knew how to get things done. She was a keen environmentalist, famous, as the Avalon Preservation Trust newsletter put it, for her 'indefatigability when pursuing an issue'. Whether she was campaigning for the creation of an Angophora nature reserve or opposing a development proposal, deep voiced, sharp-tongued Connie would fight her best fight. Once, when her son Mark had his surfboard confiscated by beach inspectors, she gave them a tongue-lashing. Later, when Warringah Shire Council threatened her with legal action Connie didn't back down. She could be a force to be reckoned with, and Trudie was very much in the same mould. But by Sunday afternoon Connie's strength and resolve was being severely tested. She was becoming increasingly frantic.

It was the day of the 21st birthday celebration that Trudie had mentioned in her letter to Narelle. But when Steve Norris arrived at the barbecue, at about 2.30pm, Trudie hadn't turned up and none of her friends had heard from her or knew where she was.

As the afternoon wore on their concerns deepened. Where could she be? And who had been the last person to see her?

At 9 o'clock that evening, Connie called the Mona Vale Police Station and told police that her daughter hadn't come home and none of her friends knew where she was. The last anyone had seen of her had been at the Newport Surf Club.

At 10.30pm that night, Charles went to the Mona Vale Police Station and formally reported Trudie missing. Among other things, he told police there was a rumour Trudie might have gone to Macksville on the north coast with friends. The police sent a message to their colleagues up north to investigate.

According to Connie, Steve Norris came to her house at about 11pm, around the same time Charles was still at the police station. He'd been to the RSL and had had a couple of beers but was by no means drunk.

'Is Trudie home yet, Mrs Adams?' he enquired.

'No, she is not, Steve.'

'Don't worry about it, she'll be right,' he replied. 'I saw her getting a lift in a car from the dance and she'll be right, she'll turn up.'

When Charles returned to the police station on the morning of Monday, 26 June, officers informed him they'd heard back from police in Macksville.

There was no sign of Trudie.

Later that day, Constable Brent Thomas and another officer went to the Adams home to gather more information. Connie, who was distraught, did most of the talking, saying the last time any of Trudie's friends had seen her daughter she'd been hitchhiking and had got into a vehicle near the surf club. She was adamant that Trudie wasn't the type to run away. All she'd been talking about lately was her trip to Bali. The world was at her feet.

Constable Thomas returned to Mona Vale Police Station and started writing 'Wireless Message 31' on a telex machine. It comprised just nine lines and was not even 100 words long. Not much to describe a life, even a young one. But the police had very little to go on, and despite Connie's assurances to the contrary, Trudie might just be another teenage runaway.

Now, all these years later, looking back at that official message, it remains both poignant and profound in its content, brevity and bureaucratic nature along with its spelling and typographical errors. It also had some factual mistakes, which weren't the fault of the police. After all, they were just relaying what they'd been told.

But one of those mistakes would reverberate down the decades.

Written in capital letters, it started:

> MKISSING [SIC] FROM 154 CENTRAL ROAD AVALON SINCE 24.6.78. LAST SEEN OUTSIDE NEWPORT SURF CLUB AT 11PM ON 24.6.78.

It went on to describe Trudy [sic] Jeanette Adams – her age, weight (nine stone), the colour of her hair (light brown), height (5 foot 4), the colour of her eyes (grey/green), her 'natural' teeth and what she was wearing, including:

> NAVY BLUE CORDUROY JEANS, BREEN [SIC] BLOUSE, BLACK FLUFFY JUMPER. GOLD CHAINEEEEEEE [SIC] GOLD CHAIN AROUND NECK, BROWN SHOES, BROWN PURSE.

It ended:

> WAS SEEN TO ENTER A GREEN KOMBI VAN WHICH THEN DROVE ALONG BARRENJOEY RD NORTH TOWARD AVALON. FEARS FOR SAFETY.

***

As Constable Thomas composed Wireless Message 31 that Monday evening, much of Sydney was sitting down to dinner, relaxing in front of the television after the first working day of the week. On Channel Nine they were watching *The*

Sullivans, a long-running and popular Australian family drama set during the World War II and the post-war years. Or maybe they were tuning in to Channel Ten to catch *Blankety Blanks*, 'a crazy fun show hosted by the irrepressible Graham Kennedy'. *Blankety Blanks* was followed by *The Rockford Files*, an American drama about a private eye. That night's episode was called 'The Deadly Maze', and the gumshoe was searching for a missing woman.

The message was broadcast via VKG, the NSW Police radio system, to police stations and patrol cars at about 7.30pm. By then, Trudie hadn't been seen for the best part of two days. It was the first official indication that something was terribly wrong.

At this stage, the public was blissfully unaware of the turmoil that was enveloping Trudie's family and friends. Earlier that day, the tabloid newspapers had been leading with another story, one that had unfolded at almost exactly the same time that Trudie was at the Newport Surf Club on Saturday night.

While Trudie, Steve Norris and their friends were dancing and drinking on the Northern Beaches, in the gritty inner suburb of Darlinghurst hundreds of young men and women had gathered to protest against the law that made homosexuality a crime. After clashing with police, dozens were arrested on the Saturday night and Sunday morning. The story was the front-page 'splash' in Monday's *Daily Mirror* with the paper reporting that 53 people arrested on the weekend had appeared in court that morning. (The same edition of the paper also carried another story reflective of the times: The NSW Country Party wanted to bring back flogging as a punishment for serious crimes.)

The *Mirror*'s arch-rival, *The Sun*, reported there were 300 protestors outside the court, supporting those arrested, including a group of women singing: 'What will we do with the cops and judges come the revolution.'

As fate would have it, one of those arrested on the weekend would go on to become a journalist. Years later, Wendy Bacon's stories about police corruption helped lay the groundwork for a Royal Commission into the NSW Police Force, which would expose rampant corruption in a number of areas – including the Northern Beaches.

And defending the protestors in court was a fiery young barrister, Peter Livesey, who would represent, or get to know, some of Sydney's toughest criminals, from murderers to armed robbers, safecrackers and the like. People like James Edward 'Jockey' Smith, who had just been charged with the murder of a bookmaker Lloyd Tidmarsh. Smith claimed he'd been framed by the cops. One of his associates at the time, a safecracker, had dropped by Livesey's office and handed over $500 in cash to help with Smith's legal fees. The safecracker lived in Terrey Hills – a dozen or so kilometres drive from the glistening beaches of Avalon and Newport and a stone's throw from Ku-ring-gai Chase National Park, a huge area of rugged bushland.

Two almost simultaneous events occurred on 24 and 25 June 1978 that would change people's lives in very different ways. One, a missing teenager from Avalon, the other a nascent protest movement in Sydney's inner city that would eventually become an annual celebration – Mardi Gras.

Just two of Sydney's tribes, blissfully unaware of each other's existence.

***

On Tuesday, 27 June, Mona Vale detectives conducted their first interview with Steve Norris. As far as they knew, he'd been the last person to see the teenager alive.

Steve told the officers he'd seen Trudie getting into a Holden panel van near the corner of Barrenjoey Road and Neptune Road at about 12.30 to 12.45am.

This contradicted what Connie had said about the car being a green Kombi and it being 11pm. As a result, at 10.26am, Mona Vale Police Station sent out a second wireless message about Trudie's disappearance:

> RE WM 31 ON 26.6.78. RE MISSING PERSON TRUDIE JEANETTE ADAMS VEHICLE NOW DESCRIBED AS 1977 HOLDEN PANEL VAN, FAWN TO BEIGE IN COLOUR, NO SIDE WINDOWS, IN GOOD CONDITIONA [SIC].

Exactly how a green Kombi turned into a beige Holden panel van is not known. Perhaps, in her emotional turmoil, Connie had been confused or mistaken about what she'd been told by Steve or one of Trudie's girlfriends.

As well as interviewing Steve Norris and Trudie's parents and friends, local detectives conducted searches near Newport Surf Club. In a police report dated 27 June a detective wrote:

> Friends of the girl Adams who have been interviewed appear to be level headed and of good character. Owing to the circumstances of the girl last being seen accepting a lift by an unknown person, her associates, Adams' previous excellent background and following interviews of both the father and mother of the girl Adams, fears must be held for her safety.

Senior police officers at Manly – the main station serving the peninsula – were notified, along with the police public relations unit. Manly Taxis – which had more than 200 cabs – was asked to broadcast a description of Trudie and the panel van to all drivers.

On Wednesday, 28 June, NSW Police contacted the two Sydney tabloid newspapers to break the story. Between them, *The Sun* and the *Mirror* sold almost 800,000 papers each day – the first edition hitting the streets in the morning, the last in the afternoon. They were read on buses and trains, and in pubs and RSLs.

That day, *The Sun* and the *Mirror* ran stories on Trudie's disappearance, the first of hundreds that would follow down the years. The *Mirror* ran the story on page three under the headline 'Police fears for hitchhike girl'. Along with the photo of Trudie she'd had taken for her passport just days earlier, the article said: 'A teenage girl is still missing more than three days after she disappeared in Sydney while hitchhiking from a dance. Police fear she may be dead.'

Next to Trudie's smiling face was a photo of another smiling woman – that of the paper's obligatory page-three bikini girl, with the caption 'Maureen Courtenay is an outdoor girl and likes the surf'. Much like Trudie really. It was standard fare at the time, the page-three girl helped sell newspapers. So did big stories, such as the disappearance of a pretty, young, white, middle-class girl like Trudie.

The Sun ran a similar article, and the *Manly Daily* spoke to Trudie's parents. 'She has been nabbed, there is no question,' Charles was quoted as saying. 'Look at the facts. She had no more than one or two dollars on her.'

'I'm sick with worry,' Connie told the *Manly Daily*'s police reporter Doug Ryan. 'Every time the phone rings, my heart jumps. The trouble with these things is we may never find her again.'

The Sun and the *Mirror* arrived at the Avalon Newsagency around lunchtime. One of the girls who worked there was Trudie's neighbour and close friend Anita Starkey. In fact, a few years before, Anita had got Trudie a job at the newsagency.

Now, instead of working alongside her, Anita was staring at the photos of her friend's face in the papers and reading the articles about the 'hitchhike girl' who hadn't been seen for days.

Even worse than that, though, were the carelessly cruel comments from customers as they fingered the papers, calling Trudie a 'stupid young girl'.

This is not real, she kept thinking. *This is our friend – one of the girls.*

Trudie had been gone for just four days and her family and close friends were struggling, fearing the worst. But already the shockwaves were rippling into the wider community.

Things like this just didn't happen in Avalon or Newport or the other little villages – for that's what they were – that made up the patch of paradise known as the Insular Peninsula.

Chapter 3

Rumours and Sightings

Within weeks of Trudie's disappearance, rumours began to circulate about her boyfriend, Steve Norris. As the last known person to see her alive, he fell under suspicion.

Steve had his initial interview with the police on 27 June, when he gave them a description of the fawn or beige panel van, and the time and place he'd last seen Trudie. Since then, the police had heard about a 'fight' or argument between them at the dance. They'd also heard Trudie wanted to split up but that Steve hadn't.

One of Trudie's girlfriends told them there had been previous fights between the couple – one or two of them serious. In a statement on 28 June, she told police that about a month earlier, Trudie had told her that Steve had come into her house while she was in bed and they'd argued heatedly.

Another friend told police that Steve liked Trudie more than Trudie liked him and Steve wanted to become more committed. She also said that Trudie had complained about an argument between her and Steve on the previous Wednesday, 21 June.

On 28 June, Steve Norris was called in to Mona Vale Police Station for a second interview. There he admitted he'd argued with Trudie in the week leading up to the dance. It had happened at Trudie's home, and her father told Steve to leave, which he'd done without incident.

He also confirmed that, six months earlier, he'd had a bad blue with Trudie, but he was adamant that, despite this, he and Trudie had still been on good terms.

Steve told police again that he'd seen her leave the dance at about 12.30am on the Sunday morning, crossing the surf club's car park and walking to the corner of Barrenjoey Road and Neptune Road. He reiterated that he'd followed her, concerned about her hitchhiking. Then, from a distance of about 100 metres, he'd seen a beige or fawn-coloured 1977 Holden panel van pull up alongside Trudie. After it drove off, she was no longer there. It had all happened in a matter of a few minutes.

Shortly afterwards, he said, he'd been picked up by an acquaintance, Gregory Rowe. And as he'd previously explained, he'd then gone to Trudie's home, where he spoke to Connie.

After being at Connie's house for anything between a few minutes to half an hour, depending on which police reports you read, Steve Norris told police he'd borrowed a pushbike and ridden to North Avalon, South Avalon, then Bilgola Beach, looking for Trudie.

The police weren't able to confirm that part of his alibi, but detectives quickly tracked down Gregory Rowe, who confirmed he'd picked up Steve Norris in Barrenjoey Road and driven him close to Trudie's home. He also confirmed the time as between 12.30 and 1 in the morning.

Connie would later tell police Norris was 'well affected by liquor', although by Steve's own estimate he'd had about five middies at the Newport Arms before going to the surf club, where he'd downed another couple of beers. Not a lot for a well-built, fit young surfer. Connie herself was known to enjoy a drink.

And perhaps this is where the green Kombi had emerged. In the early hours of the morning a mother anxious about the absence of her daughter, in conversation with the bloke she probably knew her daughter no longer wanted to go out with, words were misheard, misunderstood.

And perhaps it was here that, in Connie's mind at least, the seeds of suspicion about Steve Norris's role in the disappearance of her daughter started growing.

***

On Thursday, 29 June, the NSW Homicide Squad was called in. Four Homicide Squad officers, led by Detective Senior Constable Gary Matthews, arrived at Mona Vale Police Station. A tall, imposing figure with a bushy moustache, Matthews had been a police officer for 20 years and had been investigating homicides since 1972. His team was boosted by four local detectives taking the total to eight. They were joined by three uniformed officers from Mona Vale and up to four female police also worked on the inquiry, although it appears not all at the same time.

The same day, the investigation proper got underway, with 20 police searching the areas around Newport Beach and Bilgola Beach, which was just to the north, and some of the surrounding bush.

Trudie's disappearance was now a murder inquiry. For her already distressed family, and many friends, it was confirmation of what they already knew but didn't want to believe. Information and tip-offs started pouring in, and not just to the police.

At 4.05pm on the day the Homicide Squad arrived, the Adams home telephone rang. Connie picked up.

'The body is halfway up Mona Vale Road. It was an accident,' a man with a deep voice said. Then he hung up.

Mona Vale Road runs from the coast south-west to Pymble. The rough midpoint would be the suburb of Terrey Hills.

Ten minutes later, an almost identical call was made to the Mona Vale Police Station.

Was the information genuine? Or was it a hoax? Was it someone trying to throw police off the scent?

That evening, Gary Matthews and another Homicide officer visited Connie and Charles Adams. They wanted to acquaint themselves with Trudie's family, tell them what was going on and ask Connie about the phone call she'd received. They also wanted to reassure them that the police were doing everything they could to find out what had happened to Trudie. Then there was the difficult and sensitive issue of identification, and Gary Matthews found himself asking for Trudie's hairbrush, explaining they needed it 'in case we ever find …'

The two detectives arranged to take additional items from Trudie's room for fingerprinting. They also asked Connie and Charles for the name of Trudie's dentist, for reasons no parent ever wants to hear.

For some detectives, the hardest part of a murder inquiry is dealing with the crime scene, the blood, the smell. For others, it's witnessing, and dealing with, the grief, anguish and uncertainty of a missing person's mother and father, their siblings or friends. Particularly when there is simply no trace of their loved one.

The investigative team made a public appeal for tip-offs and leads. They were quickly inundated and overwhelmed, operating, as they were, in a pre-computer age when police documents – statements, index cards and the like – were typed and filed manually.

All the information was methodically and laboriously recorded in what police called 'the running sheets', which detailed the day-to-day information being gathered – whether from Trudie's family, Steve Norris, her friends, other police or members of the public. The running sheets were typed foolscap pages, numbered and stored in lever-arch folders.

Statements varied in length. Some, taken from people who'd attended the dance at the Newport Surf Club the night Trudie was last seen, were a few paragraphs. Others, like Steve Norris's statements, were much longer and more numerous.

As in any major inquiry, the running sheets contain information varying from vital, helpful and interesting to bizarre and a downright waste of time, including numerous false sightings of Trudie.

Well-meaning members of the public reported seeing a teenager fitting her description in various suburbs around Sydney. Others 'heard' that Trudie was in Port Macquarie, on the NSW mid-north coast, or in Surfers Paradise in Queensland. Someone rang and said they had 'sighted' Trudie at a remote service station on the Nullarbor Plain in Western Australia.

Where practical, the reports were checked out.

Clairvoyants and psychics called or sent letters, recounting their dreams that had told them what had become of Trudie.

A clergyman suggested police should use a hypnotist on any witnesses.

A young man reported he'd seen Trudie's body in the bush near Newport, but had hidden when he saw two men coming towards him. He believed one of them had shot at him as he ran away. He then told detectives he'd been on LSD at the time.

A 65-year-old man walked into Hurstville Police Station, in Sydney's south, saying he was an 'ex-dowser' (meaning he could supposedly locate underground water) and knew the location of Trudie's body. The man then produced a Gregory's street map of Sydney and a piece of string with a square piece of wood that was pointed at one end. Page 413 of the running sheet records the following: 'He opened the street directory at the Palm Beach map and held the string with a piece of wood on the end over the map and commenced to follow the last steps of Trudie Adams.'

Other leads were more tangible. And a lot more serious.

A woman reported hearing loud screaming from near the Pasadena Restaurant in Church Point on Pittwater at about 1.30am on the Sunday morning. Another person rang in reporting a panel van near McCarrs Creek Road, which runs from Terrey Hills through the bushland behind the beaches.

An observant and diligent government bus driver went to police with what must have seemed a particularly promising tip-off. He related how, for the past three Fridays, he'd been on the late bus run from Wynyard in Sydney's CBD to Palm Beach. When the driver reached Collaroy he had been followed by a white VW station wagon. 'This car just follows the bus, and speaks to female persons that alight from the bus,' he said.

The bus driver had written down the number plate of the VW, which was registered to a man named Fry, who, police quickly learnt, was a sex offender with convictions for indecent exposure, trespass and 'peep and pry', the latter basically meaning he'd been caught looking into bedroom windows. He'd been jailed for some of the offences. Granted, they were at the lower end of the scale, and the vehicle didn't match, but police wondered if his offending might have escalated.

Detectives started investigating.

Police received a report of a man driving a Jaguar who'd picked up two 16-year-old girls in Manly on 24 June, the day of the surf club dance. After some leading questions, the driver, described as a man with a 'Rolf Harris type beard', asked the girls if they'd like to make some money. He then offered to buy their panties for $20. The teenagers had declined and had been let out of the car.

Mona Vale Detectives also learnt there had been an attempted abduction of another 16-year-old, who'd been hitchhiking on Barrenjoey Road that very same day, 24 June. The driver had grabbed the girl around the neck and pulled her towards him as if to kiss her. The girl had started screaming, struggled, and escaped. She thought the driver said: 'I'll kill you.'

The running sheet recording the incident says, 'No injury sustained, no sexual advance made; however, she felt that it was implied by his actions.'

No sexual advance made? She was a 16-year-old girl, grabbed by the throat by a total stranger who'd tried to kiss her.

Reporting the matter to police with her mother, the girl didn't want to take any further action. It appears she had no desire to go through the trauma of a court case and its aftermath.

But at least she had come forward. Detectives were about to discover that many young women on the Northern Beaches had been too scared – and had too little faith in the system meant to protect them – to even do that.

Chapter 4

The Search

The two anonymous telephone calls on 29 June – one to Connie, the other to Mona Vale Police, couldn't be ignored.

Police didn't know whether it was a hoax or whether the killer was trying to throw them off the scent. In any case, they needed to take the calls seriously. Even if they didn't find Trudie, they might find other evidence. But Mona Vale Road stretched for more than 20 kilometres from the Mona Vale Golf Course near the beach all the way to Pymble on Sydney's upper North Shore. It was a huge area to cover, much of it dense bushland.

Gary Matthews' Homicide Squad colleague Detective Senior Constable Alan Herrmann set about organising a search.

On Friday, 30 June, the *Daily Mirror* reported that 'more than 100 police and 40 civilians' were walking in line along both sides of Mona Vale Road, covering a distance of 15 kilometres, looking for Trudie Adams' body as a result of the 'mystery call'.

Among the civilians were Steve Norris, Charles, Trudie's dad, and her brother John. It wasn't the first time they'd been involved and it wouldn't be the last.

Police instructed searchers to concentrate on areas near fire trials and bush tracks – anywhere that gave access to a vehicle whose driver might have been trying to get rid of a body.

Each day was planned through the police mapping section. But at 150 square kilometres, Ku-ring-gai Chase National Park is a massive, rugged area of bushland.

'Winding creeks and stretches of ocean meet rainforest and eucalypts, rocky cliffs and mangroves,' is how the NSW National Parks Service describes it. Some parts, at least in 1978, could be easily accessed from the main road by cars along the fire trails but even they were pretty rough. Smaller tracks catered for experienced bushwalkers. Other parts of the park comprise rocky sandstone ridges that tumble down through forest and scrub to Pittwater, to places like Coal and Candle Creek and Smiths Creek. Except they're not creeks, but broad, flat expanses of water with deep pockets with names like Devils Hole Bay.

Getting from some of the ridges down to the waterline can be done, in places, but in others, it's impossible.

On a sunny day, sitting on a rocky outcrop, looking down through the trees to the water below you, it's quite serene, quite beautiful. It's also isolated – there's no sound of traffic, no one to run into besides the occasional bushwalker.

On the day of the first major search, wet weather hampered those on the ground and in the air. A helicopter with Homicide detectives on board flew over Mona Vale to West Head at the northern end of the national park and Coal and Candle Creek to the west, but visibility was poor.

Meanwhile, police divers searched the waterways, including a location known as The Duck Holes, off McCarrs Creek Road, where someone had reported seeing a panel van. A tip-off from a local also led to divers searching an old flooded coalmine.

And through all of this, rumours continued to circulate about Steve Norris's involvement in Trudie's disappearance. Newspapers and television news bulletins had reported from the outset that Steve and Trudie had been seen having a fight at the dance, the inference being she'd left because of it.

Graffiti about him began to appear on walls around Avalon and Newport. Steve was understandably upset, telling a reporter from *The Sun* that suggestions about his involvement in Trudie's disappearance were not true. 'I still love her a lot and she loved me. All we talked about [at the dance] were good things as we hadn't seen each other for a few days. We didn't have any sort of argument.'

There were also rumours swirling about the real purpose of Trudie's trip to Bali, with some saying she'd intended to bring back drugs. Trudie and some of her friends had certainly smoked weed on occasion – in the letter to Narelle she said she'd asked Annette to have 'a big scoobee ready rolled' for when she arrived in Bali.

The rumours were fuelled by newspaper reports about drugs and corruption.

In early July, the *Manly Daily* reported that four people had been arrested trying to import $200,000 worth of cannabis in the form of Buddha sticks – slow-dried marijuana leaves wound around thin bamboo sticks – from Bali. Of the four, there was a woman, a 16-year-old girl and two men. One of them was a 20-year-old surfer from Avalon by the name of Clayton John Looby. Police not only seized the drugs at

Sydney airport – some of it hidden in stereo equipment – but they also took possession of Looby's diary, which turned out to contain the names and phone numbers of friends and acquaintances, many of them from the Northern Beaches. Looby lived quite close to Trudie.

The bust was the tip of the iceberg. In fact, a whole lot more dope was winding its way back to the Northern Beaches, hidden in guitar cases, battered backpacks and, clearly, stereo equipment. The Northern Beaches drug trade was fuelled by a crew of laid-back surfers who were getting the best of both worlds. They could fly to Bali, surf for a few weeks, bring back some Buddha sticks and sell them to their mates at Avalon or Newport.

In 1978, a Buddha stick in Bali would set you back a princely $1.40. You could flog them in Sydney for about $10, thus financing the trip and perhaps making a bit of cash on the side.

But there had been rumours going around that a few young women had also become involved in something more organised, sinister and dangerous. It seemed that some serious importers figured that a pretty young girl was less likely to get stopped by customs on the way through. In fact, a criminal trial had recently heard evidence of exactly that, where a drug syndicate had used 'pretty girls' to bring drugs from Bangkok using hidden compartments in specially made suitcases.

On the same day the *Mirror* reported the search for Trudie, it carried a page-two story with the headline 'Policeman jailed over drug'. The article described how a 22-year-old probationary constable had pleaded guilty to supplying $20,000 worth of heroin – 139 foil caps for $150 each – at Brookvale, which came under the Northern Beaches police command.

The judge in the case described the Manly–Narrabeen area as a 'social abscess' with regard to the drug trade. He said young people addicted to heroin from the area were constantly coming before the court.

A lot of the heroin in Sydney was being imported by the notorious Mr Asia syndicate, led by Terry Clark who, coincidentally, lived in Manly for a time in the late 1970s. It's estimated that, with the help of one or two corrupt agents in the Narcotics Bureau, the Mr Asia syndicate imported between 85 and 200 kilograms of heroin between 1976 and 1979.

Also in the headlines at the time was the arrest of a former NSW Police officer, Murray Stewart Riley, over a $43 million cannabis importation. Riley was well known for winning two gold medals in rowing in the double sculls at the Empire Games (later the Commonwealth Games). His fellow gold medallist was Merv Wood who, at the time of Riley's arrest in 1978, had risen through the ranks to become the Commissioner of NSW Police.

Wood was a controversial figure, to say the least. In 1977, when then Premier Neville Wran ordered the closure of illegal casinos, which had been operating under police protection for years, Wood protested publicly that to do it just before Christmas was unfair, saying in an interview with *The Sun*:

> Last week we decided that 16 December would be the last time casinos would be allowed to operate. Later I was told that more than 300 people were employed in casinos in Sydney and other parts of the state. I was rather shocked that these people would be jobless a couple of weeks before Christmas. The Premier agreed that these

> people should have a happy Christmas ... the proprietors were then informed and all knew they have to close their doors on 31 December.

The reaction to Wood's remarks about delaying the closure of illegal casinos – which had been bribing police – ranged from outrage to outright hilarity, with quips about the police commissioner as Santa.

At the same time as the investigation into Trudie's disappearance was taking place, a Royal Commission was underway into the murder in Griffith of anti-drugs crusader Donald Mackay. The commission was starting to expose the tentacles of the Calabrian organised crime group known as 'Ndrangheta. And it was raising questions about police corruption all over the place.

The Northern Beaches was not immune. It was said police in the area would personally pick up the takings from one of the peninsula's biggest hotels and take it to the bank 'to guard against armed robbery'. And if there was a 'drink' in it for them – drink being slang for bribe – well what harm was done?

Any way you look at it, in 1978 public faith in the police was being questioned like never before. It was against this backdrop that people on the Northern Beaches and in wider Sydney watched and waited as the investigation into what had happened to Trudie unfolded.

To be fair, the Homicide Squad was always considered to be above all the grubbiness. There might have been corruption in licensing and gaming and prostitution but they were considered 'victimless' crimes. If people wanted to drink into the wee hours of the morning long after the legal closing time, and if they wanted to gamble and have sex, who was being hurt?

Or at least that's how the argument went. It suited the drinkers and the punters and the police. But out and out corruption in Homicide and sexual assault investigations? Unlikely. It just wasn't done. Leaving aside the odd gangland killing that might remain conveniently unsolved, homicide was hardly a 'victimless' crime and nor was sexual assault. That being said, many rape victims at the time never came forward. They simply didn't think they would be believed by police, or that they would get justice from a legal system which routinely saw those who did speak up humiliated and traumatised in the witness box.

Still, Gary Matthews and his colleagues did their best with an overwhelming amount of information. With the number of lines of inquiry growing by the day, investigators tracked down Mr Fry, the man who tried to pick up young girls getting off the bus. Detectives from Flemington picked him up and took him down to the station.

The running sheet records that Fry, who was 'a student photographer', had admitted he was a 'sexual deviant' and had spent many hours each night stopping girls and making sexual advances to them, in various parts of the metropolitan area.

However, on the night Trudie was last seen, Fry had stopped to photograph a traffic accident at about 11.30pm in the inner-west suburb of Ashfield. Curiously, given his record, he processed the film and gave the photographs to the Ashfield police. They confirmed his story and estimated he would have been in the Ashfield area until 12.45am. He had a watertight alibi.

A few days later, a constable from Chatswood Police Station phoned Matthews and told him about a possible suspect, a 21-year-old man from Frenchs Forest who owned a white panel van. The man had been charged with an abduction and attempted rape that had taken place just off Mona Vale Road.

According to the running sheet, the young man 'was given a bond' – that is, not jailed – and still lived in the area. Matthews put him down to be interviewed.

In early July, detectives received information about an 18-year-old girl who had been hitchhiking along Barrenjoey Road to her home in Whale Beach. She'd told friends that the driver of a white Falcon sedan who'd picked her up had asked for sex.

The detective recorded the incident on a running sheet, saying that when the teenager refused, the driver 'masturbated himself from Mona Vale to Whale Beach', where he let her out of the car.

Some of these men might have been caught by police down the track, but some would never be identified; there simply wasn't enough to go on. Some would no doubt have married, had kids. If they were still alive today, those predators would be in their 60s, 70s and 80s.

These were just the matters being reported to the investigating police by the public. Then there were the known sex offenders on the Northern Beaches that police would need to look into as a matter of routine. Detective Matthews and his team had a list of offenders from various crime intelligence units. It ran to nine foolscap pages and contained the names of 103 men and their dates of birth. The oldest had been born in 1912, the youngest in 1960. In other words, the oldest sex offender living in the area was 66, while the youngest was 18.

It was becoming abundantly clear to Matthews that there were more than a few predators who'd been trawling the

Northern Beaches for years looking for easy prey in the form of young girls hitchhiking. The Trudie Adams murder inquiry was fast uncovering information that revealed a very different picture of the Insular Peninsula from the one usually painted of it: the rugged headlands, the glittering white sand, the tanned, fit young men and women, the surf, the sunny, carefree lifestyle.

But that vision of the Northern Beaches was unravelling, as police continued their investigations into Trude Adams' disappearance. The peninsula was transforming before them. One way to picture it is to imagine hovering hundreds of metres in the air above Newport, Bilgola or Avalon near dusk. Looking directly down, all you can see is the blue water, the light softening on the white sand, the curves of the magnificent coastline. But shift your gaze just a little and the landscape changes dramatically. Behind the homes tucked along the coast, you notice the massive dense and darkening bushland that is Ku-ring-gai Chase National Park, wild, untouched. Perhaps somewhere in there lay the body of Trudie Adams.

Chapter 5

Women Come Forward

On 30 June, the same day that police and the community searched the bush alongside Mona Vale Road, a 16-year-old girl, Lucy Russell, turned up at Mona Vale Police Station. She was by herself. She said she'd heard about Trudie and wanted to help, though she initially insisted that she didn't want to make a formal statement.

Lucy told detectives how, after having some drinks at the Mona Vale Hotel on Friday, 21 April, she'd been hitchhiking on Barrenjoey Road at about 10pm.

She'd only had to wait a few minutes before being picked up, by two men in a Volkswagen.

'I'm going to Avalon,' the passenger had said. Lucy thought they were therefore heading north.

'Good, I'm going to Clareville,' she'd replied. The man got out and pulled the front passenger seat forward so Lucy could get in the back. They then drove along Barrenjoey Road for a bit before turning off and stopping.

When Lucy asked what was going on, the passenger pointed a pistol at her. She said, 'You are going to rape me.'

'We're not going to hurt you, we just want to find out some information about some drugs that you have of ours,' he said.

The teenager protested that she didn't have any drugs but the passenger said they were taking her to see some people who might identify her.

'Do you know someone McDermont?' he asked. Lucy said she didn't and screamed, at which point the passenger climbed into the back seat with the gun and handcuffed her. Struggling, she was hit on the head with the gun. She could feel the blood running down her face.

She was then covered with a blanket and the driver stuck tape over her eyes and mouth.

About 20 to 30 minutes later, the Volkswagen turned onto a bumpy track. Lucy told police it was the passenger who clearly had the local knowledge of the area, as he was telling the driver where to go.

After the car stopped, she asked, 'You are going to rape me, aren't you?', to which the passenger replied, 'If you just sit tight you won't get hurt.'

They told her to get undressed unless she wanted 'a bullet in the head'. The handcuffs were taken off and she was sexually assaulted as she lay on a blanket on the ground.

'I'm going to shoot the gun in the air now, just to show you that it is no phoney,' the passenger said.

She heard a gunshot and said, 'Aren't you scared that some neighbours will hear?'

'There are no neighbours around here,' the passenger replied.

Getting dressed, Lucy thought she could hear running water and a crackling sound – like overhead power lines.

Bizarrely, the driver had then asked 'Would you mind if you and I went out together?'

She declined. 'Can't you find your own girlfriends?'

'No one will go out with us,' the passenger said.

Getting back into the car, she was offered a drink and given $10. Lucy asked what the money was for. 'Buy yourself some shampoo,' the passenger said before going through her handbag, finding her birth certificate and bus pass with her name and address.

The men warned her that if she went to the police or the papers, they knew where she lived and they'd be back.

Lucy was let go close to her home. But by the time she'd removed the tape from her eyes, the car had gone. Looking inside the folded $10 note, she found a receipt from Dee Why Autos for the amount of $24.

When police asked her to describe the passenger, she said he was about 35 years old, chubby, with short curly hair and was about 5 feet 11 inches (180cm) tall.

She said she hadn't previously reported the rape to police because she'd been too scared of the men. The running sheets record that Lucy declined to make a formal statement. 'She did not think her mother (who knows nothing of the rape of her daughter) would believe her and that she would leave herself open for ridicule from friends and relatives.'

Despite Lucy's reluctance to make a statement, not only had she made a brave decision to go to the police by herself, she'd provided valuable information, including descriptions of the two men who'd attacked her, the sound of running water nearby and humming power lines.

Crucially, she had also provided another piece of information for the police – she wasn't the only one who had been sexually assaulted. There were other girls – friends of hers. She would try to get them to come forward as well. A 16-year-old girl had potentially given investigators the breakthrough they were looking for.

Lucy Russell returned to the police station the following day, Saturday, 1 July. Once again she was on her own. She told police she'd thought about things overnight and decided she would make a formal statement. Not only that, she'd spoken to a friend who had, in turn, contacted two other teenagers who were prepared to talk. Lucy was opening doors.

And so it was that, in early July, investigators sat down with 19-year-old Madeleine Paine and 17-year-old Rosie Warne. They told detectives that on 19 November 1977 they'd been drinking at the Mona Vale Hotel until about 10.15pm, when they decided to go to the Newport Arms.

Like Trudie and Lucy, they'd decided to hitchhike on Barrenjoey Road. A vehicle had stopped in about five minutes, and the driver had asked them where they were going. 'Can you drop us at the Newport Hotel?' Madeleine asked.

'Sure,' the driver said.

But he then turned left one street before the road that led to the pub.

'You're going down the wrong street,' Rosie said. The driver pulled up, then both men grabbed the teenagers' hands tightly and handcuffed them.

The driver told the girls they were drug detectives from Pymble Police Station.

'We want you to come to the police station to identify a man called Roger, he owes us money,' he said.

Both women started struggling and screaming. Rosie asked why they couldn't just take them to Mona Vale Police Station.

The driver said they weren't from Mona Vale, they were from Pymble. The passenger put white sticking plaster over their eyes.

Rosie could see a little bit under the tape, and she thought that after about 20 minutes driving, they'd turned into Mona Vale Road and subsequently made a left-hand turn onto a bumpy dirt track.

After going slowly for about ten minutes the car stopped. 'What are you going to do with us?' Rosie asked. 'What do you think?' one of them replied.

When she started screaming, one of the men took her hand. He said, 'Feel this.' She could feel 'a long barrel, rounded, and it was metal'.

'If you start screaming anymore I will shoot you with it,' the man said.

Terrified, Rosie nevertheless started to scream until she heard a gunshot from very close range. 'Keep walking,' one of the men said.

As Rosie walked, she could feel bushes around her and the ground was rough and rocky. Rosie was told to sit down on what she described as something very soft like a couch but with no backrest. Like a mattress. Madeleine was forced onto a blanket a short distance away.

Rosie and Madeleine screamed each other's names.

As Rosie cried, one of the men told her to 'shut up' and to feel the barrel of the gun. He said if she didn't keep quiet she would 'get it through the head'.

They were raped.

As with Lucy, after the attacks the men sought to engage in conversation, even asking if they'd like a beer.

Then, in the darkness, the teenagers were taken by the arm through the bush back to the car. The attackers went through their handbags and found identification with their names and addresses. If they went to the police, one of the men said, they would find them and kill them. They were handed $20 each. The girls were let go outside Pittwater High School at about 3am. The car, which the girls described as a white four-door sedan with bucket seats, drove away at high speed.

Rosie told her mother the following day and was taken to a doctor. But they didn't go to the police. After all, the men knew their names and where they lived. They'd also claimed to be cops and had guns.

Madeleine and Rosie told Gary Matthews and his team they were only coming forward now because of Trudie Adams.

A pattern was emerging. Lucy, Madeleine and Rosie had all been hitchhiking on Barrenjoey Road on a Friday or Saturday night. They'd all been picked up within minutes, and within metres of the licensed premises in which they'd been drinking. It appeared the two men had been watching and waiting and that the abductions and rapes had been planned and pre-meditated.

***

A few days later, two Chatswood detectives phoned Gary Matthews about an almost identical abduction and sexual assault, one that had been reported to police. It had happened on 29 April 1978 – eight days after the attack on Lucy Russell and almost exactly two months before Trudie disappeared.

Leanne Jacobs told police she'd been drinking at the Newport Arms Hotel and had gone to the bus stop opposite the pub at about 9.30pm to get a bus to Mona Vale. 'I was going to a party,' she said.

'I was still on the road near the bus stop when a car, dark in colour and fairly small, stopped beside me and a guy in the back seat opened the door and pulled me in.'

With one man pointing a gun at her head, she was handcuffed, her eyes were taped and she was ordered to lie down on the back seat.

The men drove for some time before stopping in the bush and taking Leanne to a clearing, repeatedly sexually assaulting her on a blanket.

Unlike in previous attacks, the men called each other Harry and Peter. Afterwards, Harry had said: 'We'll get you home safely soon. I'm tired, it's late … it's two o'clock.'

They told Leanne to pick up the blankets and get back into the car. As in the other attacks, the men took her name and address. Harry fired two shots out the window, saying: 'If you contact the police I will come after you and kill you.'

Leanne was driven to her home and told to get out and not look back. She did look, but by that time her two attackers had gone.

She told police: 'I rang the door bell, mum opened the door, I said, "I've just been raped, don't put the light on or make a fuss."

'I went inside and mum woke up my stepfather and told him.

'I told my mother and stepfather that I didn't want to contact the police but my stepfather did anyway.'

Leanne told investigators she didn't think she'd be able to recognise the attackers 'but I might be able to recognise their voices'.

If so, she was prepared to go to court.

Gary Matthews and a colleague went to Leanne's home on a Friday evening to confirm the statement she'd made at the end of April.

Leanne described one of the offenders as 35 years old, about 5 feet 9 inches (175cm), with a 'tubby' build, dark curly hair and wearing glasses. Leanne also said that, after raping her, the two men had offered her money for toiletries. She'd refused.

(Years later, Leanne was re-interviewed by police and confirmed her original statement except for a couple of details. She hadn't been forced into the car, rather she'd been hitchhiking but had been too afraid to tell that to her parents.)

She also recalled hearing 'radio voices' coming from the car, similar to those in a taxi. In those days, it was possible to listen to police radio chatter. The larger newspapers had a dedicated police radio room, with a copy boy or girl monitoring messages broadcast on various frequencies. If, all of a sudden, a large number of police cars were directed to a certain street, the person monitoring would tell a more senior journalist. A good newspaper story might be unfolding. It was routine and accepted.

Of course, that meant the crooks could listen in as well, which many of them did. If you were involved in crime, it was handy to know if a police car was heading in your direction. Some crims, if they believed they were under investigation, would record what was being said on the scanners. In one case, a significant Sydney heroin dealer got his father to do it. The dealer had gone upstairs to a nightclub in Bondi Junction in Sydney's eastern suburbs, and left his car in the street. Police were watching and talking on the radio, and a police officer was recorded saying something like 'This is where we get the thing in', the 'thing' being a small amount of heroin.

The crook was arrested and charged but said he'd been framed and the heroin wasn't his. The recording made by his father got him off.

After interviewing Leanne Jacobs, Detective Matthews wrote in his running sheet entry: 'There is no doubt the report is a genuine one, as originally thought.' He and his team now knew that two men had sexually assaulted at least four young women in the bush off Mona Vale Road in almost identical circumstances.

The women had provided physical descriptions of the men – including their height, weight and build – but they were unable to identify their attackers from a photo board of suspects. Did the same two men pick up Trudie Adams on Barrenjoey Road at about 12.30am on Sunday, 25 June?

Was she shot or somehow killed resisting their attack?

Connie was already on the record saying her daughter 'would not give in to sexual advances without a fight'. Steve Norris was of the same view, saying, 'She would put up one hell of a fight ... that is what my gut tells me. She would put up a big stink. I just know it.'

All four victims had been picked up quickly, just as Steve had described with Trudie. Had the same two men, knowing there was a dance at the Newport Surf Club, been lying in wait?

Chapter 6

The Showground Ranger

In light of the information provided by the four women, Detective Alan Herrmann organised another search off Mona Vale Road on 4 July, this time involving detectives, four sergeants and more than 50 police cadets. Herrmann briefed them to look for the clothes Trudie had been wearing, including blue corduroy jeans, a green blouse, a black jumper, brown shoes, a gold chain necklace, a silver bracelet, one blue earring and 'most probably' a 6 x 4 inch (15 x 10cm) brown leather clutch purse.

He also instructed the searchers to follow the high-tension electricity wires that ran though the bush and any track or fire trail near the wires where a vehicle could gain access.

Emphasis was also to be placed on areas that contained running water, and where traffic could still be heard.

Lucy Russell had provided crucial detail – remembering the overhead wires humming as a result of the recent rain as well as the running water nearby, perhaps from a waterfall.

One of the other victims, Madeleine Paine, had also said she could still hear passing traffic at the place where she was sexually assaulted.

In addition, Alan Herrmann instructed them to look for a blanket or rug that might have been used in any of the offences that had come to light.

If anything was found, he emphasised it was not to be touched but 'left in situ and a supervisor informed'.

While engaged in this search, one of the Homicide detectives saw a 30-something man jogging through the bush. He was stopped and questioned. The man said he was training for the 1982 [sic] Olympic Games and that running through bushland 'which retains a higher degree of oxygen' was better preparation than running somewhere else like a beach.

The officer clearly thought this was bullshit and noted in the running sheet entry that the jogger had convictions for trespassing and smoking dope.

The entry ends abruptly: 'It is felt this person is a pervert.'

Meanwhile, information continued to pour in to the investigative team.

Masking tape, like that used in panel beating shops, was handed in by one of the volunteers taking part in the search.

Police received a report that a boat in Pittwater 'near Flint and Steel', a point on the Hawkesbury River not far from West Head and the open ocean, had hit an object at about 11.30am and that blood had been seen in the water.

There were reports of women's clothing off McCarrs Creek Road, near a cave.

On hearing reports that a sex worker called 'Cindy' in Kings Cross was telling people she had information about Trudie Adams, a local detective was dispatched to see if she had anything useful. She didn't. It was just rumour.

An anonymous caller said he'd overheard a conversation about Trudie and a man with the surname Franks. A man by that surname was on the list of the 103 sex offenders already being scrutinised.

A 16-year-old boy who'd been hitchhiking from Dee Why to Manly reported to a local police station that he'd been picked up on Pittwater Road on a Sunday morning. The driver had shown the teenager some hard-core porn magazines 'and asked if they turned him on'.

The running sheet states: 'He then asked [the boy] if he wished to make himself a quick $20. When the vehicle stopped at a set of traffic lights [he] jumped from the vehicle and took off. During the conversation, the driver advised [the boy] that he was not only interested in men, as he had a number of girlfriends.' He was driving a silver-coloured Toyota panel van, which had a mattress in the back.

The incident was on page 200 of the running sheets. The homicide investigation was only just starting.

More importantly, police spoke to the manager of Dee Why Autos. Although Lucy Russell no longer had the $24 receipt, police now had an identikit picture of one of the offenders. They showed it to an employee, who said it looked like a 40-year-old customer who drove a white Holden sedan and drank at the Dee Why Hotel.

It appears to be the only time an identikit picture was used, and despite media reports that police would release one, they never did.

The head of the Homicide Squad, Detective Inspector Harry Tupman, was later quoted in one of the papers as saying police didn't want to provide an identikit to the media until they were sure of the descriptions. He apparently took the view that while there was good information about who was committing the rapes, there was nothing at all in terms of hard evidence to link them to the suspected murder of Trudie, except suspicion.

***

The continued publicity about Trudie was encouraging other young women to come forward. A 20-year-old student, Claire Jamieson, went to Mona Vale Police Station on 5 July and made a statement. She told investigators that on 4 February that year she had been drinking at the Newport Arms Hotel with a friend until she decided to go home at about 10pm. Claire had walked towards Barrenjoey Road and decided to hitch. Soon after, a mustard-coloured Kingswood Holden sedan pulled up. Claire told police she'd 'just hopped into the back seat' without really looking into the car.

As the driver pulled away, the male passenger had turned around and pointed a small gun at her. Claire recalled that it looked like a pistol and she knew it wasn't a rifle.

'When he pointed the gun at me I said "you're joking" and I really thought that he was. But then he began to climb into the back seat with me and as he did I grabbed for the gun and it went off. I heard a loud bang. I don't think it hit the car anywhere.'

Claire decided it was no joke and that she would 'take a new approach and be passive so that I wouldn't get my head bashed in, and from then on I did as they told me and I did not resist them at all'. She was handcuffed.

Claire knew the Northern Beaches area well and could tell the car was being driven along Mona Vale Road. She said the passenger was giving directions to the driver and it was obvious he also knew the area.

The car made a right-hand turn onto a dirt track and stopped a couple of minutes later. The men placed what Claire thought was Elastoplast over her eyes, although she could still see down a little bit, and walked her about 100 metres into the bush.

'Then we came to a small clearing and I could just see a mattress, which I think was a three-quarter size mattress.'

One of the men told her to get undressed, which she did, and then said: 'We just want to talk to you.'

And they did for a while, in the bush, in the darkness. Claire with her eyes taped over. Just chatting.

'We all sat down on the mattress. I can't remember exactly what was said, but I know that we talked about society and how ridiculous it was that men had to chase women.'

During the conversation, the passenger offered Claire a can of beer, of which she only had a few mouthfuls.

The passenger also told Claire they had Scotch and marijuana and asked her if she wanted a smoke. 'No,' she said.

'I don't remember just how long we were sitting there,' she told police, 'but it was quite some time because I thought that nothing was going to happen.'

Then, suddenly, the driver ordered Claire to lie down. She was raped by both men.

At first, she was hysterical and screaming, until one of the attackers told her to be quiet 'or I'll shut you up'.

Afterwards, Claire told police, 'We all sat on the mattress for about half an hour and continued our conversation about society.'

The men then went through her bag, keeping her address book – names, telephone numbers, the lot. 'If you go to the police I'll pay a visit to your friends,' the passenger said. 'We've hassled people before.' He then gave her $20.

On the way back to the car, one of the men was carrying a torch and Claire was just able to make out the number plate, IUH-579, not a NSW plate but Victorian.

She was let go a few metres from her parents' home after one of the men used a key to unlock the handcuffs. After they'd gone, she wrote down the number plate on the back of her bankbook.

Like others, Claire didn't go to the police. She was worried not just about herself but about her friends, given the men had her address book. She did, however, go to a rape crisis centre where she saw 'a very understanding' female doctor.

About seven days after her ordeal, Claire went to check the mail. There, in an envelope, was her address book just as one of her attackers had promised.

Looking at the envelope, Claire 'couldn't read the postmark' and threw it away.

A check by police revealed the car number she'd written down was false. No such Victorian plate had ever been issued. Despite that, it gave police another good indication that they were dealing with violent but resourceful criminals.

For the investigating detectives, Claire Jamieson provided an insight into what might have happened to Trudie. She'd grabbed the gun and it had gone off but the bullet – well, what it had hit she didn't know. It hadn't hit her.

On 6 July, a member of the public called police saying he'd heard shots fired in the area close to the high-tension wires and a creek. Coincidentally, just a few minutes later a second man, Brian Walker, telephoned with similar information. He told police he was ringing because he'd been watching Mike Willesee's TV program, which had carried a report about Trudie.

Brian Walker was the council ranger and caretaker responsible for the St Ives Showground on Mona Vale Road, about 15 kilometres from the coast. His father had been the ranger before him. Brian had lived in the showground since he was five years old, spending many an idyllic hour or two exploring the many different tracks in Ku-ring-gai Chase National Park. And as Brian Walker knew, back in 1978 you could ride through the bushland all the way to Terrey Hills.

Brian told police he'd heard gunshots in the park around Christmas in 1977 and again in early 1978. Looking across the valley from his house in the showground, he'd seen lights, probably the headlights of a car in the vicinity of the high-tension power lines. He'd reported the gunfire to Pymble Police at the time but, as far as, he knew no one had followed it up.

With Trudie missing and numerous young women coming forward, police made arrangements to see Brian Walker in the next couple of days.

After all, crucial evidence might still be out there, just lying around in the bush, waiting to be discovered.

Chapter 7

Hot on the Heels

By early July, some of the details about the attacks on the young women had started to appear in the newspapers. The reports varied slightly, but the substance was the same. The police were hot on the trail of what had happened to Trudie.

On 5 July, *The Sun*'s front-page headline was 'Hitch Hike Girl Clue', with a subheading 'Hunt for two men'. The story said: 'Police are looking for two men believed to have raped four girls in recent weeks.' A detective was quoted as saying: 'This is our first real break.'

The Sun reported that the men used different vehicles, produced guns and took their victims' IDs and threatened to kill them.

'On at least one occasion the men fired shots to terrorise their victim into submission. The gunmen used handcuffs to bind the girls' wrists and covered their eyes with tape.'

The article said police investigating Trudie's disappearance were 'convinced the two men described by their victims are a vital link in their inquiries'. One detective said: 'We have descriptions of two men which tally to such a degree that we believe they are involved.' The unnamed officer then appealed for other women to come forward. 'Tell us now,' he said. 'It is not too late.'

The *Daily Mirror*'s Bill Jenkings told readers that police had descriptions of the two men and had launched a massive manhunt. They believed the two men 'could have been operating for months and that other girls have been reluctant to speak out'.

And in just two lines he painted a poignant picture of Connie, writing: 'Last night, Mrs Adams, who has lived through ten days of despair and disappointment, sat by the fire and waited for some news.'

Jenkings was a veteran police reporter who was close to and trusted by some of the most senior police officers in New South Wales, including Homicide detectives. It was clear he had talked to a source from inside the investigation.

By his account, and that of *The Sun*, the investigation into Trudie's disappearance was making progress, and quickly. Two men had been identified and a manhunt was underway. For Trudie's family and friends, it must have given them hope that an arrest was not far off.

This positive news – at least from an investigative point of view – prompted an unusual response from the Rupert Murdoch-owned *The Daily Telegraph*, which, along with its stablemate, the *Mirror*, were usually quick to support NSW Police against any allegations of wrongdoing.

On 6 July, *The Daily Telegraph* went uncharacteristically off-script, producing a searing editorial. It said:

> Surely what the Trudie Adams case has proved is the lack of public confidence in the New South Wales Police.

> It takes the disappearance of an 18-year-old girl to bring forward five other young girls who say they have been raped but were too frightened to report the offences to the police before Trudie Adams' suspected murder.
>
> The great problem is that the feeling in NSW is such that too many people believe the police are either inefficient or crooked.
>
> The situation has come down to such a level that any member of the public going to a police station is treated with calculated rudeness.
>
> The five girls who reported that they had been attacked clearly went through mental hell before deciding that they must speak out in order to try to aid a fellow human being.
>
> Going to the police should have been the least of their worries.

It was blistering, angry stuff, and completely out of character for the *Telegraph*.

Looking back, it feels like an article written by a senior reporter or editor, who, perhaps having had a long lunch, decided to let loose with a few home truths. Then, as they say, the faeces hit the air conditioner. A day or two later, the *Telegraph* ran a grovelling apology to Police Commissioner Merv Wood, who had pointed out the young women had all given similar explanations for not coming forward – the rapists knowing their names and addresses and threatening to kill them if they went to the police. That much might have been true, but so was the lack of confidence in the police, and that original editorial reflected the views of many members of the public.

Connie again went to the media and pleaded for whoever had made the call to her about Trudie's body being off Mona

Vale Road to come forward. 'I am appealing to them as Christians, to pinpoint the area, rather than have her lie out there like a dog,' she said.

Her emotional, tearful television plea revealed a mother bereft of hope that her daughter was alive. She just wanted her body to be found. At least that would be something. At least the family could bury her and have a place to grieve and mourn.

***

On 7 July, another report lobbed on the desk of Gary Matthews. It was from the modus operandi section revealing there'd been a rape seven years before, on 1 March 1971, involving an 18-year-old woman by the name of Jane Hampshire.

Matthews started to read. It said Jane had left the Hotel Pacific in Manly at about 10pm and had been followed by a man. She started to walk faster, but a second man with a gun had suddenly jumped out of a car in front of her, and together they had pushed her into the vehicle. Handcuffed, eyes taped, told to lie down on the back seat and then covered with a blanket before being taken to bushland where she was offered a cigarette, marijuana or whisky. 'Don't make any noise or I'll blow your brains out,' one of them said. She was sexually assaulted.

Afterwards, they drove her back to Manly. When they ripped the tape from her eyes she could see she was outside the Hotel Pacific. After sitting on the steps on the beachfront, she went to Manly Police Station at about 3.30am. While interviewing Jane, the police filled out a form. Jane's complaint was deemed 'doubtful'. The police didn't believe her.

But, as Gary Matthews noted in a running sheet entry on 7 July, 'the circumstances of this offence are identical with offences of rape presently being reported'. The modus operandi was exactly the same – but this had happened in 1971. If it started then and was still happening in 1977 and 1978, how many victims were there? What had been going on in the intervening years, and how had the perpetrators managed to escape justice? How many young women were still too scared to come forward?

What had started with an investigation into Trudie Adams' disappearance was becoming much bigger. A missing girl, almost certainly murdered, was bad enough. But almost identical rapes, starting at the beginning of the decade and still going on towards its end? How do you make sense of that?

As these crimes surfaced, the fabric of the community, which considered itself a peaceful beachside hamlet, was being forced to confront a different reality.

* * *

As this was unfolding, a fifth woman, having heard about Trudie, telephoned police and told them how she and a friend had been abducted and sexually assaulted. Not recently, mind you, but, seven years earlier – on 6 March 1971, to be precise.

The caller was Jackie Billings, 14 years old at the time of the assault, the young girl with the relative in the NSW Police. She and her then 15-year-old friend Sarah Sharpe had been picked up near Warringah Mall shopping centre.

She'd gone to a police station to report the attack soon after it occurred.

Gary Matthews made arrangements for her to be interviewed at Mona Vale Police Station, on 7 July, the same day he received the report about Jane Hampshire. Jackie's account of what had happened to her and Sarah was by now chillingly familiar.

The two schoolgirls had been 'allowed out' by their parents on a Saturday night and were heading to a café in Manly at about 7pm. Instead of catching a bus, they decided to hitchhike and 'within a few minutes' a car pulled up.

Jackie recounted how, as soon as the car took off, 'the passenger in the front seat leant over and pointed a gun at us. He ordered us to lie down on the back seat. The gun was black and it was a revolver.'

The men then handcuffed them and stuck tape over their eyes.

The driver had continued on for maybe 20 to 30 minutes and Jackie thought they may have been in Oxford Falls, Frenchs Forest or even Terrey Hills, 'because the bush area between these suburbs all connects up'.

During the sexual assault, she heard the two men talking to each other.

'I recall the guy who was raping me said doesn't it feel different with a girl. It was as if he was trying to put us off by pretending they were gay.'

The attackers then forced the young women to pose, and took polaroid photos of them.

Afterwards, they threatened Jackie and Sarah that if they told anyone, they would kill them and show the polaroid photographs to their families.

Suddenly, a shot was fired and Jackie thought the men had murdered her friend and that she might be next.

The girls were driven out of the bush and released at the Manly Golf Course close to midnight.

Jackie had confided in her mum that morning in her bedroom. When her father came in, he found his wife and his daughter crying.

The Homicide Squad detectives showed Jackie Billings a series of black-and-white photos of suspects or offenders. She picked out the photo of a well-known violent criminal who lived in the suburb of Terrey Hills just off Mona Vale Road – very close to where police believed the assaults had occurred.

Detectives were also aware that the man had three or four close associates who were serious and violent men. Between them they had convictions for break and enter, armed robbery, assault, safebreaking, escaping from jail and attempted murder. And at least two of them were known to carry not just handguns but machine guns.

With this man – and his accomplices – in their sights, it seems as though the Homicide squad was heading in the right direction. The momentum of the investigation was with them.

Chapter 8

The Mattress

On 8 July, the day after Jackie made the identification, police met with Brian Walker, the ranger who'd told them he'd heard gunshots and seen lights in the bush around Christmas 1977 and in early 1978.

At first, investigators were sceptical he could have seen anything across the valley from his home in the showground. But when they flashed a torch, they found that the light was visible through the trees, so perhaps he could have.

After pinpointing the location, Walker and detectives went to the area and immediately noticed 'a discarded mattress and a burnt oxy bottle … in the immediate vicinity'.

Inexplicably, police had left the mattress and oxyacetylene bottle where they were in the bush, despite the mattress being of obvious interest given that Rosie Warne had mentioned being forced to lie down on something that was 'very soft like a couch with no backrest'.

As for the oxyacetylene bottle, in the criminal world they were used by safebreakers – 'tank men' they used to call them – to cut open the safes that in those days could be found in any number of businesses, big and small.

The day's takings – cash, coins – were put into the safe and there they stayed until the money was taken to the bank, probably at the end of the week.

The following day, 9 July, 18-year-old Deborah Clark and her parents went to Mona Vale Station – once again, it was because they'd seen media reports about Trudie's disappearance and wanted to help.

Deborah told the police that she and a friend, 17-year-old Caroline Hitchens, had been hitchhiking at about 9pm on Barrenjoey Road near the Mona Vale Hotel on 30 December 1977. Picked up by two men in a Holden Kingswood, Deborah noticed something odd – she could smell glue.

She told police, 'both guys were wearing medium-brown synthetic wigs'.

'I nudged Caroline and tried to indicate the wigs to her but (she) didn't know what I was going on about.'

Deborah described how the male passenger had pulled a gun out and held it with the barrel facing the roof of the car.

She recounted the conversation that followed:

'I called out, "Who are you?"'

'We are police,' the driver replied.

'Have you got any identification?' I asked.

The driver then admitted they weren't police and asked them if they'd heard about the heroin bust at Frenchs Forest, a suburb a few kilometres away. Deborah said she'd read about it in the paper.

The two men handcuffed the girls and covered them with a blanket. They were driven up Mona Vale Road and into the bush in darkness.

After the vehicle stopped, their eyes were taped and Deborah was led to a spot, where, as she told police 'I trod on something that had springs in it and I knew that it was a mattress.

'I was so scared I just lay there like a board and I said to him please don't hurt us.'

'We're not going to hurt you. Just do as you are told,' the man replied.

He also said, 'I don't know why I am doing this.'

'Well, why are you?' Deborah asked.

'I don't know,' he responded.

'When he said that, he was stuttering,' Deborah told police.

A stutter, a speech impediment. It was an important clue – or at least it should have been.

After the assaults, one of the men asked the girls if they wanted a drink, saying they had some beer. Both girls said no. The men took their names and addresses and, to instil further fear, one of them said he was going to fire the gun.

'Don't point it at us,' the girls said. Deborah was pretty sure Caroline had also said, 'Don't shoot us.'

The man fired two shots, one into the ground, one into the air or maybe into the bush. The men then bundled them back into the car, drove on to Mona Vale Road and dropped them off at the home of one of the girl's friends.

It's likely the shots Brian Walker had heard from across the valley just after Christmas 1977 were the ones that had terrorised Deborah and Caroline and that the lights he had seen were the headlights of the car as the men drove out of the bush after raping two schoolgirls.

And what of Brian Walker's contemporaneous phone calls to Pymble Police?

Whoever was on duty at Pymble hadn't bothered to write anything down, let alone investigate the report. There were no records about Brian Walker's calls.

That's not all. The day before, police had found a mattress in the forest. Deborah had now specifically mentioned being assaulted on a mattress. Rosie Warne had also mentioned something similar.

But the mattress was not seized. Indeed, along with the oxy bottle, it would remain lying in the bush clearing for 30 years.

* * *

On 14 July, five days after Deborah spoke to police, two more teenagers, Kate Hamilton and Jessica Winch, came forward to report being abducted and sexually assaulted by two men. They were both 15 years old. Their account of what had happened to them was by now horribly recognisable to detectives.

They described how, on 18 March 1978, they'd gone to a hamburger place in Narrabeen and talked for a while. At about 9.30pm, they decided to hitchhike home and a man in a dark-blue VW Beetle stopped for them on Pittwater Road. Looking into the car, one of the girls noticed that the passenger seat had been removed.

After the girls got in, the driver locked the doors and pointed a pistol at them, saying he'd been ripped off in a drug deal worth $5000. He ordered them to lie down and covered them with a blanket.

Shortly after, the girls told police, the car stopped and the driver went to a public telephone box.

'If you do anything, you will get hurt,' he warned. They overheard him saying on the phone, 'We have got the witnesses so be there.'

They were then driven into the bush, along a bumpy track. After the car stopped, the driver covered their eyes with sticking plaster. Kate heard someone running towards them. Running. Not in a car, not on a trail bike, but running. As if they lived close by and, having received the phone call, had taken off, out of the house and into the bush, to a place they knew very well.

Kate told detectives: 'I could hear someone panting at the door of the car. Then a torch was shone on my face.'

A male voice said, 'We are going to have a sex session. Make it good and we won't hurt you.'

One of the men grabbed hold of Kate's arm and moved her out of the vehicle.

'I heard Jessica get out of the car too. I saw a blanket spread out on the ground … I was very frightened.'

She described the driver as about 6 feet (183cm) tall with 'fair to reddish hair' adding that he'd been wearing a medium-length black, wavy wig and dark-rimmed glasses when he picked them up.

'I knew these were fake as he removed them when he attacked me. He put them on again before he drove us back.'

Kate described the man who had run to the scene as about 39 years old, 5 feet 10 inches (178cm) with 'a beer-type belly' and a chubby face. She added that if she were to see the two men again 'I would definitely know them'.

After they'd made their statements, the police showed them a photo board of suspects. Kate and Jessica picked out two men. The first was of the same man previously identified by Jackie Billings as being 'very similar' to one of the men who had assaulted her. It was the violent criminal with a prior conviction for sexual assault who lived in Terrey Hills just over 12 kilometres up Mona Vale Road. His name was Neville Brian Tween.

The second man they identified was another violent criminal who was one of Tween's well-known associates, Ray Johnson.

While photo identification evidence can be unreliable and open to attack in court, the fact is that within the first three weeks of the investigation into Trudie's disappearance, three women had identified Neville Tween as being similar or very similar to one of the men who had raped them, threatened them with a gun, handcuffed them, put tape over their eyes, fired shots to terrify them and then taken their names and addresses, threatening to come back and kill them should they go to the police. Moreover, the physical descriptions matched that of Tween, who was emerging as the chief suspect – about 5 feet 10 inches (178cm), chubby/tubby, about 35 years old. And some of the victims had also noticed he had something like a stutter or speech impediment.

The identifications should have been a massive breakthrough in the investigation.

Chapter 9

The Net Closes In

Already, just three weeks after Trudie was last seen, a total of 11 young women had come forward and made statements recounting terrifying ordeals of abduction and rape. That number did not include Jane Hampshire. While police had the original 1971 incident report, she couldn't be located.

Police knew about all the similarities in the way the women were attacked. There was one variable though – the car used. The men had used different types of vehicles to abduct their victims, including a blue Volkswagen, a white Holden sedan, a mustard-coloured Holden Kingswood sedan and a light-coloured panel van like the one described by Steve Norris. In the one instance where a number plate had been seen it had turned out to be fake.

The police were optimistic. Why wouldn't they be? The chief suspect had been identified by three women as similar or very similar to one of the attackers. He lived close to where the offences had occurred. And, crucially, he had form, having been jailed for a sexual assault in 1975.

On 17 July, the *Mirror* had an article headlined 'Police confidence grows as net closes in Trudie case'. It went on to say that detectives believed 'the two men who have raped nine girls in the Northern Beaches area in which [Trudie] was last seen are still living locally'. Police, it seemed, were confident of breaking the case and were 'slowly but surely piecing the case together'.

At that stage, journalists at the *Mirror* didn't yet know about the two victims who'd come forward three days earlier.

Still, there seemed to be investigative momentum, and hope.

The media were reporting that an identikit was being prepared, based on the descriptions of the victims, and would be released soon.

The public had every reason to believe a breakthrough was imminent. After all, there was mounting evidence about who was responsible for the rapes. Like Trudie, many of the girls had been picked up on a Friday or Saturday night near licensed premises on, or not far from, Barrenjoey Road. They had been picked up within minutes of attempting to hitchhike. The men lived locally, or so detectives had told the papers.

Meanwhile, in between articles about the investigation's progress, the *Manly Daily* provided some insight into what other local men were getting up to. On 22 July, the paper's front-page headline was 'Probe Into Surf Hall Sex Show'.

The story reported that 'sex shows' and 'porno nights' had been 'regularly staged' in Warringah Shire Council halls, the most recent being a fundraiser held at the North Narrabeen Surf Club on 11 July for an injured rugby league player.

The league player claimed total ignorance of what had been planned but then acknowledged it wasn't new in the area.

'Porno nights are not uncommon and they are the quickest way to raise money,' he helpfully told the *Manly Daily*. 'The number of porno nights that go on in the Manly Warringah area is incredible. They've been going on since the year dot. All the sports clubs run them. They may be an illegal way of raising money but there's no better way.'

The story had come to light after a local man was asked if he wanted to buy a ticket for $20. He took his story to the newspaper telling them that for the $20 he was able to watch 'pornographic films, a striptease, sex acts between the girls, sex acts between the girls and the audience, and queue for "my turn" with the girls'.

Between 60 and 70 men were reported to have attended. The shire president was outraged and promised a full inquiry.

* * *

After all the publicity about Trudie, on 26 July, the mother of a teenage boy had called investigators with a story that must have, or should have, confirmed they were on the right track, at least in terms of the investigation into the rapes.

She told police her son had been raped by two men on 29 January 1977. The incident had been reported to Manly detectives two days later.

As it happened, Gary Matthews and his team were already aware of the case, having been previously notified by the modus operandi section.

The young man, Gavin Mark, had originally told police that he'd been hitchhiking on the Wakehurst Parkway near Narrabeen at about 11pm on 29 January 1977. Two men had picked him up in a white, two-door car and, as they drove along, had offered him a beer and a joint.

Not long after the driver stopped the car, the two men and Gavin walked away from the road and sat down. As they talked, the teenager had a drink and a smoke.

The running sheet states that 'after consuming more beer, one of the men grabbed at his fly and when he resisted, one grabbed him from behind and after a struggle the two men took his jeans off'.

Gavin was sexually assaulted by both men.

They then drove him to the vicinity of his home and warned that if he said anything they'd be back.

The teenager had told his mother the next morning and reported the assault to police.

Some of the details of the attack were strikingly similar to the rapes of the young women – hitchhiking, picked up by two men offered alcohol, marijuana and cigarettes. And like many of the women, he'd been let go close to his home and threatened.

Gavin told police he'd gone back to the area, near the Narrabeen National Fitness Camp, and found beer cans and a number of packets of Winfield Blue 25s, which the offenders smoked.

There was a peculiar twist in Gavin's case. One night in early 1978, his mother received a phone call at home. The caller asked for her son. When told he was out, he introduced himself using the name of a well-known surfing writer.

'I just rang to wish [Gavin] a happy birthday,' he said, before hanging up.

But it wasn't Gavin's birthday. Instead it was 29 January – exactly one year to the day since he'd been raped.

Gavin's mother told police she believed the caller was one of her son's attackers and detectives also believed it was a possibility.

What sort of person would telephone his victim on the anniversary of his rape and wish him happy birthday?

Detectives re-interviewed Gavin, who reiterated his account of the attack. And they showed him some photos of possible offenders. Gavin selected two photos as being similar to the men who'd attacked him. One of them was Neville Tween, the same man identified by three of the female rape victims: Jackie Billings, Kate Hamilton and Jessica Winch.

Two separate investigations were emerging. The first was the inquiry into the almost certain murder of Trudie Adams. The second was into the growing number of sexual assaults. So far, police had identified 12 victims and it's clear they thought the two lines of inquiry were inextricably linked. The detectives investigating Trudie's disappearance were on the record saying the two men identified in the rapes were a 'vital link' in their inquiry.

But there was precious little solid information about Trudie. The beige panel van described by Steve Norris had not been found despite extensive inquiries into owners of similar vehicles in New South Wales and interstate. Neither Steve, nor anyone else, had seen or even got a glimpse of who was in the panel van that night. And no one had found a trace of any of Trudie's belongings or clothes. The only thing that had turned up was the purse mentioned in the wireless message on 30 June, which had said Trudie was carrying:

> A LIGHT BROWN LEATHER CLUTCH PURSE ... THAT HAS A BLACK AND WHITE CALF SKIN INSERT ON A FLAP.

As it turned out, she hadn't been carrying it on the night and the purse had been found at home.

So the searches continued. The *Manly Daily* reported that a blanket, a balaclava and a dark jumper had been handed in. One of the search teams also found a sawn-off shotgun wrapped in a towel a few metres off a road. It had been wiped clean of fingerprints and there were no records of where it had been sold. But, in any case, the women who'd come forward had identified a handgun – a pistol or revolver – as the weapon used by the offenders.

Another young woman came forward saying she'd been attacked. And in recent days. Detectives scrambled, there was a flurry of activity, leads were followed and the 18-year-old briefly made front-page headlines. Sadly, she'd made it up. She'd been distressed and unhappy at the time and was genuinely sorry. She was charged with public mischief.

More tip-offs kept coming.

A resident of a caravan park told police about two old mine shafts, copper mines that had been closed in the 1930s. Trudie's body could have been dumped there.

An anonymous woman called to say she and her girlfriend had been raped at the Duck Ponds. She gave no details.

Another clairvoyant volunteered that Trudie had been murdered by drowning at 12.26am on 25 June, a time when in fact she was almost certainly still at the dance or just leaving.

A letter arrived for detectives from 'a thoughtful citizen' outlining a dream she'd had as to Trudie's whereabouts.

A local suggested that police look into old tank traps and tunnels dug in the area during World War II, the idea being the tunnels, some of which still existed, would be packed with explosives, thus slowing down a feared invasion by the Japanese.

There was a report someone had seen a human arm floating in the water near Lion Island, off Palm Beach. A police launch was dispatched but found nothing.

Police also investigated the attempted sexual assault of an 18-year-old student from Barrenjoey High, Trudie's old school. She'd met two men at the Newport Arms Hotel and said they'd later tried to have sex with her near the Palm Beach Surf Club. Police found that the woman had been assaulted, but not sexually, and the men involved weren't those they were looking for in relation to the rapes and Trudie's disappearance.

More searches found marijuana plants, numerous stolen cars and number plates and, according to *The Sydney Morning Herald*, 'hundreds of wrecked cars in the junk-ridden, lonely bush tracks'. But, despite intensive well-planned efforts, nothing had been found that related directly to Trudie. Finally, the searches were called off.

With no body, no sign of any clothing, and no witnesses beyond Steve Norris's last glimpse of Trudie, police had hit a wall in the case. This lack of evidence, however, stood in stark contrast to the rapes, where the statements and descriptions were starting to tally. It was around this time that it began to appear that the two investigations might separate – Trudie's disappearance on the one hand, the assaults on the other. But as the weeks ticked by, police still had not interviewed the man whom four people had now identified as their attacker.

Chapter 10

The Narcs

Trudie's mother, Connie, desperate, tried everything. When giving interviews to newspapers and radio stations, her distress was visibly apparent – in the space of just a few weeks her weight had dropped by two stone, almost 13 kilograms.

During a radio interview in July, with still no sign of any hard evidence of what had happened, Connie said: 'I'll search forever for my daughter – I won't give up looking for Trudie. We are not giving up hope. For my peace of mind I must find out if she is alive or dead. I've been living in a vacuum, it's awful not knowing, I'll search forever for my daughter, I'll find out somehow.'

Connie called Detective Matthews again and urged him to speak to Steve Otton, a young man who had made a surfing 'road movie' called *Highway One*, featuring some Avalon locals.

The movie's plot was loose, following one young surfer making a journey from Avalon to Byron Bay up 'Highway One'. The surfer's girlfriend was played with casual charm by a radiant Trudie Adams. She first appears lying on a beach eating a mandarin, laughing about the boys in the surf. Then she's up near the cliffs, a white daisy chain around her neck, with another daisy tucked behind her ear. In a later scene, she's having dinner with her on-screen boyfriend, at nearby Coal and Candle Creek.

Steve Otton, the filmmaker, had developed a crush on Trudie and taken her out to dinner a couple of times. He described her as 'a sparkler'.

Connie had told police that he'd been obsessed with Trudie, even asking her to marry him. She made it clear she wanted police to speak to Otton.

Investigators obliged and interviewed him on 1 August.

The young filmmaker told them that Trudie 'loved life and parties', was family-minded and held her parents and brothers in high esteem. He'd gone to the dance at the surf club on 24 June but had left at about 10pm because he didn't like the music. He hadn't seen her there and added that everyone he knew believed she had been killed.

He later said he'd never asked Trudie to marry him, but wished he had.

***

Detective Matthews' team continued to investigate rumours that Trudie had been involved in drugs. A number of letters had been found in her room indicating she knew some people involved in drugs, though given she was living on the Northern Beaches in the 1970s, that wasn't really surprising.

Police also discovered that a number of young men had been very fond of Trudie, among them a 23-year-old who, in the seven months to March 1977, had written her a total of 32 letters. The man had a police record, including convictions for break, enter and steal 'and drug offences involving the use of Indian hemp, heroin and LSD'. The drug offences indicated he was a user, not a dealer.

Another letter found in Trudie's room, dated 23 January 1977, had been sent to her from a male friend in Victoria named Alan, who was a surfer. He told her how he'd 'scored an ounce of grass' but how he and his mates had then been busted by the police while driving home.

He told Trudie that 'the narcs' had stopped their car because they had surfboards on the roof.

'We're really spewing about it at the moment 'cause it had been so long since we had anything. What a fuckin' bummer eh?'

The narcs had told him it was likely he'd have to have to go to court and was probably going to be fined between $50 and $200. It appears 'the narcs' hadn't been agents of the Australian Bureau of Narcotics, but most likely uniformed cops who had pulled over Alan and his mates by chance.

Alan seemed to be more afraid of his parents than any fine he might face. 'Hope the olds don't find out,' he wrote. 'I'll be in real shit otherwise.'

But the Narcotics Bureau did come to play a minor, fleeting and tantalising role in the disappearance of Trudie Adams.

The bureau had been established by the Commonwealth Government to tackle the burgeoning drug trade – heroin, LSD and marijuana. By early 1970, it was up and running, but initially its seizures were tiny. In some ways it marked the beginning of Australia's so-called war on drugs.

One former Narcotics Bureau agent, Bernard Delaney, recalled how, when he started in April 1970, people in Sydney close to the drug scene talked about 'matchbox ounces' and dollars.

The seizure of a pound of marijuana was considered a big bust.

By the time he left in 1976, Delaney and his fellow agents were talking about 'multi-kilograms of heroin and millions of dollars'.

By 1978, the bureau had gathered considerable intelligence about drug trafficking, including Buddha sticks coming in from Asia.

So it made sense for Gary Matthews to turn to their expertise for help in his investigation.

He asked the bureau to see if there was any evidence or crime intelligence that Trudie was going to make a drug run on her trip to Bali and been killed because she'd changed her mind.

In mid-August 1978, the bureau advised Matthews that Trudie's name had cropped up in the diary of Clayton Looby, the Avalon surfer charged with importing 16 kilograms of Buddha sticks worth $200,000 through Sydney Airport.

One of the Narcotics Bureau agents that Gary Matthews and his team dealt with was a junior officer by the name of Mark Standen, who'd previously worked in customs, which he'd joined in 1975.

Standen's role was fleeting but tantalising in the context of the Trudie Adams case, because, by the mid to late 1990s, Standen had risen to become one of the most powerful law enforcement officers in Australia. Over the years, he'd developed a network of informers, crooks who would provide information on the activities of their criminal rivals or associates. He would become particularly close to one of his informers – the man identified by three of the female rape victims and Gavin Mark as their attacker – and thus the chief suspect in the disappearance of Trudie. All this, of course, was in the future.

A 1978 entry in the police running sheets written by Matthews states: 'Detective Mark Standen has been spoken to on a number of occasions at his office at the Narcotics Bureau. He has informed me that he can find no association between the missing girl Adams and any of the Narcotics inquiries, apart from the original information of Adams' name being in Clayton Looby's diary.'

Not content with Standen's assessment, Matthews interviewed a 23-year-old woman who'd been arrested with Clayton Looby and pleaded guilty. The woman told him she knew Trudie only 'to say hello to' and had no information about any of Trudie's associates, although she knew Steve Norris.

To her knowledge the only involvement Trudie or Steve Norris had with the drug scene was that they smoked 'grass' on various occasions 'and that this was always shared with someone else'. She regarded any alleged involvement by Adams in drug trafficking as 'laughable' and 'was certain Looby had nothing to do with Adams' disappearance'.

In fact, Looby had told the young woman about Trudie's disappearance and had appeared 'as concerned as the other young persons in the area'.

She told Matthews that Norris was 'a gentle person, deeply in love with Adams, and would not [have] approached Adams re a drug deal and would have had nothing to do with her disappearance'.

The running sheets also reveal the possible source of Connie's fears about her daughter's involvement in drugs. Somehow she'd had made contact with a man she thought was a detective in the Narcotics Bureau.

He'd allegedly told her about something called 'The North Side Drug ring' in Sydney, feeding Connie's belief that Trudie had been killed because someone wanted her to do a drug run and 'she knew too much'.

The 'detective' turned out to be a cameraman working for the bureau, who admitted to his bosses that Connie had been calling and discussing various theories. He said he hadn't told her anything and had just gone along with whatever she said in an effort to placate her.

Nevertheless, Connie continued to harbour suspicions that Trudie somehow was mixed up in some drug deal and had been silenced. It was her 'motherly intuition' that led her to the conclusion that Steve Norris was responsible, in one way or another, for Trudie's disappearance.

When police told Connie they had accounted for Norris's movements on the night of 24 and 25 June as much as possible by talking to witnesses, she alleged the witnesses were lying.

Connie believed her daughter had met her death close to home, in Central Road, because of the behaviour of the family dog, Lucky. She said that when Trudie went missing, Lucky had faithfully waited at the end of the street for several days for her to come home.

Detective Matthews recorded that Connie believed in the dog's instinct – that Trudie had 'met harm in that street where Norris was in the habit of leaving his car'.

Later, at a birthday party for one of Trudie's brothers, Connie 'gave it' to Steve with what Steve described as 'both barrels'. He understood that Connie needed someone to blame and left.

Charles clearly didn't share his wife's suspicions, telling newspapers that people had been so good to the family. He added that their friends, Trudie's friends and Steve Norris's friends had searched all through the bushland.

'Steve and I are going to get the guy who's taken her,' he said. Nor did the police believe he was involved in any way. 'Steve was always believable,' Gary Matthews said later.

* * *

But then, almost overnight, something in the investigation changed. The earlier optimism reported in the papers that police were confident of bringing two men to justice somehow evaporated.

An article in the *Manly Daily* on Friday, 11 August, headed 'Trudie Hunt Draws Blank', said: 'Police working on the Trudie Adams case have almost exhausted their leads.' A three-day search of bushland, which had ended the day before, had yielded nothing. The story said detectives were sifting through hundreds of pages of information in a bid to find a new lead.

In all, more than 1000 personnel spent a total of 15 days looking for Trudie. At the time, it was the biggest search effort in NSW Police history.

Then, on 17 August, the *Manly Daily* ran a letter from Connie under the headline 'A Thank You from Trudie's Mother':

> My husband, myself and the boys wish to thank your paper for the way in which you have publicised and given factual information to the general public, without dramatising or colouring the facts for cheap publicity, as some city newspapers have, in relation to my daughter Trudie's disappearance.

Connie went on to thank the residents of Avalon and Manly Warringah who'd helped in the search and given her family 'such moral support and help over the past seven weeks'.

She paid tribute to the bushwalking clubs, pony clubs, surf clubs as well as 'The Godmothers, Ku-ring-gai National Park Rangers and many others …'

Her letter ended on a forlorn note. 'I have given up hope of seeing Trudie alive again and I feel it is very ironical that for the past 20 years I have been preserving the bushland area in Manly Warringah with my daughter's help and her body may still be out there.'

Much to the distress of Trudie's family and friends, a Sunday newspaper ran a front-page story saying Trudie was still alive. Connie labelled it a disgrace.

Meanwhile, she called Gary Matthews – there were many calls – and urged him to contact a clairvoyant she knew.

Clairvoyants and psychics were big at the time. British psychic Doris Stokes had been touring Australia at the time Trudie went missing and had been given huge media publicity. Stokes claimed she could talk to the dead, and stories about her ran alongside those on Trudie.

One feature story in the *Daily Mirror* was headlined 'Life Beyond the Grave'. Another article described her as 'the amazing lady who has shaken Australia with her ability to talk to the dead'. The *Mirror* reported that Stokes had 'made contact with spirits associated with an unsolved double murder' in Victoria the year before and that the chief of the Victoria Police Homicide Squad said Doris Stokes 'was most welcome to get in touch'.

Stokes spoke to some *Daily Mirror* readers, in one case telling the relatives of a missing young man she had made contact with him in the 'spirit world'.

The *Mirror*'s rival, *The Sun*, took great delight a few days later in revealing that far from being in the spirit world the young man was alive and well and living in Tasmania.

Nevertheless, a parent himself, Gary Matthews could understand the intensity of Connie's grief, and called the clairvoyant she'd suggested. The clairvoyant had nothing remotely useful for a police officer to investigate.

Some of the tip-offs received from the public were still being run to ground.

A married couple told Mona Vale Police that while travelling to Western Australia the previous month they'd stopped at a petrol station about 550 kilometres east of Perth. The wife had been struck by the resemblance of a young girl working there to Trudie. They had purposely stopped at the same petrol station for a second look on their way back to Sydney and she was even more convinced the young woman was the missing Avalon teenager.

Detective Matthews organised for a constable from the nearest Western Australian police station to go to the petrol station. He gave him a full description of Trudie, including the fact she had a mole on the lower part of her stomach.

The constable interviewed the girl, who did indeed look like Trudie, in the presence of her mother.

However, the constable checked and found she had no mole on her stomach.

A young man walked into Gosford Police Station on the NSW Central Coast one night and spoke to the uniformed officers behind the desk, telling them he'd overheard two men talking about the disappearance of Trudie Adams. The men had said they'd picked her up on Mona Vale Road and raped and murdered her.

He gave them the name of one of them, who owned a white panel van.

Within 36 hours, detectives in Parramatta found and spoke to the man who owned the panel van. He admitted that he and a 19-year-old mate had, in fact, been telling people they'd picked up Trudie and given her a lift home. But he said it was all just 'a sick joke' and they'd been boasting to show off 'in front of girls'.

The police ruled out any involvement by the two men in Trudie's disappearance, but it wouldn't be the last time that young men boasting or 'big-noting' about killing Trudie would come to their attention.

Chapter 11

The Man with the Machine Gun

On Thursday, 17 August, the NSW government offered a $20,000 reward for information about Trudie. Then, as now, rewards are usually offered as a last resort when investigations have largely run their course and the prospects of success are receding.

The reward appears to have been greeted with mixed feelings by Connie, if the newspaper reports are anything to go by. On the one hand, she was quoted in the *Daily Mirror* as saying: 'I think it's a little too late now to bring her back. I doubt whether it will help in finding her alive.'

On the other, she told the *Manly Daily*, 'It is my last chance. Someone may know something and this reward may prompt the necessary information.'

In the same article, Connie revealed she believed Trudie's body had been moved.

'She believes the body, reported by a caller to have

been dumped off Mona Vale Road early after Trudie's disappearance, was removed the same night.'

Just why she thought that is not known.

The reward, together with Connie's thank you letter and the media stories about police having 'exhausted' all leads, painted a far more pessimistic picture than the one presented only weeks earlier.

Perhaps one reason for the change was that Gary Matthews had been taken off the case. He'd wanted to stay but was told by his superiors to move on after about six weeks. It was just before the announcement of the $20,000 reward.

Matthews recalls being told words to the effect of, 'You're a homicide investigator, not a rape investigator.' Never mind that most of the detectives believed the men responsible for the abductions and rapes of young women were almost certainly connected to Trudie's disappearance. The police had announced so themselves when they broke the news about the hunt for two men.

Another factor in Matthews moving on from the investigation was that he was due to begin his sergeant's course. If he didn't do it, other less senior officers would leapfrog over him for promotion.

While Matthews was no longer working full-time on the investigation, he was still involved from time to time when new leads emerged. Some of his Homicide colleagues stayed on the Trudie Adams inquiry a little longer. But the investigation seems to have come to a fork in the road – one path being the murder of Trudie, the other the abductions and rapes.

Whatever the case regarding Gary Matthews, the investigation appears to have faltered after he left, falling between the cracks in police command. The Homicide Squad wasn't interested in investigating the rapes. It's not clear who took over the investigation of the sexual assaults – by this stage there were 12 that had been reported, plus that of Gavin Mark, and detectives believed there were a lot more women still too scared to come forward. It was a big ask for local detectives on the Northern Beaches.

By any standard, it was a complex and difficult case, with some women not wanting to go to court and police dealing with suspects who were hardened criminals who knew the system inside out.

And perhaps the police attitude to rape at the time didn't help. A couple of months after Trudie disappeared and the assault victims had come forward, the rape crisis centre told a newspaper that only 30 per cent of the women who came to them for help reported sexual assaults to the authorities.

Some were pessimistic police would believe them. Others were made to feel it was their own fault – they'd been 'asking for it' by hitchhiking or being out late. Not only that, perhaps they wouldn't be taken seriously because they hadn't fought back or screamed or called out for help. Just like Jane Hampshire, way back in 1971.

All the publicity doesn't seem to have stopped young women from hitchhiking. *The Daily Telegraph* reported that on Saturday, 19 August, two days after the announcement of the reward for information about Trudie, a 15-year-old girl had been attacked after hitching a ride on Barrenjoey Road with a man aged 20–25. She'd managed to escape by jumping from the moving car. Police issued a warning, but the incident only underlined the fact that there was no shortage of predators.

On 20 August, at the behest of investigators, Steve Norris agreed to be hypnotised to see if he could recall any further details – maybe the number plate of the panel van, for example – about what had happened on the night he last saw Trudie.

That evening, in the presence of his father, Steve went under hypnosis for two sessions, totalling 90 minutes.

The hypnotist told detectives that Norris had been fully under hypnosis and that he'd found him 'to be very truthful and recounted the same circumstances as previously stated by him'.

Inquiries continued into the owners of panel vans in New South Wales and reported sightings of Trudie, which were still coming in.

Detective Alan Herrmann interviewed a woman who claimed to have seen Trudie trying to rent an apartment in Chippendale a week before she disappeared. He showed her a clip from *Highway One*, the surf movie Trudie had acted in, and she selected Trudie as the girl most like the one she'd seen trying to rent the apartment.

Further checks revealed that the timing was wrong. Trudie would have needed to leave home at about 7.30am to get to the inner-city apartment. Connie told detectives it was a challenge 'to get Trudie to technical college on time at 10am'. In addition, it turned out she'd been doing a speed typing test at the Mona Vale Business College that morning.

Connie appeared on the top-rating daytime TV program *The Mike Walsh Show*, which was screened nationally. A woman called in, but when Connie went to see her, she turned out to be senile and said Trudie had been taken by the Mafia.

Clutching at straws, hopes raised, hopes dashed.

***

Both Neville Brian Tween and Ray Johnson were career criminals and never far from trouble. Indeed, they'd been arrested near Lismore on the NSW far north coast in October 1977 and charged with conspiring to rob a hotel and possessing guns and explosives and breaking equipment. They'd been granted bail and their case was progressing, slowly, through the courts.

Knowing his two main suspects had a court appearance in Sydney on 24 August 1978, Gary Matthews decided it would be a good opportunity to see if any of the victims could further identify their attackers.

Kate Hamilton, who had been sexually assaulted in March 1978, remembers taking the day off school.

What happened that day is not recorded in any of the 700 pages of running sheets available to the authors. But Kate later recalled: 'I saw a number of men standing outside the court in the waiting area. I recall seeing one of the men who had abducted and sexually assaulted me. I told a police lady of this fact. I recall her name was Doreen. I was certain that this was the man who had assaulted me.'

She also said that after identifying the man 'I left the court and never heard anything further' from the NSW Police.

As it happened, Tween and Johnson, already on serious charges from 1977 – and the prime suspects in multiple rapes and the killing Trudie Adams – had their bail continued that day, despite their already lengthy criminal histories.

* * *

What had happened to the 'net' that was closing in?

Crucially, there was another piece of evidence to the case against Neville Tween – a piece of evidence detectives at the time were aware of. It turned out that Neville Tween had a conviction for sexual assault. That assault bore marked similarities to the other attacks reported recently, and had occurred in the same area. The victim in this instance was a 19-year-old man called Jimmy Holten. On 11 July 1975, Jimmy had taken his mother's car to T and J Autos on Orchard Road, Brookvale, for panelbeating. While he was there he bumped into a bloke he knew called Charlie Brown – or at least that's the name he was using.

Charlie Brown knew Jimmy smoked a bit of dope and asked if he could get some marijuana for a mate. While waiting for his mum's car to be spray-painted, Brown and Jimmy jumped into Brown's Holden sedan and drove along Mona Vale Road before turning on to a bush track in Ku-ring-gai Chase National Park.

According to Jimmy, they had gone about three or four hundred yards into the bush before they came to a stop beside a fawny-coloured handkerchief hanging from a bush.

Charlie Brown told him his mate would be along shortly.

About 30 seconds later, Jimmy's door was opened by a man armed with a submachine gun with a bayonet on the front. Dressed in navy-blue overalls and wearing a motorcycle helmet, he told Jimmy to 'get out of the fucking car'. As Jimmy did, the man fired the gun into the air. He then handcuffed Jimmy's hands behind his back and ordered him to walk further into the bush until they came to a hollow.

Charlie Brown threw Jimmy a shovel and the man with the gun told him to start digging, accusing him of trying to rip off someone called Lenny.

Jimmy replied that he'd never ripped off anybody in a drug deal and never would.

'Dig, dig, you cunt, fucking dig,' said the gunman, who then start firing bullets around Jimmy's feet.

The teenager told police he started to dig a bit faster and after a while the hole was about five feet long and about eight inches deep.

The gunman ordered Jimmy to take off his clothes, put on women's underwear and to 'get down and suck [Charlie Brown's] prick and make like you're enjoying it'.

Jimmy fellated Charlie Brown while the other man put down the gun and took photographs with a polaroid camera. He told Jimmy to lie on the ground, and threw him a packet of cabanossi-type sausages and said, 'Stick three or four up your arse.'

The men continued to sexually assault him.

Afterwards, the gunman showed Jimmy nine polaroid photos. 'Right, now we have got something on you,' he said, 'so you will have to give us the money [for the alleged drug rip-off] or we will send these photos to the newspapers and put them up in factories.'

Before the gunman departed with his submachine gun he told Jimmy he knew where he lived. About 15 minutes later Jimmy and Charlie Brown also left the scene.

On the way out of the bush, Brown said: 'That cunt is mad. He picked up two sheilas hitching, took them up there and we got a lot of good pictures of them.'

Charlie Brown drove the 19-year-old back to the smash repairer in Brookvale where his mother's car was waiting to be picked up. Later that night, after Jimmy returned home, a man he believed to be the gunman appeared outside his house and called out 'You know what I want.'

Jimmy told the man he'd give him his money on Monday. Scared, he retreated inside only to hear a loud bang. In the morning he found his car window had been smashed and one of his tyres let down.

Jimmy Holten didn't tell anyone about what had happened in the bush until he was arrested by NSW Police on an unrelated and minor matter seven days later on 18 July, at which point he told detectives everything about his ordeal.

He took the detectives to the spot in the bush where the sexual assault had happened where police found parts of a safe, handcuffs, a spent 9mm cartridge shell, some Indian hemp in a jar, some cloth money bags, two company finance books and a stash of alcohol. Crucially, they also found women's clothing – a bra and a pair of pink underpants.

Jimmy described Charlie Brown as about 6 feet 2 inches (188cm) tall and of a slim build with thick red hair and a beard. He described the gunman as about 5 feet 8 inches (173cm) and of solid build. Jimmy hadn't been able to see his face because of the helmet, but said he had long ginger hair.

When police at North Sydney Station asked if he could identify either of his attackers from some photos, he identified 'Charlie Brown' as Garry James Batt who had a lengthy criminal record. Police then worked out that Batt's accomplice was named 'Nev'.

Having found parts of a stolen safe, police called in detectives from the CIB's Breaking Squad, saying they had a suspect in mind but all they knew was that his Christian name was Nev and he was in possession of a machine gun.

One of the Breaking Squad officers assigned to the case was Bob Inkster, who remembers it to this day.

'It immediately rang bells with the people in my office and they knew of such a person. (They knew) it had to be Neville Brian Tween, he was that well known and particularly in relation to the machine gun. It was obvious to us.'

At 6am on 20 July 1975, Bob Inkster and other armed detectives burst into Tween's home in Booralie Road, Terrey Hills, not far from where Jimmy had been subjected to his terrifying and humiliating ordeal.

Police aimed their Remington shotguns at Neville Tween's head as he came out of his bedroom, naked. Their search of Tween's house turned up a motorcycle helmet, blue overalls, a .22 rifle, another rifle with ammunition, a jar containing Indian hemp, a polaroid camera and nine photographs of the teenager being sexually assaulted.

'Gotcha,' exclaimed Inkster.

But not for the first or last time, Neville Brian Tween managed to work the legal system to his advantage.

He knew Jimmy Holten was terrified about giving evidence. In what appears to have been a plea-bargain negotiated by his lawyer, well-known Sydney solicitor Leon Goldberg, Tween and Batt pleaded guilty to a lesser charge of indecent assault

They were jailed for just six months, a sentence that disgusted Bob Inkster. And he wondered where the two men had obtained the women's underwear they made Jimmy put on. It wasn't something safebreakers or drug dealers would usually carry around or were likely to buy. From Inkster's policing experience, it was more likely something they'd kept as a trophy.

Chapter 12

A Jail Confession

The team investigating the disappearance and murder of Trudie Adams was gathering plenty of information and evidence about Neville Tween and the rapes. They knew his criminal past, including the 1975 assault on Jimmy Holten.

By July 1978, they had not only identified Tween but also two of his associates – Garry Batt, aka Charlie Brown, and a hardened and violent Sydney crook, 32-year-old Raymond Johnson, born on 31 January 1946, and not to be confused with a couple of other men with the same name who also had colourful reputations. Kate Hamilton had picked Johnson from a photo board as Tween's accomplice in one of the rapes. Johnson was also sometimes known as Christopher Clayton. His criminal history had started at the age of ten and included robbery, assault, drugs, resist arrest and possession of explosives and firearms, particularly shortened firearms and pistols.

As if all that information wasn't fertile ground for investigation, there was more. Because, as early as 7 July 1978 – less than two weeks after Trudie disappeared – Neville

Tween's name had been front and centre in Gary Matthews' investigation. On that date Detective Alan Herrmann had taken a signed five-page statement from a taxi driver, 35-year-old Andrew James Kingston.

He told the detective he'd been watching the Channel Nine news the night before when newsreader Brian Henderson had mentioned that a number of young girls had been coming forward, saying they'd been raped in Ku-ring-gai Chase National Park.

Kingston said he felt he had no choice but to speak to the police and, furthermore, he was prepared to go to court to give evidence.

Kingston said that in mid-February 1978 he'd been charged with fraud offences – bogus investment deals that netted him $30,000 – and spent several months in the Metropolitan Remand Centre at Long Bay Jail. For the first couple of weeks he'd kept to himself, and had been reading a book in the exercise yard one day when another prisoner approached him and said, 'You really are a bookworm.'

Apparently associating someone reading a book with someone who might know a thing or two about the law the man, a New Zealander by the name of Len Evans, asked him for advice about applying for a 'no-bill' – an application to the Crown for the charges against him to be dropped before going to trial.

Although Kingston had no idea what a no-bill was, Len Evans went into some detail about what he'd been charged with – demand money with menaces – and why he was an innocent man. Kingston recalled that over the following four to five weeks most of their cell mates were transferred, 'leaving only the two of us and therefore we associated constantly'.

After a couple of weeks the subject of girls had come up in conversation while they were in the exercise yard, and Kingston recalled Evans saying words to the effect of:

> If you want to pick up women, you have to show them something different, show them some excitement. Me and Tweeny used to have a good thing going. We used to cruise up and down the highway and look for hitchhikers and when we saw a girl hitchhiking we used to pick her up and make her sit in the back seat. And as soon as we got going again we used to stick a gun in her face.
>
> Then we used to make her lie down in the back and put the cuffs on her. Then we used to take her out to a little dirt road we knew which runs into the Ku-ring-gai National Park. We used to have our own private spot there.
>
> There we used to get the girl out of the car and give it to her and when both of us were finished with her we would smoke a bit of grass and then we would make her suck us off. After that we used to sit around and talk for a while and maybe have a few drinks, and then we used to put the girl back in the car and take her back to the highway.

Kingston told Herrmann he remembered the conversation with Len Evans because he'd never heard anything like it before in his life.

Although five young women had come forward with details about their ordeals and some of the details had been described in the media on 5 July, a lot of the information Kingston provided to police could only have come from someone familiar with, or involved in, the assaults.

And police now believed that Tween had committed the offences, teaming up with his different associates. In the frame were Ray Johnson and Garry Batt and now, Len Evans.

Kingston said he'd asked the Kiwi how it was that he and Tween had never been arrested, to which Evans had replied:

> We just talked to the girls for a while and after that they were alright. As a matter of fact what we were doing was what everybody else would like to do and the girls like it.
>
> As a matter of fact we have done it four or five times and we got away with it each time. The only trouble we used to have with the girls was to show them that we really meant business and what we did as soon as we got them out of the car we'd fire a shot or two in the air and after that there would be no problems.

Kingston told Herrmann that at this point of the conversation they'd been interrupted by another prisoner. However, two or three days later, he and Evans had got talking again, this time about cars, with Evans saying that good crooks never used the same vehicle twice, either selling or dumping them. He said he and Tween usually took their cars 'to our spot in the Ku-ring-gai National Park'.

According to Kingston, Evans said that on one occasion he and Tween had gone into the bush to test out a few handguns and been sprung by a ranger who told them to 'clear out'. Despite that, Evans and 'Tweeny' had gone back to the same spot not long after when they 'picked up two girls and took them up there and did our thing'.

He then recounted – according to Andrew Kingston – how he and Tween had picked up the girls somewhere around

Crows Nest, handcuffed them to each other and taken them into the bush. Evans had said: 'When we were finished with them one of them asked me why we do this and I told her that we were only doing what all other men would like to do and she agreed.'

Kingston said that around 20 April 1978, while he and Evans were in the exercise yard, Evans told him, 'Tweeny's been here to see me ... He's got a few problems at the moment with the law but he is still doing his thing. He told me he'd done another couple of Ku-ring-gai jobs in my honour.'

Kingston said he understood what Evans meant by 'a Ku-ring-gai job' because every time they talked about the park it was in relation to the rapes of young woman.

It appears there were no further conversations between Kingston and Evans because, in late April 1978, two months before the disappearance of Trudie Adams, Kingston was assaulted for being a 'police spy' and placed into protective custody.

He told Detective Herrmann he'd only decided to speak to police when the Channel Nine News reported that 'a number of other girls had come forward to complain about having been abducted and taken to Ku-ring-gai Park in exactly the same manner as told to me by Len Evans'.

Kingston said, 'I am prepared to give evidence if required at any court and assist police in this matter. I am only too aware of the type of persons involved and the danger to me and my family, I could not let this information go without telling police, although I do honestly fear reprisals if my identity became known.'

Andrew Kingston needn't have worried. Police did not call on him to give any evidence. His statement lay, untouched, in police files for years.

Unknown to him, there was evidence to corroborate the fact that Tween and Evans had indeed been together at the time of the rapes in 1971. It involved a chance meeting between two men who had been to the same school in Leeton, in south-western New South Wales.

Brian McVicar attended St Joseph's in Leeton in 1953 with Neville Tween, then known as Neville Tiffen. But McVicar had chosen a different path to his one-time school mate. He'd joined the NSW Police.

He hadn't seen the boy he knew as Neville Tiffen since the 1950s. But there he was one day, walking down George Street, in Sydney.

McVicar never forgot their conversation. It went something like this:

'Hello, Neville, how are you going? It's Brian, Brian McVicar.'

'My name's not Neville.'

'Sorry?'

'My name's not Neville – you're mistaken.'

'Oh, come on, Neville, I went to school with you.'

'No, you're mistaken.'

At which point Neville Tiffen/Tween turned on his heels and walked away.

McVicar was not one to give up and followed him to a hotel in George Street.

He knew who Tween was, or more accurately what he'd become. As an aspiring detective, he'd seen his photo in one of the regular circulars that alerted police to active and serious criminals.

McVicar rang the Consorting Squad.

Under certain circumstances, it was an offence for convicted crims to be in each other's company. To 'consort' together, say, in a pub. The Consorting Squad spent a lot of time in pubs – duty called – but they also got plenty of work, and plenty of good intelligence.

Police documents record that following McVicar's call, the squad 'sighted Tween and Evans in the Bourke Hotel in George Street', in the middle of the CBD.

It was 10 March 1971. Tween was charged with two offences, including goods in custody – the goods in question being a handcuff key.

The rapes of Jackie Billings and Sarah Sharpe had taken place four days earlier. The assault on Jane Hampshire, the first one reported, on 1 March.

As for Andrew Kingston, who volunteered to go to court to testify against Len Evans, it's not clear, but it appears that police never spoke to him about Evans or Tween again.

Chapter 13

The Grave

On 14 September 1978, Gavin Mark, who'd been sexually assaulted by two men in January 1977, and had identified Tween from photographs, was taken by police to the Sydney Central Court of Petty Sessions.

That day, Tween and Ray Johnson were before the court on the charges relating to their arrest near Lismore the year before. They'd been charged with conspiracy to rob a hotel and with possessing guns and explosives. Once again, police were hoping for a more positive identification.

The running sheet records that Gavin 'was unable to identify either as being the persons who attacked him'. It then goes on to say: 'The offenders who attacked him have not been identified and this inquiry is to be held pending further information.'

This was despite the fact that, on 25 July, Gavin Mark had picked out a photo of Tween, something that was recorded in the police running sheets. And there's no question that he got a good look at the men, sitting down with them, drinking beer and smoking dope.

So, on the one hand, a positive ID, but on the other, trying to pick out the men as they milled about outside court, the ID was negative.

Was the young man fearful at court, knowing he might be close to his attackers, one of whom, after all, had the coldness, callousness and cruelty to phone his home on the anniversary of his rape?

And the process itself was odd. Even if Gavin had picked out Tween, a good defence lawyer would have argued in court that the identification was tainted – useless – because he had previously been shown a photo of Tween. The outcome was, for whatever reason, that Gavin's failure to identify the two men at the courthouse seemed to bring an abrupt halt to his case.

On any assessment, Neville Tween was leading a very charmed life. All the fingers were pointing at him and his associates in regard to the sexual assaults of young women and men on the Northern Beaches.

A day later, on 15 September, two more women, Beverley Gilbert and Sharon McDonald, came forward to police and gave statements. They'd been abducted and sexually assaulted in January 1978. The MO was the same – they'd been picked up on Barrenjoey Road, taken to the bush, assaulted while lying on a mattress and then offered drugs and given $10. One of the girls said she remembered bright lights and what sounded like a film camera.

Why were the attackers offering their victims money? Police believed it was a ploy used by the two men 'to stop evidence of force' being used in court should they ever be apprehended. In other words, they'd argue that by accepting money, the women were willing participants.

Then, in late September, three months after Trudie disappeared, Brian Walker, the park ranger who had alerted police to shots being fired across the valley from the St Ives Showground, contacted detectives again. He'd made a disturbing and rather macabre discovery in the bush.

He told investigators he'd been riding his motorbike along a fire trail off Mona Vale Road when he'd noticed a sports coat hanging off a branch of a tree. He'd stopped to have a closer look.

As he walked into the bush he started to get a chill up his spine – in front of him was a large hole. At about 6 feet (183cm) long, 2 feet (61cm) wide and 3 feet (91cm) deep, it was just the right size for a grave. And near the hole was a long-handled shovel, a crow bar and a green plastic sheet.

The houndstooth sports coat hanging on the branch was charcoal, grey and black. The hole was meticulously dug with Brian Walker noting the corners had been neatly cleaned out. He thought whoever had been digging the grave had heard him coming on his trail bike and run off into the thick bush. He felt the owner of the jacket was not very far away at all, and watching.

He was a fair way into the bush. It was very quiet.

Summing up the situation, he jumped onto his bike and left the scene as fast as he could.

He didn't go to the police, not immediately. Instead, he consulted a friend and together they revisited the site the following day. The 'grave' had been filled in and covered with leaf litter and twigs so that if you didn't know it was there you wouldn't notice it.

Walker's friend had advised him to keep quiet, but after some thought he contacted the team that had been investigating Trudie's disappearance.

Detectives dug it up, helped by Walker, but there was nothing there. A few days later, detectives, accompanied by six uniformed officers, searched the area around the grave and both sides of the fire trail for a distance of over a kilometre.

The grave made the front page of the *Manly Daily*, along with a photo of one of the officers standing in it.

There are all sorts of stories about drug dealers burying their drugs, or cash, in the bush and coming back to get it. Or, in some cases, forgetting where they buried it. Tween's co-offender Garry Batt admitted he'd once buried about $3000 in the Ku-ring-gai bush but then couldn't locate it. But this was a grave. The question is, who was it for, who might still be lying there, never to be found, if Brian Walker had not scared off the person digging it, the noise of his trail bike heralding his imminent arrival at the scene?

How many other graves had been dug in Ku-ring-gai Chase National Park, by the man in the houndstooth jacket?

* * *

Judging from the running sheets, it seems that by the end of August 1978 all the Homicide detectives had returned to the CIB in the city and the full-time part of the investigation was over. The investigation into the rapes? It's difficult to say. Some of the women didn't want to go to court and the photo identifications would no doubt be challenged in court. But to say all leads were exhausted just doesn't seem right.

Intriguingly, sometime during this timeframe, around July or August, Gary Matthews received an out-of-the-blue phone call from Neville Tween's solicitor, Leon Goldberg. He was to the point – he said Tween and Ray Johnson knew they were being investigated over Trudie Adams but they had nothing to do with it. Furthermore, Goldberg said, they would not be interviewed. They had nothing to say and would be saying nothing. At that stage, the names of the two suspects had never been made public. Indeed, the information that the police had Tween and Johnson in their sights was tightly held. Their names are mentioned just once in the 700 pages of running sheets, when Gavin Mark was taken to court to try to identify them. Gary Matthews later said he believed there had been 'a leak' from within the NSW Police. Someone had tipped Tween off that he was under investigation. Matthews also thought that not all the leads in the rapes had been properly followed up because officers were diverted to other cases.

So Neville Tween and Ray Johnson knew they were suspects in Trudie's disappearance, and Tween's lawyer had called the cops to get them to back off. A disturbing turn of events, by any measure.

Given that they seemed to be aware of police suspicions, you might have expected the two crooks to lay low. But on the night of 5 October 1978, Tween and Johnson popped into the sights of police in the western Sydney suburb of St Marys.

A local resident called police to report seeing two men lurking suspiciously close to the St Marys munitions works, which produced high explosives and ammunition. Two police cars were dispatched to investigate. A police statement of facts from the time outlines what happened next.

'As the two police crews approached the vicinity, they had radio conversation, and as they neared the location (the munitions works) two motor vehicles decamped from the bush.' The police gave chase to a Ford Falcon until it hit a fence and came to a standstill. The driver then 'decamped' on foot, running through the backyards of nearby homes.

The Falcon turned out to be registered in Johnson's name. And a search of the vehicle turned up Johnson's wallet and a radio scanner, which was tuned in to listen to the police frequencies.

The other vehicle was a stolen Torana, with different number plates front and back. It sped off but hit a tree, at which point the driver 'made good his escape'.

In the vehicle, police found a .22 'Uberti' brand revolver, fully loaded, along with a portable radio scanner and two full face masks. On the ground nearby they found Tween's wallet and a brown wig.

Two days later, on 7 October, members of the public found a fully loaded .357 Magnum revolver, together with ammunition, a wig and a false beard, along the route taken by Johnson.

Deborah Clarke and Caroline Hitchens and Kate Hamilton and Jessica Winch had reported the men who had attacked them in December 1977 and in March 1978 were wearing wigs and false beards.

And Leanne Jacobs had told police that during her abduction and sexual assault in April 1978 she'd heard what sounded like 'radio voices' coming from the car. Detectives believed it was a scanner tuned in to the NSW Police's radio frequencies.

Johnson, out on bail for the 1977 Lismore offences, was arrested eight days after the car chase, on 13 October 1978. Tween proved more elusive. He was picked up a month later while driving a Ford Transit van fitted with a radio scanner of the same type found in Johnson's car, the scanners being only three serial numbers apart.

The Torana had been stolen from Muirs Motors on Parramatta Road, Ashfield on 5 June. Remarkably, both men were granted bail.

It's unclear if any of the information about what was found in or near the vehicles used by the two criminals at St Marys in October was passed on to Gary Matthews or any of the Homicide detectives working on the Trudie Adams case or the rapes.

Whether any information was passed on to officers at Mona Vale or Manly is not known. If the police involved in the St Marys chase did alert someone at CIB – which should have happened – it appears that nobody joined the dots.

In any case, by the end of 1978, things had settled down for Neville Tween. The Lismore and St Marys charges were still hanging over his head but he hadn't been approached by a single police officer in relation to Trudie Adams or the rapes. There'd been no police raid of his home in Booralie Road, Terrey Hills – a brisk 3.6-kilometre walk from where the attacks had taken place. And as far as we know, he was not put under surveillance.

* * *

Towards the end of 1978, the newspaper stories about Trudie and the sexual assaults became less frequent. They continued to appear every now and then when a tip-off, no matter how unlikely or trivial, emerged, but public interest was waning and the media responded in kind.

One lead did arise at the very end of December 1978, although it didn't make the papers. A couple of young men had been boasting to their mates about killing Trudie Adams. They were saying they'd picked her up and tried to have sex with her but that she'd jumped out of their car and been killed accidentally. They also said they'd buried her somewhere around Palm Beach.

The two men were part of a group that used to gather casually at the Roselands Shopping Centre in Sydney's south-west. They'd told the story numerous times to different people within their circle, some of whom had repeated it to their friends and partners. One version of the story involved them being outside the surf club and watching Trudie and Steve Norris having an argument. In this version they said they'd seen Trudie hit her boyfriend with her purse in the car park. Shortly after, they'd picked her up.

But Trudie, as the undated wireless message had earlier confirmed, wasn't carrying a purse that night. To Detective Gary Matthews this was crucial.

Nevertheless, inquiries continued sporadically into 1979 but Matthews dismissed the stories as young men big-noting, relying in particular on the fact that Trudie wasn't carrying a purse.

Some facts did later emerge in relation to the Roselands group, which left seasoned investigators deeply troubled and suspicious. One of the young men in the group owned a Falcon panel van and used it to visit his girlfriend on the Northern Beaches. Another young man owned, of all vehicles, a green kombi – the same type of vehicle originally identified in Wireless Message 31 as the one Trudie was last seen getting into.

***

In May 1979, a newspaper article in *The Sunday Telegraph* headed 'Drug ring killed my girl to silence her – mother' saw Connie going public with her theory that Trudie had somehow got caught up in the drug trade:

> The police have known about the drug involvement in Trudie's case for months but they've done nothing about it … There is big money involved and I'm sure Trudie was killed because she refused to act as a courier on a drug run for the syndicate … I also think she told them she was going to tell everything she knew.

Reading that story now, more than 40 years later, Connie's anguish and desperate desire for an answer is heartbreakingly apparent. In it she reveals that she's bought a new Labrador pup 'to replace Trudie's old German Shepherd, Lucky, who died at Christmas'. The final sentence in the story quotes Connie as saying, 'Old Lucky just kept walking the streets looking for Trudie until her heart gave out.'

The following day there was a one-paragraph story in *The Sun*, saying, 'Sydney Homicide Squad detectives say there is no evidence to support a Sunday newspaper report which suggested missing teenager Trudie Adams was the victim of a drug smuggling ring.'

It was around this time that Trudie's friends, family and the wider community must have started to question whether they would get any answers at all. Leads were drying up, and police were failing to uncover any new evidence. Would the people who loved Trudie ever find out where she was and what had happened?

As well as Trudie's disappearance fading from the public gaze by the late 1970s and early 1980s, the multiple rapes of the young women received even less attention. It was almost as though they were a stain on the golden sands of the Northern Beaches. Best forgotten, swept away by the tide.

It's not clear what police did about the rapes, if anything. There was no breakthrough, nothing to report.

PART TWO

Chapter 14

A Life of Crime

Neville Brian Tween had been in the frame almost from the beginning of the police investigation. But Tween was nothing if not elusive – he was also a man of many names.

He'd been born Neville Brian Tiffen, the name by which the NSW Police officer Brian McVicar had known him at school. Then, over the years, he'd used the aliases Neville Brian Burn, Neville Brian Fraser, Neville Brian Tween, John Andrews, Dale Evans, Neville Brian Anderson and then, finally, John David Anderson.

And just as he'd changed his name, he'd also falsified his age on 'official' documentation, in order to confuse the authorities.

Tiffen had been born in Western Australia on 29 June 1940. But he also claimed at various times to have been born on 29 June 1941 and 29 June 1936.

He began life in Perth but grew up in the rough and tumble goldmining town of Kalgoorlie. His family were dirt-poor, and he had two older half-siblings. Tiffen was his stepfather's surname.

At the age of nine, he first came to the notice of the police in Kalgoorlie when he appeared in the local Children's Court charged with break, enter and steal and attempted stealing. He was cautioned, ordered to pay restitution of 21 shillings and sixpence and placed on probation.

This was to be the start of a long criminal career that would span almost six decades – eleven prime ministers from Ben Chifley to John Howard. By the end, there would be close to 100 criminal charges – from stealing to break and enter, possession of firearms, possession of explosives, safebreaking, robbery, attempted bribe, drugs, assaulting police, sexual assault, fraud and escaping from prison. Not many crims have that sort of pedigree, if you can call it that.

Although he beat some of the charges against him, he spent time in jails in New South Wales, South Australia, Victoria and New Zealand.

By the time he was 13 he'd moved to Leeton, in south-western New South Wales, where he went to St Joseph's and played in the school's Aussie Rules team. Although he wasn't a big bloke, by all accounts he was pretty nippy around the packs.

But even way back then there were whispers in the playground. Neville Tiffen always seemed to have lots of lollies and some of his old school mates remember him throwing handfuls into the air. They wondered where he got the money to buy them.

He left St Joseph's as abruptly as he'd arrived, and in 1954 he appeared in Leeton Court of Petty Sessions for break, enter and steal. Early the following year, he appeared in Hay Children's Court, once again for break and enter and in April 1956, he was back in the Leeton Children's Court charged with stealing, assaulting police, resisting arrest and goods in custody. After that the patience of the courts ran out for young Neville and, in 1956, he was sent to Mount Penang Training School for Boys near Gosford on the NSW Central Coast.

As we now know, many boys' homes back then were brutal institutions. And according to those who remember Mount Penang, there wasn't much 'training' unless that included beatings and buggery.

One former resident of Mount Penang, Mark Merriman, recalled the horrors of the place with clarity. He described being 'beaten like a rabid dog' and 'kicked, punched, knocked out'. He was taunted for being Aboriginal, endured regular beatings and was forced to perform physically demanding menial tasks. And that was in the 1970s, long after Tween had passed through.

Merriman calls Mount Penang 'the monster factory, because that's all they turn you into, is a monster … You've got no other way. If you're going to be treated like an animal, how are you going to come out?'

When Neville Tween did come out, his criminal record speaks for itself. Back on the streets, he appeared in court in Leeton in April 1957. Three months later he was hauled before the Bendigo Court of Petty Sessions in Victoria; ten months after that, in May 1958, he appeared before Deniliquin Court for break, enter and steal. He was 17.

By July 1959, he'd made his way to Perth, where he was charged with stealing and receiving. A few months later, he was back in Sydney; a newspaper report dated 24 November 1959 detailed how he had stolen a safe and a total of £511 from two butcher shops, as well as another £771 from a bowling club.

Detectives told the court he had taken some 'essence of aniseed' to one of the robberies in case of dogs. Just a few drops would keep the dogs quiet, the court heard. It appears that the robberies resulted in Tween's first serious jail term, about three years. He was 19.

Tween's criminal history is remarkable, with an arrest record running to 20 foolscap pages. It's instructive to look at his progress through the system – his dealings with police, the courts, lawyers, prisons. His CV, if you like.

After the relatively minor crimes of his youth, Tween started to get serious.

Hundreds of pages of documents from the 1960s, 1970s, 1980s, 1990s through the early 2000s record his interactions with police, his court appearances, legal representation and prison records in New South Wales, Victoria, South Australia and New Zealand. There are also numerous confidential police intelligence reports about him that reveal a resourceful, innovative, vicious and cunning criminal.

Yet it seems – whether by luck, experience or bribery – he beat more charges and spent less time in jail than he should have, at least until the very end of his life.

From early on Tween became well versed in police methodology, engaging in counter surveillance using scanners and other methods. He kept a solicitor virtually on tap and he moved with the times. When stealing, safebreaking and robbery became harder due to better security, he increased his drug dealing and made a lot of money. And, unlike some crims who spend what they steal, Tween invested his cash in property, and shares in mining companies like BHP and Poseidon. One lawyer who knew him said he had a corrupt stockbroker on side.

At some stage in the early 1960s, Tween moved to New Zealand – perhaps because he was getting too well known to law enforcement in Australia. In 1963, he was jailed in New Zealand for five years for burglary. At the time, he gave his occupation as 'hairdresser'. Records show that in April 1964 he and Len Evans were both in Mount Eden prison. They were then both transferred to Christchurch prison for 12 months.

As a rule, Evans didn't much like his fellow inmates, judging from a letter written by New Zealand prison authorities that described him as 'an intractable and very difficult inmate – quarrelsome with other inmates, defiant and uncooperative with staff'.

At one stage, Evans was sent to a psychiatric hospital. For some reason, the cantankerous Kiwi took a shine to 24-year-old Neville, who was two years his junior, and he became Tween's first major partner in crime.

But Tween was not one to be pinned down. He escaped from Christchurch prison on 2 June 1964. Possibly thinking his old stamping grounds in New South Wales might be a bit too hot, he settled in Melbourne, ostensibly getting a job at the Holden factory in Dandenong under the name of Dale Evans.

But doing real work in a car factory wasn't for him. In November 1964 – while still on the run from New Zealand authorities – he was arrested by Victoria Police and charged with possession of explosives and fuses.

When they searched his house they turned up pamphlets dealing with oxyacetylene welding and cutting, plus a photograph of a Chubb safe. In his coat pocket were ten consecutively numbered ten-shilling notes, and under the carpet, four partly burnt ten-shilling notes.

There was a list of grocery shops, some of which had been robbed, and in his car they found a sawn-off .22 rifle with seven rounds in the magazine and one in the chamber, ready to go. A number of his moneyboxes contained 970 threepences and 500 sixpences.

Tween told the court he'd been saving the coins for years and had left all the money behind while he went to New Zealand.

He represented himself at trial, but lost and was sentenced to three years jail. He appealed and again represented himself before the full bench of the Victorian Court of Appeal, comprising three judges. In its 1965 judgment, the court said that at trial and during the appeal Tween 'conducted his case with considerable ability', though they described his explanation for the burnt ten-shilling notes and the huge numbers of coins as 'improbable' in a classic case of judicial understatement.

The more likely explanation was that the notes were burnt while he was using the oxy bottle for safebreaking. The hundreds of coins were more likely to be the change found in the safes of grocery stores.

After Tween's appeal was rejected in August 1965, he did his time in Victoria before being sent back to New Zealand to serve out the remainder of his sentence for burglary and escaping from custody. From there he was deported back to Sydney in late 1970.

* * *

By the time he returned to Sydney, Len Evans had also got out of jail and moved to Australia. Evans and Tween were seen together in the hotel in George Street within days of the rapes of Jane Hampshire, Jackie Billings and Sarah Sharpe in early March 1971. Soon after that, Tween failed to turn up to court in Sydney on two charges of goods in custody and attempting to bribe police. He bolted to Adelaide – almost as if he was spooked by something. Is it possible that he was tipped off that one of the rape victims had a relative in the NSW Police?

After a series of safe robberies in and around Adelaide, he was arrested on 16 September 1971.

An undated and unusual confidential South Australian police report gives a unique insight into Tween's relatively sophisticated offending, the amounts of cash he was stealing and also his standing in the criminal milieu – inside and outside of jail.

The document is headed 'Profile – Breaking Offences', and is essentially a detailed history of his modus operandi and his influence on other wannabe 'tank men'.

It reveals how Tween rented a flat in Adelaide under the name John Anderson and bought two cars – one in the name of Anderson, the second in another alias. Meanwhile, he rented a lock-up garage at the rear of a home occupied by an elderly couple.

On his arrest, the document described the garage as containing 'the greatest collection of breaking implements ever assembled in Australia', including 'thermic lances, oxy gear, TNT blocks of explosives, gelignite, fuses, detonators, electric detonators, a machine gun, pistols, rifles, safes, burnt money, PMG [Postmaster-General, later split up into Telstra and Australia Post] working overalls, ladders, gas lights, drills, ropes, balloons with bell wire attached'.

The machine gun was identified as having been stolen from the Merrylands Army Depot in Sydney. Tween used both the bell wire and balloons and the thermic lances for safebreaking. He was reported to have also been in possession of water pistols containing ammonia (used for squirting in the faces of guard dogs and police) and 'every other imaginable tool associated with breaking implements'.

Then there was Tween's safety deposit box, which contained 'money, passport, bank books, miner's rights, false driving licence, false car registration papers, licence to navigate a vessel, marijuana and seven envelopes containing master keys to the following [seven] hotels …'

It then states how Tween and his associates would meet in the rented lock-up garage, change clothes, select their breaking implements, and prepare to rob major hotels, gaining entry using a master key and either blowing open the safe or carrying it away.

Tween would obtain the master key for the hotels, or get one cut by previously booking in to and staying at the hotel he intended to rob, or by bribing an employee.

Police estimated that Tween's 1971 South Australian spree had netted him $100,000 in cash, which he invested in 'various businesses including dance studios, delicatessens, other businesses on a commission basis'. He also used considerable amounts of the money to buy shares in the mining companies BHP, Peko Wallsend and Poseidon.

Tween was sentenced to three years in jail.

Meanwhile, Len Evans had followed his old mate to South Australia and the same document says that while Tween was in jail, Evans was arrested in Adelaide after 'a lengthy hostage taking, shooting at police episode when another machine gun was confiscated'.

Evans was also convicted. Once again they were banged up together, two peas in a pod. By this time Tween had become friendly with other prisoners and conducted 'schools' within Yatala Labour Prison, where he taught other inmates 'how to cut and open safes by use of oxy or explosives'.

One of the prisoners Tween got to know was Bruce Douglas Sandery, who, upon his release, went to New South

Wales and brought back guns and explosives for Tween. Sandery went on to become a major heroin dealer before being murdered in 1988, his body found in sand hills near Sydney airport. His killing remains unsolved. Other inmates went on to commit safebreaking offences in Victoria and South Australia.

While in prison, Tween also made a life-changing decision to marry his parole officer, Dulcie Wegener, which police believed was 'a marriage of convenience for the purpose of influencing the Parole Board and to have "someone on the outside" to run errands for him'.

The relationship turned out to be a bit more than that.

Having served his sentence in Adelaide, Tween was extradited back to New South Wales on 1 October 1974 to face charges relating to stealing the machine guns from the Merrylands Army Depot. Remarkably, given his record, he was released on bail the following day.

He promptly returned to Adelaide and visited Len Evans in Yatala Labour Prison.

The document states that Tween apparently 'collected a large amount of money from South Australia and obtained from Evans the location of the other machine guns'.

As for his investments in various businesses, not all of them went as planned.

He had loaned a large amount of money to the owner of an Adelaide dance studio but Tween lost his copy of the contract. The studio owner refused to repay the loan.

On 8 October 1974, the dance studio burnt down. A petrol can was found in the office. Perhaps unnecessarily, the document states: 'Arson was suspected.'

So it appears that Tween had left jail in Adelaide on 1 October, been bailed in Sydney on 2 October, gone back to Adelaide to visit Evans, collected his hidden loot and weapons and – without much doubt – burnt down the dance studio on 8 October.

Busy week.

And, mixed into all of this, was the Merrylands Army Depot break-in, which had happened years before but which, only now, was coming to its legal conclusion.

After being found guilty of stealing the machine guns from the depot in Sydney, Tween's conviction was quashed on appeal on the basis that the trial judge had misdirected the jury.

The police intelligence document states that with plenty of cash left from his Adelaide robberies, 'Tween paid approximately $35,000 for a home in Sydney'.

The median house price in Sydney was about $32,000. This was in the days when you could still pay in cash, no questions asked, particularly if you had a friendly bank manager willing to accept a small 'commission'. Tween, by now known widely as John Anderson, probably also paid cash for the grey-coloured 1972 Holden panel van, HCA-634, he bought on 16 December 1974 and registered in the names of John and Dulcie Anderson.

As 1975 began, Tween had a new wife, a new house, a new car. A new start? Unlikely.

Chapter 15

Lawyers, Guns and Oxy Bottles

Being under suspicion for a crime didn't bother Neville Tween, or stop him from committing another one. There was robbery, safebreaking, money laundering – the list goes on – and, of course, drugs. Marijuana and heroin in the earlier years, ecstasy and cocaine later on, as demand dictated. It was an extraordinary range of crimes for one man. Confidence, bravado, call it what you will.

But then again, he'd been at it since the age of nine. It was his occupation.

On his return to New South Wales, Tween wasn't out of trouble for long. On 11 July 1975, he and Garry Batt sexually assaulted Jimmy Holten in Ku-ring-gai Chase National Park, firing machine gun bullets around his feet while telling him to dig his own grave.

A week later, when Holten was arrested on minor matters, he informed police he could give them some bigger fish to fry.

The next day, police put Tween and Batt under surveillance. They were driving around to various North Shore second-hand car yards in a Holden panel van, HCA-634, which was 'officially' registered as a 1962 model – not the 1972 model Tween had bought on his return from Adelaide.

No doubt they were looking for a new vehicle to replace the one in which Batt had picked up Jimmy Holten. That was cut short by the NSW Breaking Squad bursting into Tween's Terrey Hills house.

Tween and Batt, who'd first met at Mount Penang in 1956, received an extraordinarily lenient six-month sentence for their sexual assault of the 19-year-old, partly because Holten was terrified of Tween and didn't want to go to court.

When Neville Tween emerged from jail around 1976, nothing changed.

Except it appears the NSW Police had decided he'd been getting away with a bit too much and was out of line. As well as the machine gun charge, there'd been the assault on Holten and the safebreaking. The police determined it was time Tween was taken off the streets for robberies they believed Tween and Ray Johnson were carrying out in Sydney and around New South Wales.

It took a while, but around September 1977, no less than six detectives from the Sydney CIB were assigned to investigate a series of robberies. One of them received a tip that Tween and Johnson had left Sydney, and were armed and heading up the north coast.

The detectives followed their movements for some days, but lost them. Then, on 4 October 1977, a detective saw Tween and Ray Johnson go into the Cecil Hotel in Casino, on the NSW north coast. The two men stayed inside for a while before leaving and heading for Lismore, with Tween driving.

Unbeknown to them, police in a number of vehicles were following, while others up ahead were setting up a roadblock. They were stopped, handcuffed and taken to Lismore Police Station. A search of the Holden panel van Tween had been driving revealed firearms, explosives, electric detonators, wire, an oxy bottle, hoses and two walkie-talkies hidden in panels in the back. Interestingly, the Holden panel van had the same number plates – HCA-634 – but was once again recorded as being a 1962 model.

Police put Tween and Johnson in separate rooms for questioning.

When they asked Tween why he had the firearms, he replied, 'I've got enemies, I have to protect myself.' Asked why he had the oxy bottle and cutting equipment, he allegedly said: 'If I think of a good excuse you'll be the first to know.'

The police then spoke to Ray Johnson, who reportedly said, 'You blokes are too good for me. I didn't think that anyone could find that gear behind the panels.' He went on: 'I'll tell you what I can, provided there's no records of interview. Neville told me he'd kill me if I made one.'

Johnson – not normally talkative in the presence of police – went on to say that one of the .22 pistols was his and the other belonged to Tween and that they'd both secreted the explosives and other gear in the panel van.

Both men were charged with possession of the guns, explosives and breaking implements.

The next day, police spoke to Johnson again, who allegedly admitted he and Tween had been 'casing' the Cecil Hotel in Casino to break in and do the safe, with their oxy gear. When police told him he would also be charged with conspiracy to break in to the Hotel, Johnson said, 'Don't tell Neville I told you; he'll shoot me.'

According to the arresting detectives, when they told Tween what Johnson had said, he replied, 'That weak bastard. Alright, we were going to do it, but we didn't. If he [Johnson] keeps his mouth shut we deal with everything at the lower court.'

As to what Johnson had allegedly said about the plan to rob the Cecil Hotel, Tween said, 'That weak little bastard has already told you; there's no need for me to say another word.'

Taken before a magistrate, Tween and Johnson flatly denied making any admissions at all and said they'd been 'verballed'.

During the subsequent court case, Tween's lawyer, Leon Goldberg, reiterated that Tween and Johnson had been verballed – that far from saying things like 'you blokes are too good for me' the detectives had simply fabricated the confessions.

At the time, police 'verbals' were increasingly under scrutiny, with some officers both planting evidence and fabricating confessions, although it took a long time for many judges to accept that sworn police officers could possibly do such a thing. It was sometimes called 'noble-cause corruption'.

In other words, police broke the rules, and the law, to put dangerous criminals they believed had been committing crimes – but against whom they didn't have quite enough evidence – behind bars.

In the 1970s, there were no telephone intercepts (not legal ones, anyway), no listening devices, and little to no CCTV. There were no tracking devices, no mobile phones or red-light cameras, no computers of any great use to law enforcement. The police officers who charged Tween and Johnson had little doubt the career criminals had in recent times been committing armed robberies and had access to weapons such as machine guns. There was a high chance an innocent bystander might be killed.

Given the vehement denials relating to the 'confessions', NSW Police sought the advice of Jim Semmler, who was a lawyer in the office of the Solicitor for Public Prosecutions.

'The file at first glance appears massive,' Semmler wrote. 'However, a lot of Mr Goldberg is on file.'

The ubiquitous Mr Goldberg was something of a legal legend around Sydney's criminal courts. Never mind the fact that he sometimes slept in his own car, he was the go-to man for serious villains.

He made it crystal clear that 'no admissions had been made and that immediately after the alleged admissions, both [Tween and Johnson] made a statement to the Magistrate that they had not made any admissions'. Goldberg also said the equipment found in the car Tween and Johnson were using was not even good enough to blow the safe at the Cecil Hotel.

In his report to police, Mr Semmler said that in light of the matters raised by the defence, it seemed to him that the Crown case on the conspiracy charge was extremely weak. He also noted there was a significant disagreement among detectives involved in the case, with two officers having told him they were 'not satisfied with the investigations carried out by other police' regarding alibi evidence presented on behalf of Tween and Johnson.

The alibi evidence Goldberg had supplied was that the two accused had been on their way north to work on a salvage job on a ship called the *Cherry Venture* and they'd intended to use the equipment found in the car on the ship's propeller.

It was an unlikely tale, although both men had a long-standing interest in boats. Indeed, Ray Johnson eventually came to be known by some as 'Captain Pugwash', after a cartoon character of the era, although there wasn't much funny about Johnson.

Once again, remarkably, both men were released on bail.

Numerous court appearances and adjournments regarding the case followed, though so slowly that Tween and Johnson remained at large during 1977 and 1978 – the years when the majority of the abductions and rapes on the Northern Beaches were committed.

In fact, there was a pattern to the rapes that matched Tween's time behind bars.

In 1971, there'd been three sexual assaults – Jane Hampshire and Jackie Billings and Sarah Sharpe – but the attacks stopped after Tween moved to South Australia and was jailed. However, after his release and return to Sydney in late 1974, Jimmy Holten was attacked on 11 July 1975. After Tween was put away for that matter the abductions ceased.

Tween was released in 1976 and the team investigating Trudie Adams' disappearance knew the Northern Beaches abductions and rapes had started again at least as early as 19 November 1977, and had continued until at least 29 April 1978. They'd stopped after Trudie's disappearance, at which point Tween moved from Terrey Hills to the NSW Central Coast.

Then there were the possible co-offenders. Right from the beginning of his criminal carreer, Tween had preferred to work with a partner, another man.

There was his old mate from Mount Penang, Garry Batt, nicknamed Dinga or Ding-batt. They'd been inmates together in the mid-1950s when Batt was just a skinny kid with bright blue eyes and hair that stuck straight up on his head.

Tween had a nickname back then, too – Tubby.

They'd run around together for years, graduating from minor misdemeanours to more serious stuff, like safes and drugs.

Police knew Garry Batt was involved in the 1975 attack on Jimmy Holten because he'd pleaded guilty. However, it was unlikely he'd been involved in the abductions and rapes in 1977 and 1978 because, after doing time with Tween, Batt had decided his friend was 'as mad as a meat axe'. In fact, he'd disappeared to such an extent off the law enforcement radar that many police believed he'd been murdered. Most likely by Tween.

Other associates included Len Evans, who was a suspect in the 1971 abductions and rapes. Like Tween, he was a violent and erratic criminal and they'd been working in cahoots with each other in South Australia. Thanks to Andrew Kingston's 7 July 1978 police statement, in which he detailed what Evans had told him about Tween's and Evans' sexual activities on the Northern Beaches, investigators had known about their possible involvement in the abductions and rapes within days of Trudie's disappearance.

And then there was Ray Johnson, Tween's other significant partner in crime from the 1970s to the early '90s. Garry Batt says that back in the day he knew Johnson by the nickname 'rugged', or 'rug' for short. With a crop of curly hair and a scar on the left side of his forehead, Johnson was a well-known and violent Sydney criminal in his own right, who'd been found guilty of safecracking and numerous other offences.

There was no shortage of leads. And if police suspicions were right, Tween and Evans had probably committed the attacks together in 1971, while Tween and Johnson were most likely responsible for the attacks in 1977 and 1978.

As police records reveal, Tween had been under police surveillance in those same years – late 1977 and 1978 – the very time the rapes were taking place.

But the surveillance was the result of his arrest in Lismore, with police trying to shore up a conviction on the conspiracy, explosives and firearms offences. On 28 December 1977, covert surveillance officers saw Tween outside his house at Booralie Road, Terrey Hills. They also saw a grey Holden panel van, HCA-634. Just two days later, Deborah Clarke and Caroline Hitchens were abducted and raped.

On 10 January 1978, surveillance police saw Tween driving a grey Holden panel van. Despite official records listing it as a 1966 model, it was almost certainly the same car as before.

Then, later that month, Beverley Gilbert and Sharon McDonald had been abducted and sexually assaulted.

Police surveillance of Tween continued. On 1 April 1978 he was observed driving a grey Holden panel van HCA-634 in Southern Cross Drive, Zetland. This time it was listed on official records as a 1972 model.

On 18 April that year, police again saw Tween driving the same vehicle with the same number plates, though official records were showing it as a 1965 model. Just three days later, two men picked up Lucy Russell in an old blue Volkswagen and sexually assaulted her in bushland.

On 24 May 1978, just a month after the abduction of Lucy Russell, police surveillance had recorded the presence of a blue 1960 Volkswagen in the driveway of Tween's Booralie Road home.

Of course, at this stage, police had no inkling Tween might have been involved in multiple rapes – that only became apparent after Trudie's disappearance in late June.

Physical surveillance is a difficult, time-consuming and incredibly expensive undertaking because it involves multiple undercover cops, multiple vehicles and huge amounts of overtime.

Unlike the movies, rarely does it happen 24/7, seven days a week for an extended period.

Nevertheless, it appears that NSW Police were very keen to nail Tween over a conspiracy to rob a hotel and possession of firearms and explosives, which is all well and good.

The question is: What surveillance of Tween was carried out in the second half of 1978, after Trudie Adams disappeared and Homicide was called in to link up with detectives on the Northern Beaches? Were surveillance officers brought into play after it became evident Tween, Len Evans and Ray Johnson might be responsible for multiple rapes and murder?

It appears not. If they were, no record of it has ever been made public.

Chapter 16

Tony Yelavich Disappears

It seems that many of the charges flowing from the arrest of Neville Tween in 1977 and 1978, including conspiracy to break and enter and possessing firearms, explosives and wigs, were not finalised in the courts until 1981. While he was eventually convicted in the 1977 and 1978 matters, in both cases some charges, including conspiracy and 'possessing means of disguising face', were dropped. In fact, throughout his long criminal record there are several notations against a number of charges saying: 'The Attorney-General has decided not to prosecute.'

Tween successfully appealed his sentences and non-parole periods. In the end, it appears he was jailed in March 1981 and served a total of about three years.

In typical fashion, on his release, he went straight back into business, this time selling drugs on the NSW Central Coast, among other places.

Tween was on NSW Police records in the late 1970s as selling heroin, perhaps sourcing it from the notorious Mr Asia drug syndicate. Another more likely source of supply was the much-feared New Zealand criminal Godfrey Jonassen Sadaraka, known in Australia as John Sadler. In jail for murder and described by police as 'a psychopath', Sadler ran his Sydney heroin business from inside Parklea Prison in the 1980s, and was known by inmates as 'The General'. According to those who knew him, he made a fortune, with close associates distributing the drugs on the outside.

It appears Tween was one of them.

Tween was still married to Dulcie, the parole officer he'd met while in jail in South Australia. The union had been judged a 'marriage of convenience' by the South Australian authorities. By now, Tween and Dulcie had two children together. But, by Dulcie's own admission, it wasn't a conventional marriage. She told police her husband came and went as he pleased, and a lot of the time she had no idea where he was, what he was up to or who he was with.

It's not clear when they finally parted, but in around 1984 he moved to Toowoon Bay, near The Entrance on the NSW Central Coast with his new partner, Susan, whom he'd met on 14 February 1978 – Valentine's Day. She was 19 years old and had a two-year-old daughter, Kylie. Neville Tween was almost 38.

Not that long out of jail, it appears he wasn't flush with cash although he owned a little two-bedroom beachfront shack – the first of a number of property investments he would make over the coming years in the area. One of Tween's associates in the heroin business was a young man, Ante Yelavich. Better known as Tony, he was 17 years younger than Tween. Exactly when, or where, they met is not known.

Tony Yelavich was not your typical heroin dealer. Or at least, he shouldn't have been. Described as 'bright, charismatic and attractive', he'd grown up in Manly, where he surfed and played rugby league at school. As a court later heard, he 'had a happy family life and he was the apple of his father's eye. He took care of his appearance, perhaps before it was common or fashionable for the average Aussie male.'

'Women were drawn by his looks and by his charm. He was sociable, charming and personable, he had the gift of the gab.'

Sadly, Yelavich had started using drugs, including heroin, in about 1975, when he was 17 or 18 years old. One thing led to another and he became a dealer and then an importer, bringing in, from Thailand and Bali, Buddha sticks and heroin that he secreted inside surfboards.

Yelavich had first been arrested in Perth and was in and out of custody during the 1970s before being charged in 1981 with more serious heroin offences.

Skipping bail, he'd moved to Queensland. There he took to carrying a pistol and continued in the drug trade. Judging from official records, business must have been brisk.

But whereas in the beginning he'd been cautious – he was never charged over the importations – he was now becoming careless, flashy. He acquired a luxury Gold Coast apartment, and bright red Porsche for which he paid cash. He started dating a young, good-looking blond woman called Andrea Wharton, who also used heroin.

The law, in the form of the Australian Federal Police, caught up with Tony Yelavich and, in March 1983, he was jailed in Sydney for just over two years.

Being banged up in jail presented some difficulties for his business and for Andrea's heroin habit, but they were not insurmountable.

One of his associates in jail, according to NSW Police documents, was none other than James Edward 'Jockey'

Smith, who had initially been convicted of the 1977 murder of Sydney bookmaker Lloyd Tidmarsh.

And Jockey Smith, in turn, knew Neville Tween. It had been Tween who in 1978 had dropped by the office of Jockey's barrister, Peter Livesey, with $500 in cash to help with legal expenses. Smith's conviction for the Tidmarsh murder was later quashed by the NSW Court of Appeal, but by the 1980s, he was still inside for the attempted murder of a police officer.

Yelavich made arrangements to keep his customers satisfied.

One of them was a young woman from the Northern Beaches whom we'll call Suzanne. She'd started using heroin in 1982, when she was 17.

From jail, Yelavich arranged for Suzanne to meet up with Neville Tween and Ray Johnson.

It would prove to be a long-term relationship in more ways than one. As Suzanne would later reveal: 'Both these men supplied me with heroin and I used some and sold some. At this stage, I also began to sleep with Neville for drugs and money.' This arrangement had lasted for about five years.

'A short time after this I also began to sleep with Ray for drugs and money. This arrangement lasted on and off again for about 12 years.

She said: 'Neville was either living on the Central Coast or at least up there a lot. He also spent a lot of time in Sydney in Terrey Hills. Ray was living on the Central Coast.'

Revealingly, she said that both men 'asked me repeatedly to set them up with young girls for them to have sex with for money or drugs'.

Suzanne obliged, introducing a 17-year-old girl, Sandra, to Johnson, who was then approaching the age of 40.

Another young girl, a 20-year-old, whom we'll call Joyce, was introduced to Neville 'in exchange for drugs and money'.

The trail of destruction that followed Tween and his associates continued. Sandra died of an overdose and Suzanne herself went to jail for six months, spending her 20th birthday behind bars in Bathurst Prison.

While she was there she had a visit from Tween who brought along Joyce and some heroin. As Suzanne recounted: '[O]n this visit, I received about 1 or 1.5 grams of heroin. I don't remember who exactly gave it to me, or much else of this incident.'

The heroin delivery was hardly a surprise – Suzanne had received a letter from Tween making a reference to 'giving her a magazine'. Suzanne said this was code for heroin. Then, as now, getting drugs into prison was not all that difficult.

After her release, Suzanne continued to see both Tween and Johnson for sex, drugs and money, although Tween 'eventually faded out of the picture'.

So began a chain of events that would once again bring Neville Tween to the attention of the NSW Police. Because, in February 1984, while Tony Yelavich was still in custody, his girlfriend, Andrea Wharton, disappeared. Her car was found at Coolangatta airport.

Yelavich had tried to keep her supplied with heroin, obtaining it from the New Zealander John Sadler, or perhaps even from Tween, but evidently something had gone terribly wrong.

As a court later heard: 'It was rumoured that Andrea had been killed after she lost or used or sold a large amount of drugs in her possession which belonged to a major crime figure.'

Curiously, her mother later received a letter allegedly from Andrea saying she planned to stay away for a month. The letter was postmarked Darlinghurst.

As with Trudie, Andrea's body has never been found and no one has ever been charged with her murder.

There was no suggestion Tony Yelavich was involved in Andrea's death – he was devastated when he heard the news that she had disappeared, but there was little he could do.

***

Tween's dealings with Yelavich did not go unnoticed. Once again, and now going by the name of John Anderson, he was on the radar of the NSW Police. According to a confidential law enforcement document, Tween was a target of the NSW Drug Squad, which was looking into the distribution of heroin on the NSW Central Coast.

But Tween was never charged with any offences. According to the confidential report, the investigation failed due to Tween's 'awareness of law enforcement scrutiny … and the use of anti-surveillance tactics'.

Think about that: 'awareness of law enforcement scrutiny'.

Years later, a NSW detective, Jayson Macleod, was investigating Tween and spoke to a surveillance officer from the 1980s. 'He told me straight up their jobs were regularly compromised,' Macleod said. 'An occasion he specifically referred to was where they were lying in wait outside … a premises where Neville was residing. They were there during the night-time and Neville walked out the front of the premises [in the morning] and looked down the street and gave the surveillance operatives a wave. He knew they were there. Inside information [was] getting back to him, absolutely.'

Tipped off about Trudie. Tipped off about the surveillance. And according to one former law enforcement officer, Tween himself had spoken about something he had called 'The Union' – a small clique of corrupt NSW Police he turned to in troubled times.

Of course, Tween didn't limit himself to the Central Coast or heroin. Another police document details how Tween and Tony Yelavich popped up in information supplied to police in 1985, which related to drug dealing 'in various areas around Sydney', including a licensed club in Punchbowl and a hotel in Milperra, west of the Sydney CBD.

Other individuals named in the same report included well-known Sydney criminals Robert Arthur Chapman, Arthur Joseph Loveday and Peter Fulcher, a member of the Mr Asia drug syndicate, which became the subject of a Royal Commission of inquiry that started in 1981.

Peter Fulcher was a Kiwi. He went to jail for conspiring to import heroin but, according to the Royal Commission, was also involved in forgery and armed hold-ups. Intriguingly, page 74 of the commission's 900-page public report lists one of Fulcher's aliases as Peter John Anderson.

Terry Clark, the murderous head of the Mr Asia syndicate, had lived in Manly in the late 1970s before moving to McCarrs Creek Road, Church Point, just around the corner from Neville Tween, and the same McCarrs Creek Road that had popped up from time to time in the police running sheets for the Trudie Adams investigation.

Clark, the Royal Commission later found, murdered three of his own drug couriers or syndicate members and arranged for the murder of at least two others. When he was told, allegedly by a corrupt Narcotics Bureau officer, that one of his drug couriers had been blabbing to the cops, he took the courier into the bush off Mona Vale Road and bashed him.

Another syndicate member, Gregory Paul Ollard, turned up dead in Ku-ring-gai Chase National Park. Shot by Terry Clark in September 1977, Ollard's remains were discovered in the park in 1982 as a result of the Royal Commission's inquiries.

Clearly, Tween was mixing in some very heavy-duty criminal circles. Whether he and Terry Clark ever met, or whether Tween sold Clark's heroin, is unknown. Maybe they just passed each other, like ships in the night, while buying bread and milk at the Terrey Hills shops.

* * *

Tony Yelavich was released from prison in 1985. It didn't take him long to re-establish his connections with the drug trade, specifically Neville Tween.

On the evening of 2 September 1985, just weeks after he got out of jail, Yelavich jumped on his pushbike and left his house on Pittwater Road, Manly.

It was about 6.30pm. He told his parents he was going to a friend's house, although earlier in the day they'd heard him on the telephone arranging to meet someone outside the Manly Pacific Hotel on the beachfront.

Formerly known as the Hotel Pacific, the Manly Pacific was where Jane Hampshire had gone for a drink on 1 March 1971 before being abducted a few hundred metres away and then raped.

Yelavich never turned up at his friend's house. Indeed, 28-year-old Tony Yelavich, like his girlfriend, Andrea Wharton, and like Trudie Adams, disappeared off the face of the earth.

Like them, his body has never been found. But his pushbike was. As counsel assisting the Coroner into Tony's disappearance said: 'Strangely, Tony's bicycle did return [home]. It was quietly placed inside the front gate of his house some time that night. It was noticed there around 4.30 to 5.30 the next morning.'

So someone had taken the trouble to return the pushbike, in the same way the person who abducted Claire Jamieson in February 1978 had taken the trouble to return her address book by mail. And like how one of the men who abducted young Gavin Mark had taken the trouble to telephone his home to remind him of the anniversary of when he was raped.

At 8am on 4 September 1985, Yelavich's father, Ivan, reported his son missing at Manly Police Station. He made no bones of the fact he believed it was drug related.

The initial investigation into Yelavich's disappearance was run by Manly detectives. Almost immediately, police found three letters in the missing man's bedroom, written to him while he was in jail. The letters were from Neville Tween. One mentioned that he (Tween) was 'holding some furniture' for Yelavich, which he could claim upon his release. Police had no doubt that furniture was code for drugs.

Months later, the Homicide Squad joined the investigation. Friends and associates were interviewed. Some were more willing to talk than others.

Peter Bombala had known Yelavich since school and they'd played sport and socialised together. They'd scored drugs together, with Bombala driving Yelavich to the Central Coast to buy heroin from Tween. Around that time, Bombala had also met Ray Johnson.

Bombala told police Yelavich had talked about the meeting at the Manly Pacific and that he was going there at about 11pm to score an ounce of heroin from Neville Tween.

From the prison records, it was established that Ray Johnson had visited Tony in jail on 12 April 1985. A prison officer nominated another visitor as being Neville Tween, but no formal statement was taken from him by police investigating Tony's disappearance. Another was Leon Goldberg – who made nine legal visits.

A detective who re-investigated the Yelavich case years later stated: 'For unknown reasons the investigation stalled in 1986, even after it was clearly highlighted that Neville Tween was the principal suspect.'

Just like the investigation into the rapes seemed to stall.

And, like the investigation into Trudie Adams, the inquiry into what happened to Tony Yelavich seems to have sprung a leak.

In May 1986, Neville Tween arranged to have a meeting with a senior detective from the same squad that had had him under investigation, without success, two years earlier.

According to documents on the public record, Tween knew he was a suspect and wanted to 'explore the basis of the suspicion he was involved in Tony's death'.

He met with a detective sergeant in a car park on 30 May 1986. A second meeting took place on 3 June.

To be fair to the detective concerned, on 11 June, he made an entry in the relevant running sheets to record the meetings. He said he had never met with Tween before or since.

The incident is revealing, because a known criminal doesn't cold-call a senior detective. Tween obviously knew this man, or someone close to him, well enough to ask for assistance, and for the officer to turn up at short notice.

There must have been something in it for the detective. But what? Maybe it was a two-way street – the detective would give Tween a heads-up and Tween might give him something in return. Such as information or money.

Whatever the cops had on Tween, it didn't amount to much. There's no record of him being formally questioned. The body of Tony Yelavich has never been found.

It later emerged that some exhibits in the case couldn't be located. The letters written by Tween to Yelavich alluding to drug deals had disappeared from the files. Gone.

And the car park detective who met with Tween? By the time the coronial inquest into Yelavich's death took place that officer was, the court heard, 'himself now disgraced after being implicated in corruption and evidence fabrication'.

Chapter 17

Neville Makes a Friend

In 1989, 11 years after Trudie Adams disappeared, her mother, Connie, died at the age of 52. Just as she'd feared, and as she had told the newspapers years earlier, she never found out what happened to her daughter. According to her husband, Charles, she died from a broken heart.

Neville Tween's drug activities, meanwhile, were continuing without any interference from law enforcement.

In September 1988, information was provided to the NSW State Drug Crime Commission – the forerunner of the NSW Crime Commission – about some people taking a scuba diving course who 'did not appear to be genuine divers; however, they had been paying cash for all types of gear, including an underwater scooter, radar direction finder, hand-held sonar device and honing devices'.

The report went on to say the people doing the scuba diving lessons owned a 'Star' class cabin cruiser, which was fitted with satellite navigation equipment.

The people named in the confidential document were Neville Tween, aka John David Anderson, and his old mate

Raymond Johnson. Others were named as well and the report noted that apart from one individual 'these people do not appear to work but are referred to as entrepreneurs'.

Given Tween's lengthy criminal history and police intelligence that he was heavily involved with drugs, you'd think someone in policing circles might have decided that he needed to be thoroughly investigated.

It didn't happen.

By this time, Tween was developing a serious drug habit of his own, with cocaine his drug of choice. Nevertheless, for all intents and purposes, he moved into the 1990s as a budding property developer and a 'family man', even if his home had a lot of security other families didn't need, including roller shutters, sensor lights and alarms.

He was also forging a close relationship with a rising law enforcement officer – Mark Standen – whose behaviour would later lead to serious questions about how Tween had escaped arrest for so long.

Standen was the former junior Narcotics Bureau officer who, back in 1978, had been asked by Gary Matthews to make inquiries about Trudie and accused drug trafficker Clayton Looby. By all accounts, Standen's career should have ended around that time. In May 1979, he and two of his colleagues had found 18 silver foils of hashish during a raid on a house in Sydney's east. A few weeks later, Standen flushed the drugs down a toilet, falsified entries in the bureau's logbooks and destroyed a signed confession by the owner of the drugs.

When Standen was questioned, he claimed he and his colleagues had done this because the drugs weighed less than 500 grams so charges for drug possession couldn't be brought under federal laws.

When the Royal Commission into the Mr Asia syndicate looked at corruption within the Narcotics Bureau, the Royal Commissioner himself, Justice Donald Stewart, commented that Standen's actions were dishonest.

This hadn't stopped Standen's rise. In 1980, he joined the Australian Federal Police, despite the AFP's Commissioner, Sir Colin Woods, accepting a recommendation that Standen not be employed.

During the 1980s, some of Standen's AFP colleagues say they noticed he had become an enthusiastic gambler. One of them recalls him regularly running off from after-work drinks to place bets.

Red flags should have been raised but, somehow, Standen not only survived in the Federal Police but flourished. By the early 1990s, he had been seconded to the National Crime Authority (NCA), a powerful and secretive body set up to fight organised crime, and in particular drug trafficking. The NCA had the power to hold secret hearings, and compel witnesses to answer questions and produce documents. Within the walls of the NCA, there was no right to silence. Where necessary, the authority worked with the Federal and State Police forces.

Intelligence holdings reveal that NSW Police had been after Tween and Johnson, unsuccessfully, during the years 1984 to 1989. They also state that the career criminals were involved not just in the distribution of drugs but with the importation of heroin, cocaine, cannabis and hashish.

The up-and-coming Mark Standen, his Federal Police career on the rise, moved to The Entrance with his family in 1991 or 1992. Tween and his family lived about a kilometre away. By this time Tween was buying and developing property. In addition to his beach shack in Lakeside Terrace, he had bought, or would soon own, another four properties, three of them in Hutton Road in The Entrance about 90 minutes drive north of Sydney.

In correspondence with the authors, Standen said it was entirely coincidental that at this time he received 'an investigative referral from the then National Crime Authority that was related in part to Anderson [Tween]'.

Standen said he saw no reason not to move to the area just because Tween lived down the road.

He said that when he received the referral it was the first time he'd ever heard of Neville Tween. Shortly after, he said, he made himself known to the career criminal and formed the view he was 'a retired, old-school criminal looking for a quiet life on the coast'. According to Standen, his relationship with Tween developed from there.

How Standen could say he thought Tween was 'a retired, old-school criminal looking for a quiet life on the coast' beggars belief. Official documents clearly show that Tween and Ray Johnson were targets of the NCA in relation to drugs, money laundering and fraud between 1991 and 1996, a period during which Standen worked there. Indeed, in 1993 he became the NCA's chief investigator

Specifically, between 1991 and 1993, Tween was a person of interest in what was known as Operation Amigo, which had been set up to investigate the activities of two well-known drug traffickers by the names of Bruce Richard Cornwall and Barry Richard Bull, who were suspected of involvement in a traveller's cheque scam with a potential loss to Westpac of $32 million.

By early February 1992, the NCA believed that Tween had been cashing bond certificates to the value of $305,000. One of the transactions had been carried out on his behalf by a relative of Barry Bull.

A document relating to Operation Amigo says that Tween had come to their attention through both his bearer bond activities and 'suspected drug importations off the Western Australian coast in 1992'.

Standen must have known – or should have known – about Tween's interstate and international travels, which pointed to one thing – drug trafficking. In July 1990, Tween flew out of Australia on Singapore Airlines, returning 18 days later. In June 1991, he flew to Buenos Aires, returning about a month later. In September 1991, he once again flew to Buenos Aires, returning to Sydney some two weeks later. Then in February 1992, he flew to New Zealand for a week.

By April 1992, investigators at the NCA were aware that Tween was most likely involved in the illegal importation of narcotics through the port of Fremantle in Western Australia. It knew he had been telephoning the Mitsui OSK line, a shipping company that had three relevant ships, the *Karina Bonita*, *Joana Bonita* and the *Maria Bonita*. It was most likely he had been using the *Karina Bonita*, which sailed from Buenos Aires to Australia, stopping in Brisbane, Sydney, Melbourne and Fremantle.

He had visited Perth three times, coinciding with the *Karina Bonita* being in port, calling the shipping line as well as four dive shops in Perth suburbs.

Both the NCA and the AFP Eastern Region Drug Unit knew this, but it's unclear what happened to this intelligence or what law enforcement did about it.

Tween was strongly suspected of importing cocaine and his movements were being monitored by early 1992 but nothing happened.

The timing coincides with when Mark Standen was working in the AFP and then the NCA and when he said he first met Tween on the Central Coast.

Because of the controversial nature of the relationship between Standen and Tween, it's worth setting out in some detail. While Standen at first claimed Tween was retired, in later correspondence with the authors, that story changed.

He said that, in fact, after receiving the NCA referral around the time he moved to the Central Coast, he arranged for Tween's telephone calls to be intercepted and directed that surveillance on him be conducted. Presumably, for that to happen, he didn't regard Tween as being 'retired'.

Standen said that after 'getting a feel for the situation', he orchestrated a direct approach to Tween, driving to the Central Coast with a female AFP officer and parking about 100 metres from Tween's home. He later recalled that he had been in constant contact with the Telephone Interception Branch (TIB) in Canberra, who kept him updated on calls to and from Tween's house. Once, when the TIB confirmed to Standen that Tween was home, he said he rang the intercepted home telephone and Susan, Tween's wife, answered. When he asked for John, Susan asked who was calling and he replied that it was Mark.

'Mark who?' Susan queried, to which Standen replied, 'Just Mark.'

When Susan said that John wasn't home, Standen said, 'If I leave my number will you get him to call?'

'Okay, but I don't know when he'll be back,' she replied.

Standen claimed that law enforcement officers listening in heard Tween calling several friends to ask if any of them knew a Mark.

'TIB could tell by the background chatter that Susan and Anderson were worried because I had asked for John and not for Neville.

'A short time later [the female AFP officer] and I saw Anderson leave the house and walk to a nearby pay phone. He rang my mobile.

'The conversation was roughly as follows: Is that Mark?

'Yes, is that you John?'

Tween said: 'I'm sorry Mark, but I'm having trouble placing you, where do I know you from?'

'You don't,' Standen says he replied.

'My name is Mark Standen and I'm a detective sergeant in the Australian Federal Police.'

Tween replied: 'Oh, why are you after me? I've got nothing to say.'

When Standen responded that he needed to talk to him, Tween replied, 'About what?'

Standen says he reiterated that they needed to meet and suggested they do so at a café in the main street of The Entrance, saying he could be there in 10 minutes. Standen said that the phone call was the first time he and Tween had spoken.

Standen and his colleague then met with Tween in person.

Standen says: 'It was the first time we had ever set eyes on each other and the above phone call was the first time we had ever spoken.'

He also described Tween as very nervous and that he spoke 'circuitously and in riddles'. However, after some time, Standen said he was able to turn the conversation in the direction he was seeking.

Tween was 'exceptionally polite and respectful' to him and the other AFP officer, according to Standen.

'That demeanour never changed during the time that I knew him.'

Standen didn't say it in his letter to the authors but he was in the process of getting Tween to 'roll over' and become an informant on some of his criminal associates. Or, in the more colourful and far less flattering language of old-school crims, to become 'a fuckin' dog'. A law enforcement source who knew Standen well for many years confirmed that Standen cold-called Tween and rolled him over.

Tween would remain Standen's 'man' for almost 15 years. However, it's unclear who obtained the most benefit.

Former senior detectives have raised doubts about whether Tween should ever have been used as an informant in the first place, given he was the chief suspect in so many unsolved major crimes. There were the murders of Trudie Adams and Tony Yelavich, and the abductions and sexual assaults of at least 14 young women, not to mention the importation of cocaine by ship from South America first flagged in the early 1990s.

Standen said he was completely unaware that Tween was the chief suspect in the Trudie Adams case until September 1994, when Tween was arrested by NSW Police on the Central Coast and charged with cultivating and supplying marijuana. The cops had found a warehouse with a sophisticated hydroponic set-up containing 1200 marijuana plants, some mature, some seedlings.

When Tween appeared in Wyong Court, Standen was there. Standen said a NSW Police officer had casually mentioned in conversation that Tween was a person of interest in Trudie's disappearance.

'He put it no stronger than saying that Anderson [Tween] was known to frequent the area from which Trudie was believed to have gone missing and that he drove a white panel van.' Standen said he gave it no further thought.

The *Central Coast Express* carried a short article about the original bust on 21 September 1994. Under the heading 'Man on drugs, pistol charges', the story revealed that Tween had been charged with cultivating cannabis in West Gosford and had been arrested by local detectives on the previous Saturday. The article also said Tween had been granted conditional bail to appear before Wyong Court on 25 October.

Standen says he was 'disappointed' when Tween was arrested for growing dope and told him so. As the local paper noted, Tween got bail. Again. Remarkable for a criminal with his history, unless of course Standen put in a good word for him as one of his informants. He went to jail the following year in May 1995, serving just 18 months before being released around November 1996.

He served his sentence in the minimum security Cessnock Correctional Centre, 'minimum' being the operative word. According to one of his regular prison visitors: 'The only thing you couldn't do was leave.'

As for Tween being the chief suspect in the rapes of so many women, Standen says the first time he heard anything about this was almost two decades later, in 2011, which is simply unbelievable, on a number of fronts.

For a start, when investigators cultivate or register an informant, one of the first things they do is find out about the person's criminal history and what intelligence holdings there are about them.

The NSW Homicide Squad and detectives in the Northern Beaches area knew Tween was a suspect in the murders of Adams and Yelavich and the 14 sexual assaults on women in the Northern Beaches area.

Other NSW officers also knew of Tween's reputation. In 1993, NSW Police Detective Inspector Brian McVicar, who'd gone to school with Tween, had nominated him as a possible suspect in the serial killings of seven backpackers whose bodies had been found in the Belanglo State Forest south of Sydney. Although Ivan Milat was ultimately convicted and jailed for life for those murders, during the early days of the investigation, police officers, as a matter of course, put forward the names of a number of serious criminals with a history of violence.

In an information report to the task force, McVicar raised Tween's history as a suspect in the disappearance of Trudie Adams as well as the rapes. A detective sergeant from North Sydney provided similar information to the task force, including that Tween and Ray Johnson were suspected of raping a number of women in the 1970s.

This was at the same time Mark Standen became chief investigator for the National Crime Authority and, apparently, had Tween working for him as an informant.

As one source simply said of Standen's claim that he didn't know about the rapes until 2011: 'Mark's lying.'

Numerous people have condemned Standen's relationship with Tween as corrupt, including former NSW detective Michael Kennedy, who investigated Tween's and Johnson's involvement in drugs in the 1980s when police were having a problem with heroin in Bankstown. Kennedy, who went on to become an academic at the University of Western Sydney, described their relationship as 'unholy'.

Some senior detectives believe Standen protected Tween for years in return for information – and money. Standen denies this and says there was nothing corrupt about their relationship.

However, he did say to the authors: 'I accept that opinions will vary as to whether it was appropriate, but that will be partly due to people not knowing all the facts'. He went on to describe his dealings with Tween as 'justifiable in the unique circumstances based on what I knew at the time, the job I had to do and the proximity of our homes in a very small neighbourhood'.

Standen and Tween were certainly neighbourly. The way Standen tells it, his socialising with Tween was just 'unavoidable'.

Two of his children went to the same local primary school as did Tween's.

Then there were the dogs.

He told the authors: 'Between our respective homes there was a dog-friendly reserve where my kids and I exercised our German Shepherd. The Andersons used the same reserve to exercise their dog. My kids and I also frequented the public tennis court that was only 80 to 100 metres from Anderson's home.

'Socialisation was unavoidable, and, as I perceived no threat to my family from Anderson, I merely compartmentalised my work and social interactions.'

In addition to school, dogs and tennis, there was the scuba diving. He said that when he and his son Matthew wanted to learn how to dive, they went to a local dive school at The Entrance where Susan Anderson, who was a keen underwater photographer, was a member. The three of them went on a dive together.

Standen's brother, Glen, did some landscaping at the Andersons' home and got on well with the family, Susan in particular. 'At the time she [Susan] was in the early stages of starting a lingerie home-party business.'

She invited Glen to participate. And, according to Mark Standen, his brother, Glen, and Susan and John Anderson, aka Neville Tween, attended a meeting with an accountant together to set up the business.

Explaining the relationship further, Mark Standen said that the Andersons asked him to their home to counsel one of their children who was a little 'wayward' and wasn't responding well to their attempts to control him. 'I visited him at their home a number of times and established a good rapport. There was some improvement in his behaviour. This placed me in good stead with their family.'

At one stage in the 1990s, Anderson and his wife, Susan, were renting a house in Lakin Street, Bateau Bay on the Central Coast, but, having bought a new home, were planning to move out.

According to Mark Standen, coincidentally he and his family needed somewhere to stay, somewhere with a high fence to contain their Rottweiler, which 'did not get on well with other dogs'.

'Susan knew of our dog problem … she let me know the house [in Lakin St] would soon become available for rent.'

John Anderson and his family moved out, Mark Standen and his family moved in. As to a suggestion they'd actually lived under the same roof for a time, Standen said: 'At no time did any member of my family live in the house at the same time as the Andersons.'

Despite initially admitting that his social contact with Tween had been relatively frequent and unavoidable, when Standen later wrote to the authors, he sought to put more distance between himself and the man numerous NSW detectives have described as 'evil'. He claimed any planned meetings between them were for professional purposes.

'We were friendly and had a legitimate basis for so being, but I only saw him three to eight times a year if that. It was not as though we were best mates and hanging out together.'

Former NSW detective Michael Kennedy believes Standen's relationship with Tween was born out of ignorance and naivety on Standen's part. He said Tween would have seen Standen coming and played him as a long-term investment.

Kennedy also believes Tween should never have been used as an informer because of the awful crimes for which he was the chief suspect.

'It's a relationship that [was] fraught with danger,' Kennedy said.

'You're dealing with people who have no conscience about what they do. They are ruthless. The ends justifies the means. They have no regard for human safety or human life.'

He said informers like Tween 'either pave the way for their own industry or you'll end up being used by them when they do something really nasty'.

'I think Standen was totally compromised.'

As for being a family friend, Mick Kennedy was blunt.

'How the fuck could you even let him in your house knowing what he's done?'

Jayson Macleod, the former NSW detective who was one of many who investigated Tween, had a similar view.

He said he'd never seen anyone accused of so much crime who'd managed to escape police attention for such a long period.

And avoid police attention was exactly what Neville Tween continued to do. It appears his close relationship with Mark Standen was serving him very well indeed.

Chapter 18

At Home with Neville

One person well placed to observe the relationship with Mark Standen was Kylie, the daughter of Susan, Neville Tween's wife. When Kylie was young, she called Tween 'Uncle Neville', but once she started to grow up, she was encouraged to call him Dad.

Kylie recalls: 'They [the Standens] lived down the road from us. If my dad [Tween] and Mark weren't catching up, my mum and [Standen's wife] were … I remember Mark being around quite a bit, whether it was to come over for dinner … He had barbecues with us, he was at events like birthday parties, he was at my son's naming. You know, he was *there*, he was very much a friend of the family.'

Kylie recalls that Standen even copied Tween's home renovations. 'In our house at North Entrance they built a big screen enclosure and then Mark did the same, similar, but it was covered and more enclosed.'

But Kylie said that her stepfather never explained the relationship. They were just 'friends'. When she found out Mark Standen worked for the National Crime Authority it didn't make sense. In one of a number of interviews with the authors, she said 'I knew that my dad [Tween] … wasn't down the straight and narrow. So for me to even consider that [he] was friends with a police officer, let alone someone as high up as Mark, that was impossible to me. Why would he have friends who were police officers? And then my only reasoning as to why someone of his stature would be friends with a police officer was because he was a crooked cop.'

Kylie also remembers the day the cabin cruiser *The Sea Wolf*, attached to a Land Cruiser, had arrived at their house in the mid-1980s when she was about ten years old. 'We did a lot of deep sea fishing on that boat … We used to come home with so much fish – whiting, deep sea perch, everything.' What Kylie had no way of knowing at the time was that law enforcement had identified Tween as a drug importer who was using the boat for more than just fishing.

Tween's 18-month stint in jail in 1995 and 1996 over the hydroponic marijuana crop had slowed him down, but those who knew him at the time remember a man who still had lots of cash. Kylie remembers being embarrassed when he opened his wallet, chock full of notes, in the local supermarket. 'Everyone could see all the money and we always used to be, like, Dad, calm down!'

Despite the cash, he was never a flashy dresser – far from it – with stubbies and a T-shirt more the go. Kylie recalls: 'He never flaunted anything. He could have got a Mercedes … [he was] a millionaire dressed like a pauper. [It was] stubbies and a T-shirt with his brick mobile phone pulling one side [of his shorts] down.' If he happened to wear a surf brand shirt it would usually be because someone had bought it for him.

Nor were there any Rolex watches or jewellery or gold chains or flashy sports cars, although he did have the nice house with a pool on the beach at The Entrance. According to Kylie, he didn't much go to the pub either, preferring to drink at home.

But while he might not have known much about the finer things in life, he liked French champagne and Grange Hermitage, which he drank like it was a $20 bottle of plonk from the local bottle-O.

As for his taste in drugs, well, it was top shelf. In fact, Tween's behaviour was becoming erratic as a result of his cocaine use. Former barrister Peter Livesey knew Tween during the 1980s and early 1990s, although he had no inkling he was suspected of being involved in multiple rapes or of being an informer and was mortified when he found out. Livesey remembers going out on the town in 1992 with Tween and Jockey Smith, whom Livesey had defended in the late 1970s on a charge of murdering bookmaker Lloyd Tidmarsh. It was the only time the three men had socialised together.

Livesey said that Smith 'got the shits' because Tween kept referring to him in an increasingly loud voice as 'Jockey', which Smith didn't appreciate, having recently survived an attempt on his life that left him seriously injured. Indeed, he'd gone to the Central Coast to lie low.

Livesey recalls that later that night they went back to Tween's home where Tween decided they should keep drinking and carrying on. His wife, Susan, had other ideas. According to Peter Livesey, she was angry – and pushed her husband hard enough that he fell to the ground, knocking himself out. Despite being injured, Jockey Smith carried his mate into the house.

Kylie remembers the same incident and remembers 'Jockey' in a different light from the way he was publicly portrayed. 'Whatever people say about Jockey, I only ever saw a kind man.' She said he showed concern and care for her when her stepdad was on one of his binges.

It was during her early to mid-teens when Kylie first had an inkling that her stepfather was not your normal suburban dad. It probably started with the very large marijuana plant in the backyard, which he would show off to visitors. He told Kylie it was a tomato plant. She wondered why he would be showing it off to visitors until, going to school one day, she looked up pictures of marijuana plants in the school library and figured out there wouldn't be many tomatoes on the bush in the backyard.

It was all a little confusing, because at school at the time, Kylie and her fellow students were being told that marijuana was 'a gateway drug' and to 'just say no'. There was even an anti-drugs campaign featuring Healthy Harold, the giraffe. By the time she was in her teens, she began to realise that her stepfather was into more than marijuana. At times, Kylie's relationship with Neville could be volatile and there were times where she briefly left home. One time she was staying with some of his friends 'who were renting a house off us' a couple of doors down, she recalled.

'Something happened one day, they [the friends] had coke and I walked in … and they sat down and explained to me what it was. And they said, do you want to try some and I was like, okay, so yes I did.

'And then all of us got high and they got chatty and that's where I learnt that they'd actually got it from Dad. I was snorting his stuff, you know, and I'm like, this is interesting.' She said it was an experience that opened her eyes to where the money was coming from.

'That's why he's got so much money when he doesn't work.'

Later, Tween even supplied Kylie. She said it sometimes happened after he would shout her and her friends a meal at the local Chinese restaurant.

'We would all have dinner, but I would get the drugs off him for my friends …' He didn't always carry the drugs with him but 'he just had access to them at cheap prices, supplying us the pills was more a favour to me. It was almost always ecstasy as we couldn't afford the other [cocaine]. We still had to pay for them, just a quarter of the price.'

So much for Healthy Harold.

Bit by bit, Tween's behaviour was starting to become unpredictable due to his increasing drug habit. Kylie remembers waking up to a commotion after the home alarm system had been triggered. 'We had perimeter alarms so if anyone stepped foot on the property they broke the beam and the siren went off. It wasn't loud, like a little whistle, only we could hear it in the house.' The person in the yard couldn't see the lights come on inside the house because the external shutters would be down on all the windows.

Tween went outside and found a teenage boy who was probably looking to snip a few buds from the plant in the backyard.

Kylie remembers seeing the boy lying on the ground, with his feet and hands tied behind him 'like he was hog-tied'.

She said he was crying 'please help me, please help me' – he thought he was going to die.

Kylie recalls something else.

'I remember Dad took a Polaroid of him.'

Tween told Kylie he'd caught the teenager trying to break in to the family's back shed to steal fishing rods, but she realised the marijuana plant was still there and that maybe the kid was 'just trying to get a little smoko for himself'.

After gagging him with 'one of his dirty socks', Tween put the boy in the boot of his car and left.

And that was the last time she ever saw the teenager. By the time Kylie left to catch the bus to school, Tween hadn't returned. 'I don't know where he went, what he did.'

Things made a bit more sense to Kylie when she later discovered her stepdad's porn collection. 'I've seen some of the porn videos he left around the place and they were actually quite violent, a lot of them included tying people up and rape scenes and holding them in cells … a lot of those scenarios. And men and women … and a lot of bondage.'

Kylie also remembers Tween forcefully advising her against hitchhiking, telling her that 'young girls like you that go missing, they'll never see you again … [You'll] never see us again. They'll take you, they'll hurt you.'

Another night, around 1992, she was woken at about 4am by noises inside the house. She walked out of her room to see Tween holding a gun. 'What's going on?' she asked, only to have Tween turn around 'and now the gun's pointing at me, like loaded and ready to fire'.

Off his head on cocaine or something else, he was terrified his old mate Ray Johnson was in the house and going to kill him. 'Uncle Ray, he's under the lounge, he's trying to get me.'

'I remember my mum coming out … and my mum actually said oh your father's fucking losing it, Kylie, or something like that, like he's going crazy.'

Reefing up the lounge, Kylie said: 'There's no one under the fucking lounge, you idiot.'

Tween calmed down. 'I'm better now,' he said, before going back to bed. It was one of the few occasions she saw him with a gun.

Tween may well have been right that Ray Johnson was trying to kill him. The two men had had a massive falling out about a large amount of cash that had gone missing around the same time Mark Standen was cultivating Tween as an informer in the early '90s. Perhaps Johnson also suspected his partner in crime of rolling over.

Kylie said she was in Year 10 at high school when it all came to a head. She was woken up in the middle of the night by her mum, who told her to pack her bags because they were going to Western Australia. Her mother had said: 'This might be the last time you ever see your [stepfather].'

It was in Western Australia, Kylie says, that Tween told her about the missing money; she recalls it being about $1 million dollars.

'He told me the story about Ray being involved and him believing Ray stole the money [but that] he was now accountable for the money so he's going to suffer the consequences ...'

Kylie flew back from Western Australia 'in absolute tears' and going to her Year 10 formal thinking Tween was dead or was going to be very soon. Then, just as suddenly as she had left for Perth, he turned up at home, unharmed. Kylie said he'd either got the money situation 'sorted' or something else must have happened.

Perhaps this was one of the disputes Tween spoke to Mark Standen about later, where a handful of corrupt NSW Police referred to by old-school crims as The Union sorted out disagreements between criminals – no doubt for a fee.

Standen himself says it was Tween who told him about The Union.

It had come up when Tween was explaining a 'serious dispute between two criminal groups over a cocaine importation' to which Tween was a party. He had mentioned that a senior NSW Police officer had acted as a mediator between the groups.

Standen said he knew the names of the criminal group members but not the name of the police officer.

'I pressed him [Tween] for details on The Union,' Standen told the authors. 'But he refused to discuss them although, perhaps inadvertently, he once said something which suggested one [of the corrupt police] may have been stationed at Chatswood.'

The dispute between the groups had involved 'two close former associates' of Tween's, one of whom used to be 'very close' to him and heavily into firearms. It was a description that fitted Ray Johnson to a tee.

Kylie remembers another incident, when she was older, which happened at a factory. Tween had been 'on a bender' and was off his head on drugs. 'He was chasing me naked with a knife,' she said. 'It's only lucky that I'm faster than him and I had a car which was keyless entry.'

She made her escape, but she's not even sure he recognised her or whether he would have done anything had he managed to catch up.

Amid the madness, there were some good times, in particular in the house on the beach at The Entrance.

'I used to come home from school in summer, walk through my front door, into my bedroom, get into my swimming costume ... walk straight through the house, dive into the pool, swim up to the other end, get out, go through the gates, go up the sand dunes and go down the beach, bodysurf, come back, rinse off in the pool and go back inside. That's what I used to do I loved it.'

That was when Tween owned properties in Hutton Road, including one next door to the family home. He'd installed a fully self-contained granny flat in the rental and could access it through a gate in the Colorbond fence. He called it the 'Den of Iniquity' and it was where he went to drink, smoke dope, do coke or talk to his mates when he needed some privacy. Former barrister Peter Livesey also recalls Tween referring to the 'Den of Iniquity'.

One thing Kylie remembers well about her stepdad is that he absolutely loved animals, particularly his dog, Bonnie, which he took everywhere, including in his Mitsubishi Magna, though not in his newer, more expensive Kluger.

'He used to take her for walks, whether he used her as an excuse to go for a walk to meet with Mark [Standen] or not … he loved her.'

There was another time when Tween was driving with her out in the bush and he spotted something on the road.

'He's pulled to a stop because there was a black snake across the road and he wasn't going to run over it 'cos he didn't want to hurt it.' He stood in front of the car throwing stones at the snake to get it off the road.

'A massive animal lover. He'd be cruel to a person before he'd be cruel to an animal.'

Kylie knew that for a fact.

Chapter 19

Hopes Raised

In August 1995, in a blaze of publicity, the NSW Police announced they had made a breakthrough in the Trudie Adams case.

It was revealed that 30 detectives on Task Force Loquat had been digging away for months and finding new leads.

'[Police] now firmly believe Trudie died at the hands of not one killer but a group of mates who pack raped her after grabbing her off the street,' reported the *Telegraph-Mirror*.

The police didn't say it publicly, but they were looking at the Roselands Lads – whom, back in 1978, Gary Matthews had dismissed as just 'big-noting' themselves by boasting about killing Trudie.

The *Telegraph-Mirror* reported on 21 August, in an article headlined 'The 17-year secret of Trudie's killers', that NSW Police believed 'they were close to solving the mystery of Trudie's abduction'. Not only that, there was a possibility of 'finding her remains in bushland on Sydney's Pittwater Peninsula'.

A Channel Nine reporter claimed the 'dark secret' of those responsible for Trudie Adams' murder would 'once and for all be revealed'. A police officer told the reporter it was a 'breakthrough' and that police had 'very reliable information'.

For Trudie's family and friends it seemed as though, at last, there might be some answers and some justice. She may have disappeared 17 years earlier, but for many, thoughts of Trudie were never far from their minds.

Trudie's friend Anita Starkey, who was working in the Avalon newsagency when Trudie disappeared and had read all the awful headlines, had dreamt about her good friend for quite a few years after. 'I'd just dream that she'd be somewhere, and she'd be there and I'd go, Trudie, and I'd hug her. And I'd say, "Where have you been, we've been looking for you." And she'd say, "I'm fine, I'm fine, everything's fine."'

Trudie's brother John told the media, he was 'impressed and heartened' to learn that police had reopened the case.

Her former boyfriend, Steve Norris, asked by police to be part of the carefully planned publicity was interviewed about the breakthrough on the TV news.

'I always thought one day something would come up somewhere, somewhere along the line,' Steve said. 'But this surprises me … 17 years is a long time.'

There was real hope this time. In the television interviews you could see it in his eyes.

The chief police reporter for the *Telegraph-Mirror*, Les Kennedy, told readers the key to the new inquiry was the vehicle involved – a mid-1970s lime-green VW Kombi – that had been 'overlooked' in the original investigation. The new information had come to light 'by chance earlier this year while police were making inquiries into a number of unrelated matters on the Northern Beaches'.

In fact, the genesis of the new inquiry was a tip-off that went back to 1992, at a time when Detective Senior

Constable Ian Lynch was in the Homicide Squad. One day, while working on another murder, Lynch bumped into a colleague, Detective Senior Constable Gary Jubelin. Just chatting, Jubelin happened to mention that an informant of his had given him some potentially explosive information about the unsolved disappearance of Trudie Adams.

According to Jubelin's source, police had taken the 'wrong path' in the original investigation back in 1978.

At the time, police had focused their efforts on the beige-coloured panel van described by Steve Norris. But this new source – whom police identified as Witness A – said that Trudie Adams had actually been abducted in a green Kombi van and she knew the men who owned it, and was prepared to name names.

According to Witness A, seven men had been involved in Trudie's disappearance – not two, as had been reported in the media in the weeks after Trudie disappeared in 1978.

Witness A identified three of the men as brothers Ray, Emile and Sam Khoury, and the others as a mix of drifters and hangers-on. Together, the men formed a loose group that investigating police dubbed the Roselands Lads after their stomping ground, the Roselands Shopping Centre.

Police obviously didn't say it, but Neville Tween, Ray Johnson and other associates were no longer in the frame. This was a completely new, unrelated set of suspects.

***

The emergence of the Roselands Lads is one of the most perplexing aspects of the various investigations into Trudie Adams' disappearance because it's at this moment that police theories about the case begin to vary wildly.

There were those who believed there was every chance Trudie had been picked up in a green Kombi van by a group of men who hung around a shopping centre in Sydney's west.

Others dismissed the theory, believing the evidence pointed to it being a beige panel van, and the killers being the two men who had been attacking women in the area for years.

However, the more Detective Ian Lynch looked into the Roselands Lads, the more intrigued he became by the green Kombi. But because of other cases and commitments, he only worked on the Trudie investigation part-time. Lynch knew that several men had bragged about killing Trudie Adams in the months and years after her disappearance. Furthermore, one of the Roselands Lads had been going out with a girl who lived near the Northern Beaches in 1978, so it was plausible they were in the area at the time. In addition, Ray Khoury had owned a green Kombi van when Trudie vanished. And Ray, along with his younger brother Emile and another man, had been charged with raping a woman in the green Kombi in 1980. A jury had found the three men not guilty.

On 16 October 1992, Lynch and Jubelin went to the Orchard Tavern in Chatswood on Sydney's North Shore, where they had their first official meeting with Witness A, who had lived in Sydney's west in the early 1980s with her truck-driver boyfriend, Keith Patrick Hurney.

Witness A and Hurney had been going out for three years and were planning a future together. One day in September 1983, while the couple were getting buzzed smoking some weed, Hurney glanced at a local newspaper with an article about Trudie Adams' disappearance.

According to Witness A, Hurney's eyes lit up 'like a Christmas tree' when he saw Trudie's name. Witness A asked him why, saying, 'I want the truth, Keith, what have you done?'

Whatever Witness A thought Keith was about to say, the story she heard next must have been far worse. According to evidence later given in court, he told her he'd actually been at the Newport Surf Club the night Trudie disappeared. He'd been with a group of five or six guys and seen Trudie leave the dance. He said they'd hassled her as she left the surf club, asking her repeatedly if she wanted a lift. When Trudie said no, he said the mood in the pack of men turned and became physical. The group of men had dragged Trudie into a green Kombi van and started to attack her.

'They started raping her in the car,' he said.

He claimed the group of men drove up the peninsula towards its northernmost point, Palm Beach. He went on to say that Trudie struggled and opened the van door and jumped out then 'hit her head on a telegraph pole and split it open … We went back and scraped her off the telegraph pole. She was dead.'

Hurney's story shook Witness A to her core, and though she wasn't in the habit of talking to police, she decided this wasn't something she could ignore.

A few days later, Witness A went to Ryde Police Station and told them everything she knew.

She didn't hear anything back from them for months. Then, one afternoon, Hurney came home in a rage, saying the cops had been to his work asking questions about Trudie Adams. He said: 'If the Khourys find out about this they'll fuckin' kill me.' According to Witness A, he said: 'Do you want to see me go to jail, do you?'

She told police he'd then physically assaulted her. 'I got a black eye, bruised ribs and I was sore for days.'

Lynch and Jubelin were sure Witness A was not making the story up. But that didn't make it true. It was hearsay – something related to her by Hurney. On the other hand, they wondered if this might be the clue the original investigators had overlooked or dismissed all those years ago.

Detective Lynch requested the five volumes of running sheets on Trudie Adams' disappearance from Mona Vale Police Station and started methodically trawling through them, page by page, finding the very first telex message – Message 31 – circulated by Mona Vale Police at 7.27pm the Monday after Trudie vanished. It said Trudie was:

> SEEN TO ENTER A GREEN KOMBI VAN WHICH THEN DROVE ALONG BARRENJOEY RD NORTH TOWARD AVALON.

For Lynch, the mention of the Kombi was an immediate sign he might be on the right track. But when he read the second message sent out just 15 hours later, which changed the description to a 1977 Holden panel van, fawn to beige in colour, he wondered what had happened overnight. Which wireless message had the right description?

As Ian Lynch continued to go through the running sheets, names jumped out at him. Some of the men Witness A had mentioned had come to the attention of Gary Matthews and his team as early as 1978.

The first mention of any of the Roselands Lads was in December 1978, six months after Trudie's disappearance. Someone had told investigators they'd heard that a guy called Garrian (Garry) Carr had been telling people he'd murdered Trudie Adams. In 1978, Carr was 22, a drifter with no job, living with friends. He hung out at the Roselands Shopping

Centre, where he had a reputation for talking shit and for carrying around a black steel cash-box full of newspaper clippings of crimes. When people asked what was in the steel box, Carr would laugh and reply that it was filled with 'dark thoughts, brother'.

Police had made inquiries about Carr's whereabouts, but it appeared from the running sheets that they didn't find him.

Four months later, in April 1979, Carr once again came to the attention of investigators when an informant told them he'd heard that 'two male persons' called Garry Carr and Gary Ireland were involved in the 'disappearance of the girl Trudie Adams'. In 1978, Carr had owned a 1976 Holden panel van.

The two – Garry and Gary – were friends who had gone to school together, and could usually be found together at the shops or the pub. The informant had told police he'd heard that one of them had a girlfriend who lived near the Northern Beaches.

The story went that on the night Trudie vanished, the two men had gone to visit the girlfriend. When they couldn't find her, they went to the Newport Surf Club instead and saw Trudie arguing with her boyfriend outside the surf club before hitting him with her purse.

There was a note in the running sheets saying that 'further inquiries are being made'.

Gary Matthews had long been taken off the case full-time, although he did look into new leads as they emerged. Neither he nor his Homicide Squad colleagues gave the story about Carr and Ireland much credence.

Five months later, police spoke to a bus driver called Alf Sergi whom they considered 'reasonably responsible'. Sergi told them he'd heard Carr and Ireland talking at the

Roselands Shopping Centre about being involved in Trudie's disappearance. But Alf Sergi hadn't believed them, forming the opinion 'they were skylarking and scaring local girls.' Sergi also told police he'd heard them give varying versions of what they'd done, from throwing Trudie out of the car, to raping her and then running over her with the car, to shooting her and burying her body.

When Detective Lynch tracked down Garry Carr and Gary Ireland in 1995, they vigorously denied any involvement at all in Trudie's disappearance.

Ray and Emile Khoury were 'known' to police but only in relation to minor matters and neither had ever been convicted of anything. Their brother, Sam, described himself as 'the family drug addict' and over the years had been charged and convicted of using and possessing heroin, along with driving offences and an assault.

According to Witness A, the three brothers had been there the night Trudie had vanished.

However, all of them categorically denied any involvement in the matter. Ray Khoury had indeed owned a green Kombi on the night Trudie had disappeared, and in 1980, Ray and Emile Khoury, along with a number of other men, were charged with raping a woman in the back of the vehicle. Later, in court, they claimed the sex with the woman was consensual, with one of them describing her as the 'town bike'.

All were found not guilty.

* * *

If police were trying to rattle the Roselands Lads with all the publicity in August 1995, their strategy worked. Detectives had placed intercepts on a number of their phones and were listening in to their conversations.

Ray Khoury was concerned when he saw the publicity, and, while he was worried about his phone being bugged, he called Garry Carr to talk about 1978. Police listened in as he said words to the effect of: 'I didn't even know you at that time, Garry,' which wasn't true.

Ray Khoury also called his friend, Alf Sergi, the 'responsible bus driver' who'd been one of the Roselands Lads back in the late 1970s and had told police the boys were just bragging.

By 1995, when Ray rang him at home on Monday, 21 August, the day the news broke about the new investigation, Sergi had a new career – he was a NSW Police officer. 'Hey, Alf, it's Ray. Have you read the papers?' he said. 'It's all over the news. The police have reopened the Trudie Adams investigation.'

Ray told Alf he had nothing to do with the 'Trudie Adams business' but he was 'worried because the green Kombi's been mentioned and they [the police] want to talk to me'. He added that, 'If they come here I think I will tell them to fuck off, I had nothing to do with it.'

Three days later, on Thursday, 24 August, Alf Sergi heard a horn beeping outside his house and saw a dark grey car he didn't recognise.

Ray Khoury was in the driver's seat and was accompanied by two other men.

This time, Alf Sergi told Ray he couldn't associate with him or anyone else.

When Ray pleaded, 'Come on, Alf,' Sergi stood firm, telling him not to telephone or come around, saying, 'Ray, I'm a police officer … it puts me in a bad position.'

Ray made one last appeal, saying he didn't hang around 'with those wankers' – Carr and Ireland – and that he only knew them from Roselands. 'I don't want to get you in trouble but I want to sort this out, I've got nothing to hide,' Ray said. 'I owned a green Kombi – that's all.'

On 29 August, detectives from Strike Force Loquat interviewed Ray Khoury, who told them he didn't know anything about Trudie Adams' disappearance. And while he didn't tell them to fuck off, like he'd threatened, Ray did make it clear he was sick of the 'rumours'. 'What do you want to do?' he said. 'Do you want to make stories out of nothing? I mean, what do you want me to say?'

Investigators also interviewed Garry Carr and Gary Ireland. By this time Garry Carr had been diagnosed with schizophrenia, and told police he remembered going to a dance on the Northern Beaches in Ray's green Kombi. He denied raping or killing Trudie Adams, saying the allegation sounded like 'fabricated evidence'.

He did concede he and others might have spoken about Trudie but said that 'if we were then it's taken out of context', claiming it was 'probably my friend big-noting himself'.

Gary Ireland, who was working as a labourer, also admitted to talking about Trudie Adams, when he was 'young and stupid' but said, 'If they took it as fair dinkum then that's not my problem.'

Keith Hurney admitted in an interview with police he'd said what Witness A had claimed but that none of it was actually true. 'I was only big-noting myself and I said it in a laughing manner.'

He said the story he'd told Witness A had been told to him by Ray Khoury at Khoury's house … about a week after the original disappearance. Re-interviewed, Hurney repeated this version of events, saying Khoury had 'boasted involvement' in picking up Trudie Adams outside a dance with some friends. Khoury had claimed Trudie's body was buried at Palm Beach.

Despite their best efforts, Detective Lynch and his colleagues on Strike Force Loquat never got to the bottom of the green Kombi mystery. Lynch re-interviewed witnesses, including the two uniformed police who'd originally gone to the Adams home to talk to Connie and Charles. They confirmed that Connie did most of the talking but neither could recall the origin of the information about the Kombi van.

It was more likely than not it was Connie who had told police her daughter was last seen in a green Kombi van and that she had thought Trudie's boyfriend Steve Norris had told her. Indeed, in the weeks after her daughter had disappeared, Connie had asked one of Trudie's girlfriends why Steve had changed the description of the car. For his part, Norris said that he had no memory of telling Connie it was a green Kombi and he was a man who knew his cars. He maintained, like he always had, that it was a beige panel van.

In the end, Task Force Loquat was inconclusive, despite formal interviews with all the Roselands Lads. Lynch and his colleagues had done their best, locating and interviewing the men who'd been heard to boast about killing Trudie. In December 1995, Lynch was promoted and sent to the Major Crime Squad South, while the investigative brief into Trudie's disappearance remained at the offices of the Major Crime Squad North for further work.

Lynch believed more needed to be done on the investigation into the spate of rapes on the Northern Beaches. 'At this point a body of work remained outstanding concerning a group of suspects believed responsible for a number of rapes that were reported to police investigating the Miss Adams disappearance in 1978,' he said.

For Trudie's family and friends, Task Force Loquat proved to be a bitter pill. Hopes raised so high in August 1995 were once more dashed and, yet again, Trudie disappeared from the front pages and the TV news.

Chapter 20

A Reward for Neville

By the time Neville Tween was released from jail in November 1996, having served his time for the hydroponic marijuana crop, Mark Standen had left the National Crime Authority and moved on to the NSW Crime Commission, another powerful and secretive body that had been set up to fight organised crime and seize the assets of big-time criminals, particularly drug traffickers.

Standen was an assistant director at the commission, which meant he was involved in investigating some of the biggest drug dealers and organised crime figures in Australia.

It appears he took his informant, Neville Tween, with him. Official documents outlining the NCA's interest in Tween from 1992 through to 1996 state that there are no 'holdings' on Tween after 1996, the year Standen joined the Crime Commission.

And it appears the NCA's lack of success in bringing Tween himself to justice over his cocaine importations through Fremantle in the early 1990s might be explained by the fact that he was providing some useful information – on occasions – to Standen and the authority.

Including information about one of Australia's biggest drug traffickers, Ian Hall Saxon.

In 1989, Ian Saxon and others had imported a massive 10 tonnes of cannabis into Australia and sold it, making millions. Saxon was arrested in 1990 by Mark Standen, then in the AFP. The drug trafficker was jailed but famously escaped from Sydney's Long Bay Jail in 1993 and went on the run. A reward of $250,000 was offered for information leading to his capture, which finally happened in San Diego in the United States in 1995. Mark Standen made the trip to the US to witness Saxon's arrest and bring him back to Australia. It was a coup for Standen, perhaps the high point of his career, because Saxon was a very, very big fish indeed.

According to former law enforcement sources it was Tween who provided the crucial tip-off about Saxon.

The career criminal, the chief suspect in so many brutal rapes and at least two murders, was allegedly rewarded, being paid just over 50 per cent of the reward money: $127,500. Tween must have laughed all the way to the bank.

Standen himself won't say directly that Tween was an informer or that he was involved in the Saxon case.

But needled by allegations that Tween had never provided him with any useful information, Standen said: 'I will provide some limited and generalised information to address some of the concerns …'

He told the authors: 'If it were the case that he [Tween] had been a registered informant and that he had been paid rewards, let's say, for argument's sake, $127,500 from a federal agency with the knowledge of a state agency', then criticism that the career crook had never given him any good information would be demonstrably false.

'Rewards were approved by committees based on results. I did not make reward decisions,' Standen said.

'You will note I have not stated that [Tween] was a registered informant or that he was paid any rewards, but I hope my point is clear enough.'

What's clear enough is this: The recapture of Saxon boosted Standen's career and probably paved the way for his appointment in 1996 to the NSW Crime Commission. If true, Tween had come through in spades, something Standen wasn't likely to forget.

***

As the 1990s drew to a close, Kylie found herself a single mother raising a young boy and times were tough. In 2000, her stepfather, Neville Tween, made her an offer she couldn't refuse. It involved a scam aimed at laundering some $90,000 of his dirty money.

Kylie remembers how he made false Queensland drivers licences because they were easier to forge than those issued in New South Wales. Armed with the $90,000 in cash, Kylie and Tween went to numerous Thomas Cook exchanges in Sydney in the course of a day, using the fake IDs to get travel cards and putting $9000 on each – just under the $10,000 reporting limit.

She had ten IDs in her name and would memorise their details before she went in to the Thomas Cook exchanges. Tween paid Kylie $100 a card, which allowed her to make $1000 in a day.

All was going well until they tried a Thomas Cook in the Queen Victoria Building in the Sydney CBD. 'We get there and the guy turns around to us and says oh, hang on, we're just having a problem with something else and I remember sitting there going, nope, I don't like this,' Kylie recalled.

'Then I get a tap on the shoulder and it was the Fraud Squad.

Tween was handcuffed, but not Kylie, and they were taken to a nearby police station.

In the cells, a relative bailed Kylie first. Tween told her to contact a well-known female criminal lawyer.

'Like, I thought I was going to jail; I had a one-year-old son.' She needn't have worried. When Kylie and Tween went to court she remembers one of the police officers coming up to have a bit of a chitchat. According to Kylie, he said something like 'about the money, where the money came from, we'll just say that you showed us receipts for the transactions'.

Tween must have felt life was pretty good. He was earning money from drugs, fraud and, apparently, the taxpayer via a $127,500 reward.

Kylie's charge of goods in custody – the cash – was withdrawn. On a second charge, making a false statement to obtain between $5000 and $15,000, she was given a good behaviour bond with no conviction recorded. The magistrate commented that Kylie had been used, roped into the scam by her stepfather.

Tween's knack of getting off the hook on criminal charges continued, and he was also given a bond.

* * *

By 2004–05, Neville Tween and Mark Standen were both preoccupied with cocaine, albeit for different reasons.

Tween was still successfully importing it from South America, which he'd been doing on and off since 1992

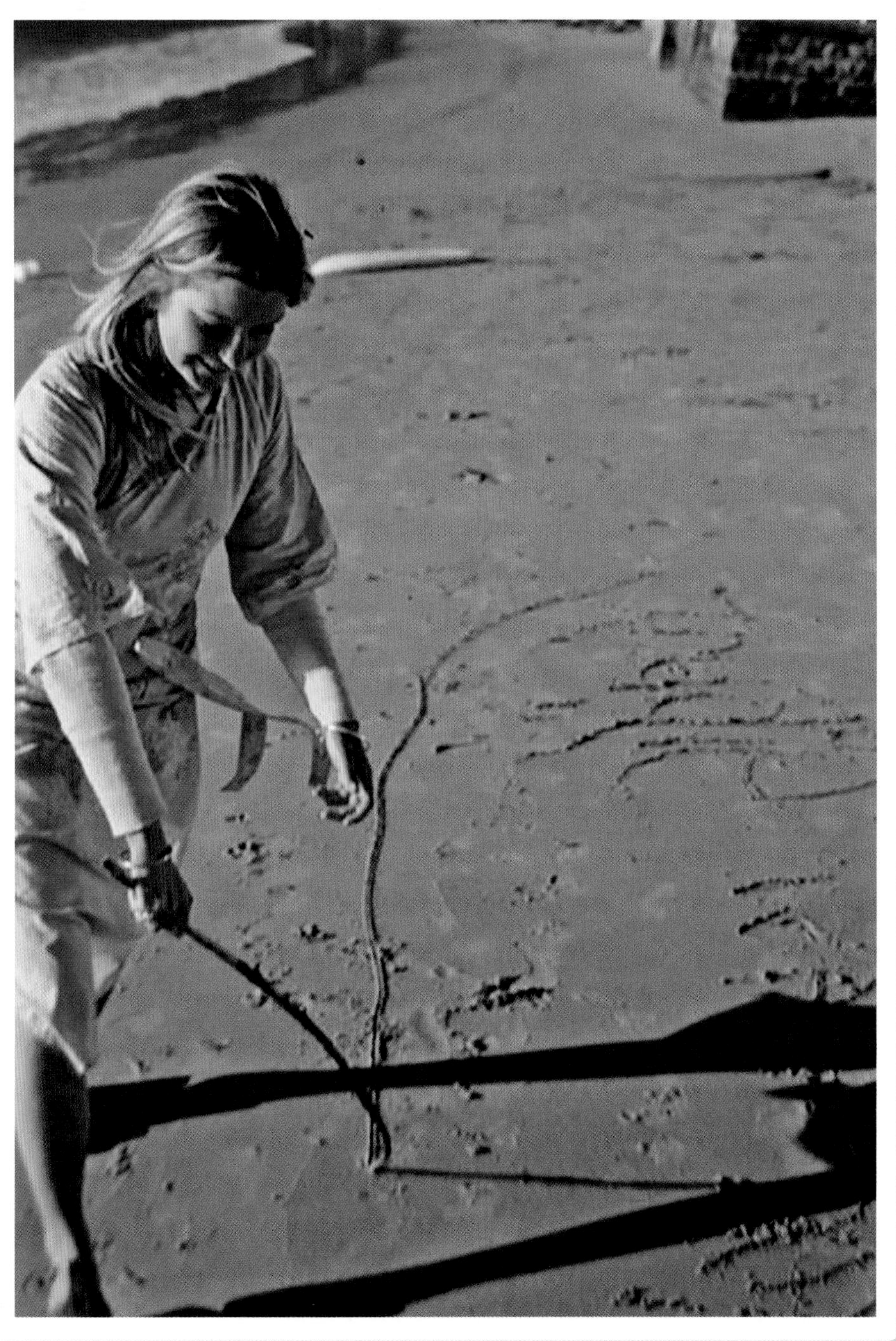

A line in the sand … a carefree Trudie Adams at Palm Beach c. 1977. © *Steve Otton*

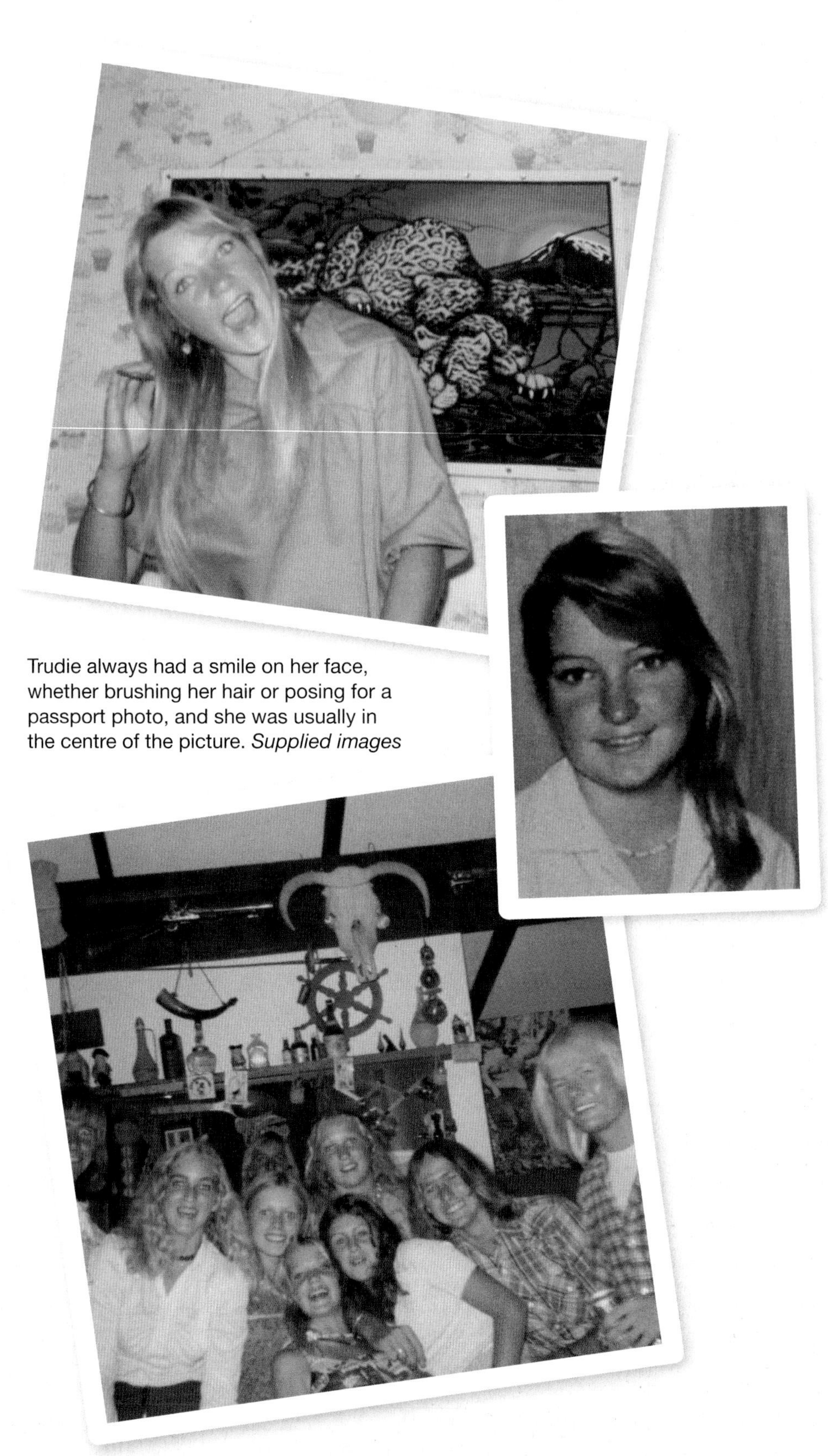

Trudie always had a smile on her face, whether brushing her hair or posing for a passport photo, and she was usually in the centre of the picture. *Supplied images*

Trudie had a close-knit group of friends on the Northern Beaches. Years later, they would describe her as the glue that held them together. *Supplied images*

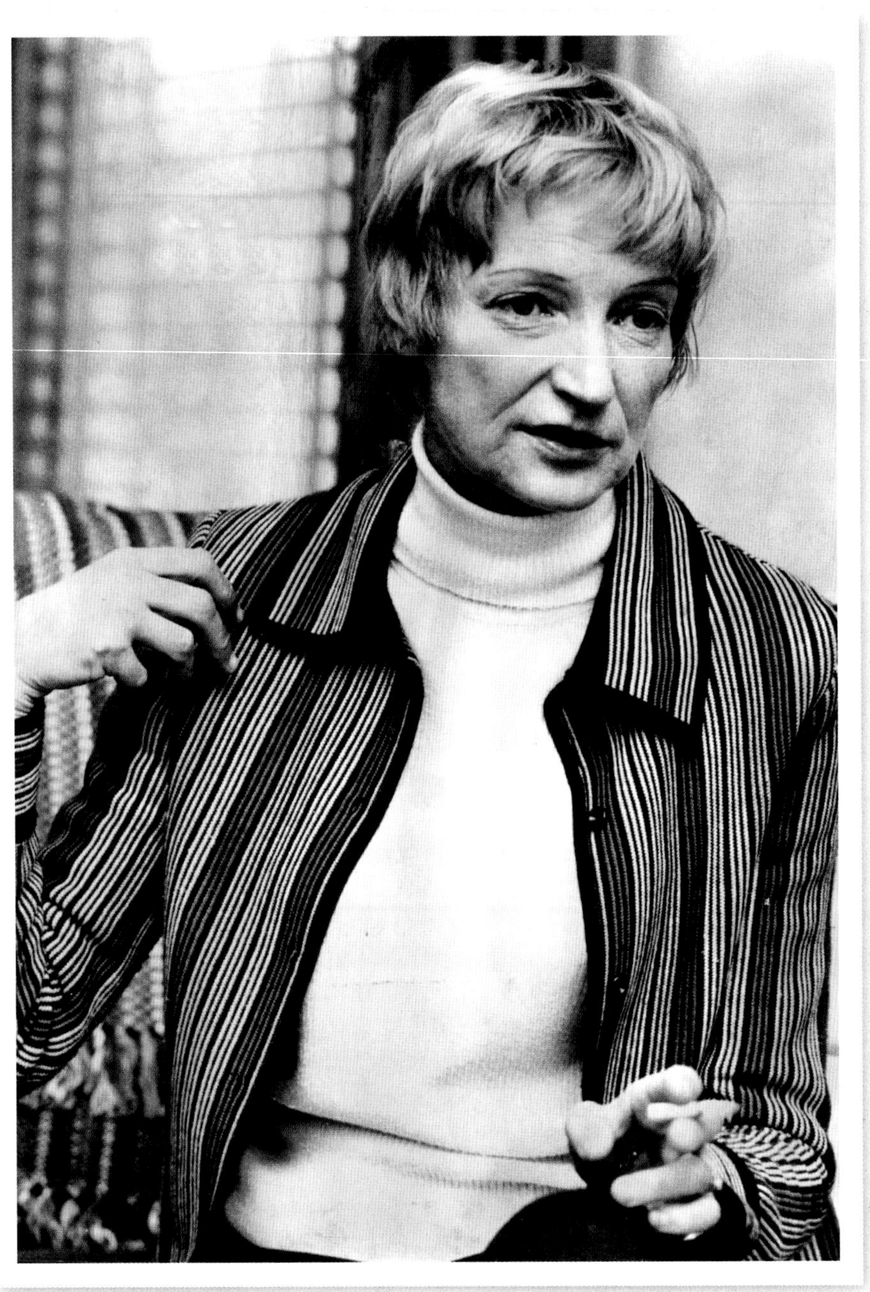

Connie, Trudie's mum, was an early environmental activist. She died in 1989, not knowing what had happened to her daughter. *News Ltd / Newspix*

Steve Norris, Trudie's boyfriend, stands on Barrenjoey Road on 5 July 1978, just days after her disappearance. She was last seen hitching a lift after the surf club dance.
Barry McKinnon / Newspix

A panel van similar to the one Trudie was seen getting into on Barrenjoey Road stands outside the Newport Surf Club, on Sydney's Northern Beaches, in 1978. *Barry McKinnon / Newspix*

The mystery of the green Kombi has never been explained. *Brief of Evidence, 2011 Coronial Inquest*

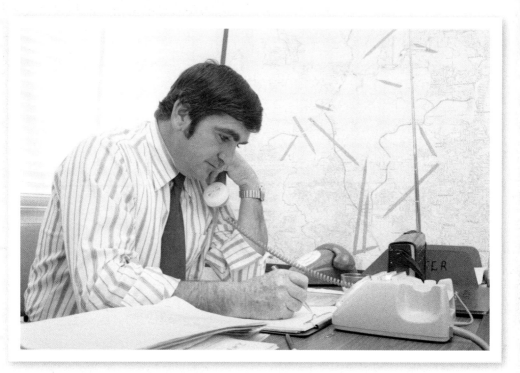

Detective Alan Herrmann was responsible for organising the search for Trudie; it was as comprehensive as it could have been, given the size of Ku-ring-gai Chase National Park.
Leo Thomas / The Sydney Morning Herald

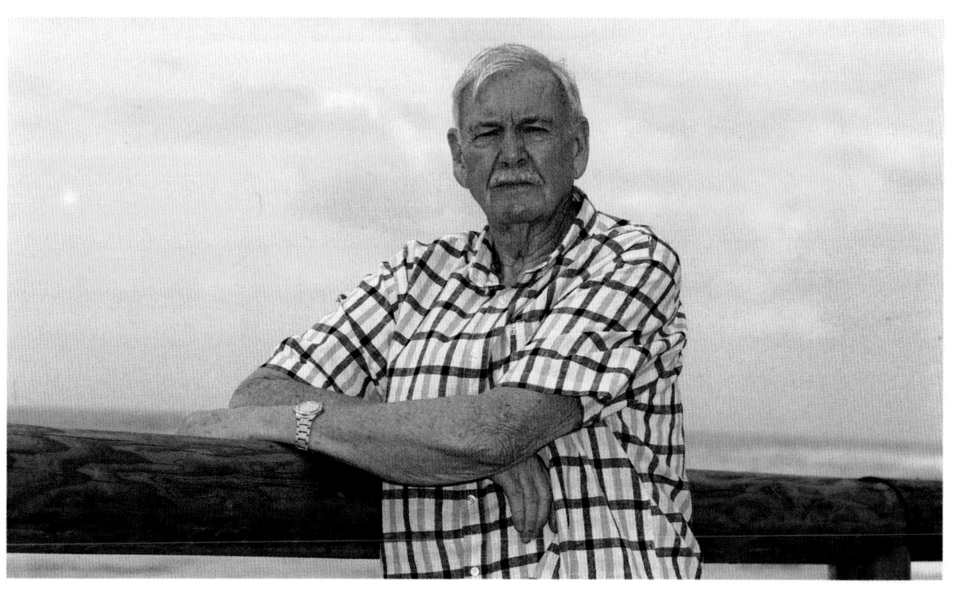

The lead Homicide Squad investigator, Gary Matthews, in retirement. Matthews was taken off the case in 1978, being told, 'You're a homicide investigator, not a rape investigator.'
Jason O'Brien Photography / Newspix

The search for Trudie was, at the time, the biggest in NSW Police history. It extended over 15 separate days and involved more than 1000 police, park rangers, bushwalkers and volunteers.

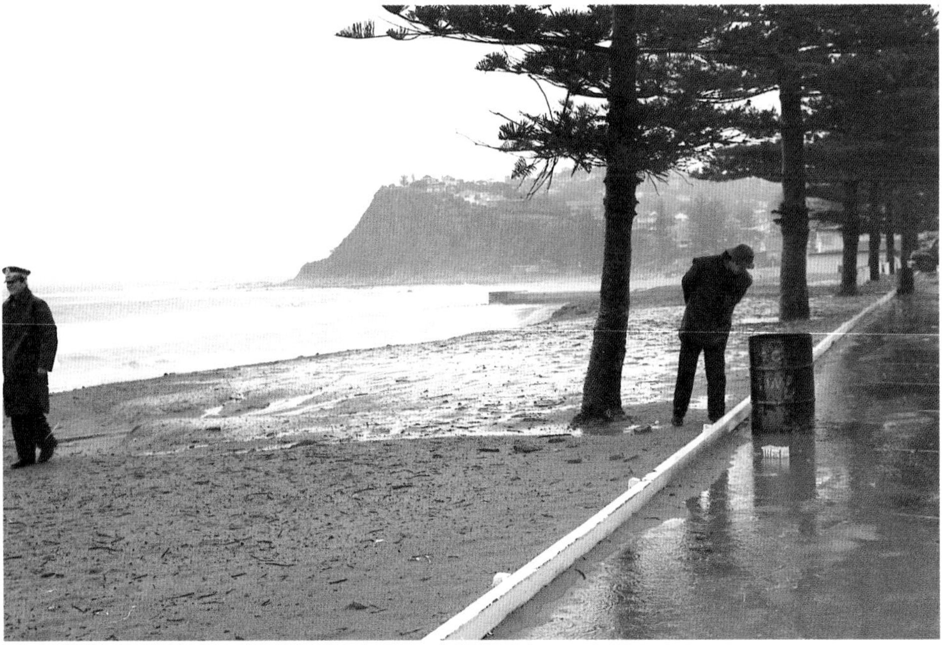

Police looking for clues at Newport Beach, 29 June 1978.
John O'Grady / The Sydney Morning Herald

Searching bushland around Terrey Hills, 7 July 1978.
David Bartho / The Sydney Morning Herald

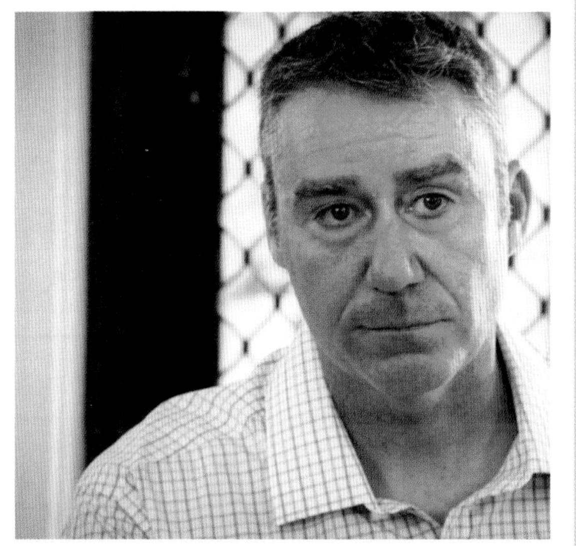

Detective Jayson Macleod was dismayed when he looked at the crimes of Neville Tween – he wondered how Tween could have got away with so much for so long. © *WildBear Entertainment*

Detective Ashley Bryant told the 2011 Coronial Inquest that there were leads that needed following up. *Fiona-Lee Quimby / The Sydney Morning Herald*

Detective Gavin McKean reinterviewed witnesses and carried out a lengthy and comprehensive review of Trudie's disappearance, the rapes and the suspects. He gave evidence at the 2011 inquest. *Jane Dempster / Newspix*

Neville Tween in 1953, at St Joseph's College, Leeton, with the rest of the school's footy team. He's in the front row, big smile, to the left of the trophy.

Neville Tween's mugshot from the 1970s.

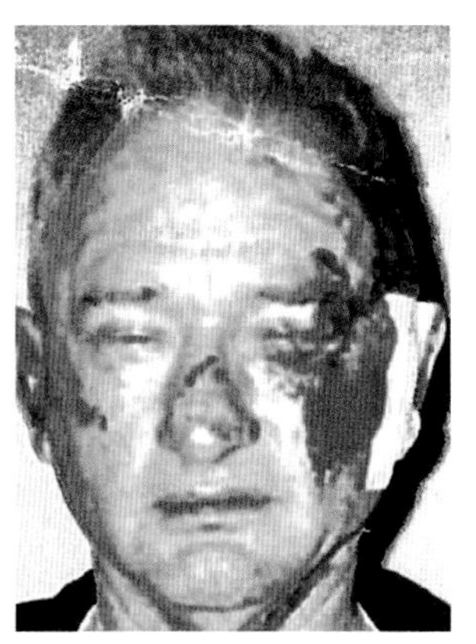

Ray Johnson, Tween's partner in crime, after being confronted by NSW Police and resisting arrest.

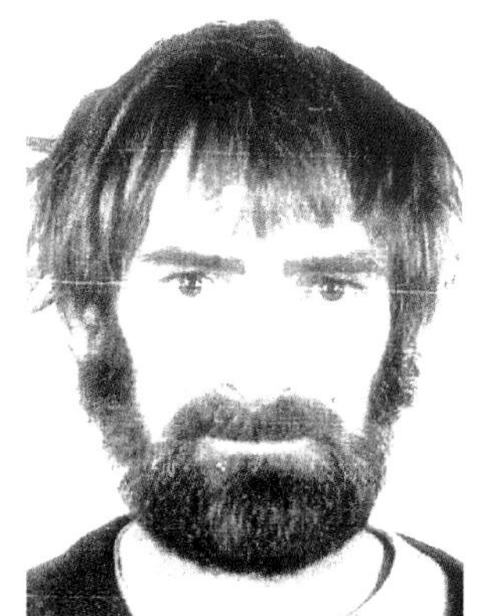

Garry Batt was another of Tween's accomplices, until he decided that Tween was 'as mad as a meat axe'.

Ante 'Tony' Yelavich, a heroin dealer from the Northern Beaches, disappeared in 1985 while on his way to Manly to buy heroin from Tween. Andrea Wharton, Tony's girlfriend, also used heroin; she disappeared in 1984. As with Trudie, neither of their bodies has ever been found. *Supplied images*

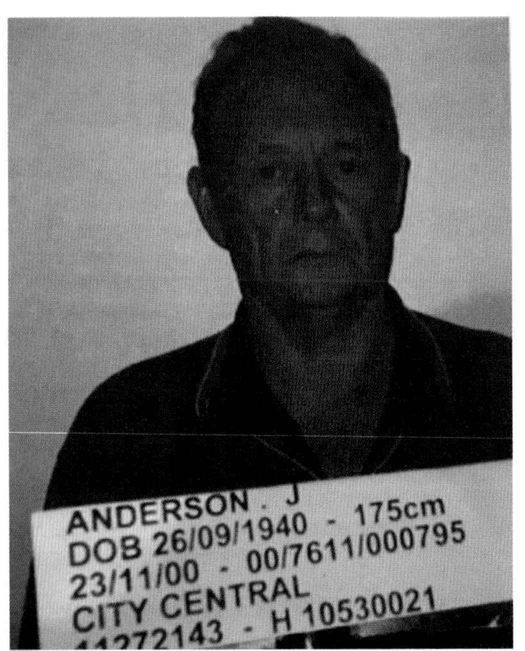

Neville Tween, by now known as John Anderson, in 2000. Note the DOB in the mugshot: 26/09/1940. To confuse the authorities, he changed his date of birth several times over the years – he was actually born on 29/06/1940.

During a routine inspection in 2006, law enforcement officers discovered Tween's cocaine attached to the hull of the *Tampa*. As later evidence revealed, it wasn't the first time he had imported the drug. *Handout photo released by Australian Federal Police / AAP Image*

NSW Crime Commission chief investigator Mark Standen being led into court in 2009 to face drug charges following his arrest the year before.
Lindsay Moller / Newspix

In 2008, James Kinch, Standen's informer and co-conspirator, was arrested in Thailand, where he languished in jail for years before being extradited to Australia.
Supplied

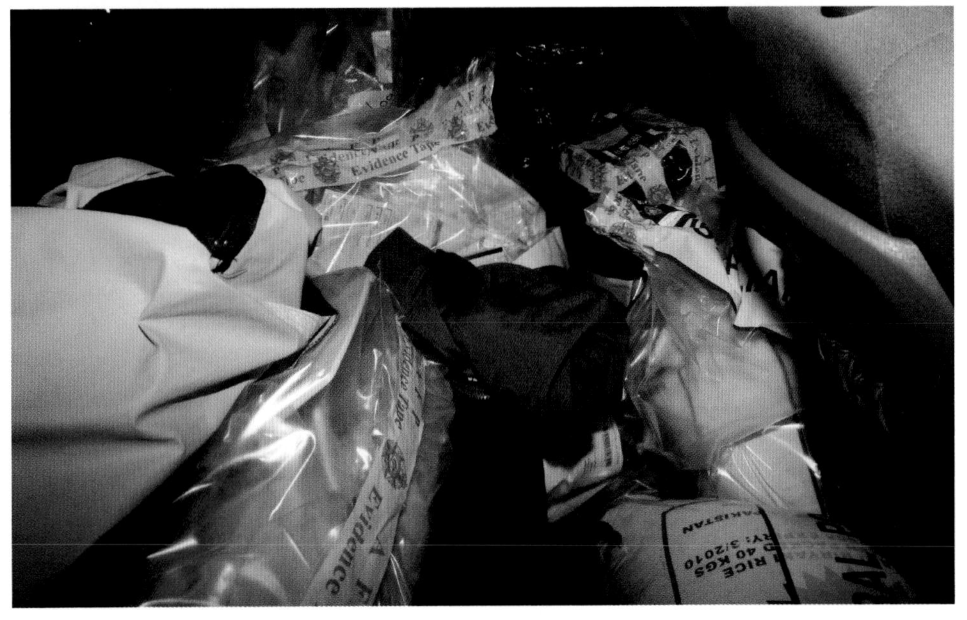

Both Standen and Kinch were accused of being key players in a conspiracy to import hundreds of kilograms of pseudoephedrine, yet no drugs ever arrived – just bags and bags of rice. *Sam Mooy / Newspix*

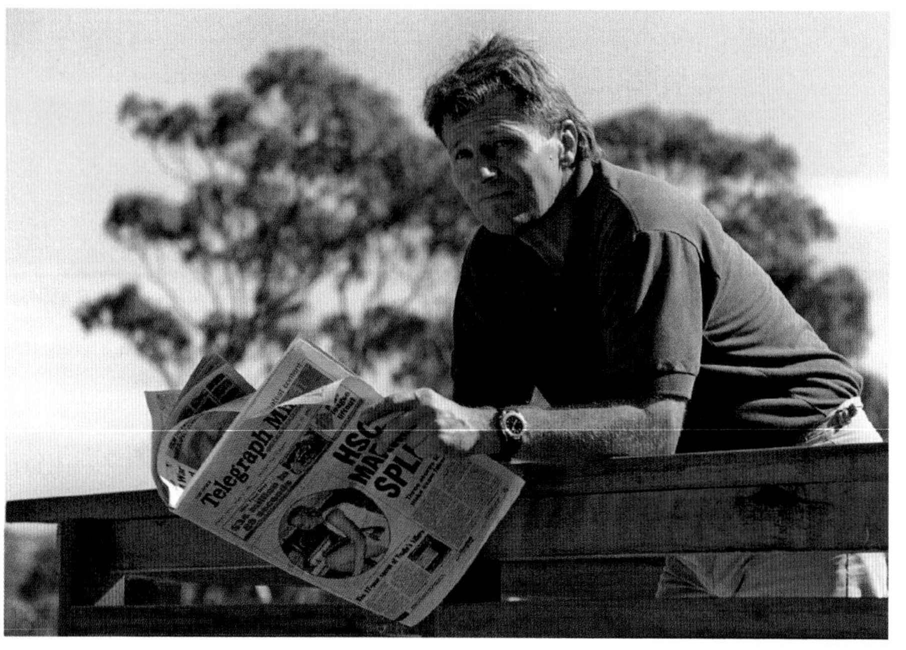

In 1995, NSW Police reopened Trudie's case, and the story made front-page news again, although this time they had a completely different set of suspects in their sights. Steve Norris (pictured) hoped that finally, 17 years later, there would be a breakthrough, but those hopes were soon dashed. *Marc Vignes / Newspix*

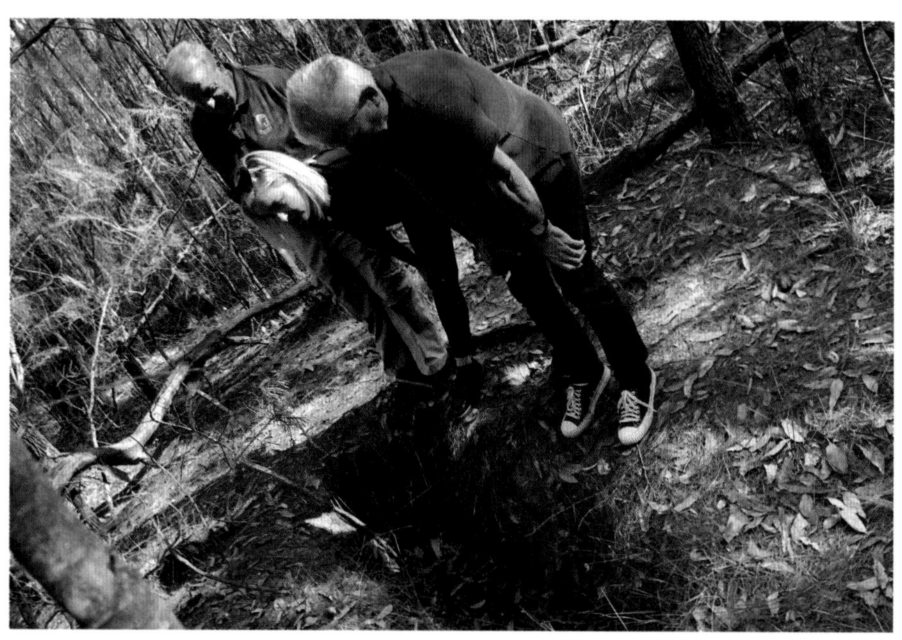

Park ranger Brian Walker and the authors look into a 'grave' that Walker had discovered in Ku-ring-gai Chase National Park in 1978. At the time of writing, it was still there. © *WildBear Entertainment*

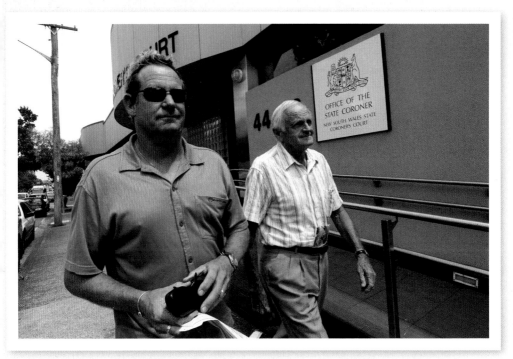

Trudie's brother John and her father, Charles, along with a number of her friends, attended the 2011 Coronial Inquest into her disappearance. *Brad Hunter / Newspix*

Neville Tween, aka John Anderson, leaves the inquest in a police vehicle. Back in 1971, one victim of sexual assault on the Northern Beaches couldn't initially identify her attacker but told police, 'I remember that the driver had snaky type of eyes.' *Craig Greenhill / Newspix*

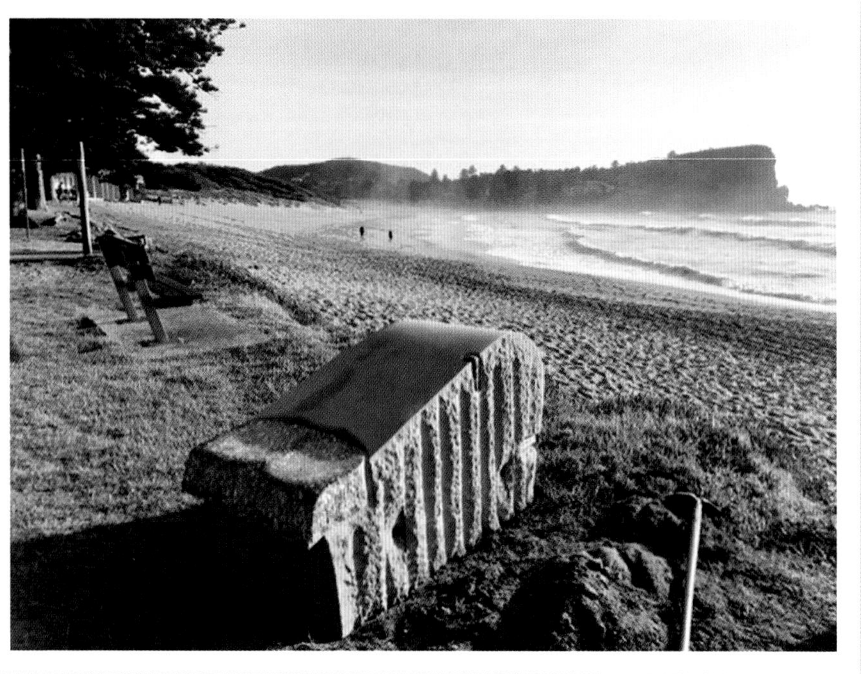

For years, Trudie's friends tried to have a plaque or memorial created in her honour. In 2019 – 41 years after she disappeared – it finally happened: Trudie's whale stone, a beautiful sandstone and blue crystal granite sculpture, was installed on Avalon Beach.

according to the National Crime Authority, which had alerted the Federal Police in the same year.

Standen was probably at the peak of his influence at the NSW Crime Commission. And while he and the commission often got significant results – arrests of major criminals and the seizure of millions of dollars in assets – some NSW and Federal Police regarded him as a 'cowboy' with little regard for the strict rules of running major operations or indeed informers. By all accounts, he wasn't big on paperwork and there were niggling rumours about his gambling habits.

In 2004, the Crime Commission launched one of its most controversial operations, which involved selling 7 kilograms of cocaine on to the streets of Sydney.

It came about through an informant known as 'Tom' who wanted to do a deal. Tom led Standen to a 7-kilogram stash of cocaine buried at Wahroonga, which was then taken to the Crime Commission offices in Sydney's CBD. Standen allowed Tom to re-package the drugs for sale on the street, the idea being that Tom would lead the commission to other major dealers down the track.

At this stage, Standen didn't have the authority to conduct what's called a 'controlled' operation to legally allow the sale of the cocaine. However, he obtained the authority from the commission's boss, Phil Bradley, just hours before Tom started selling the cocaine in various Sydney suburbs.

Only 1 kilogram was ever recovered. The rest went up the noses of thousands of Sydneysiders.

When details of the undercover operation emerged in court, the magistrate hearing the case described the decision to allow the sale of cocaine around the city as 'jaw-dropping'. It also emerged that the Federal Police had pulled out of the operation because supplying cocaine in this way wasn't permitted under federal laws.

Standen's reputation as a 'cowboy' was enhanced, particularly after he gave evidence that he'd looked up Google and couldn't find any deaths related to cocaine, so it was not a life-threatening drug.

Having worked in customs, the Narcotics Bureau, the AFP, the NCA and then the Crime Commission, there was no way Standen could not have known cocaine could be deadly.

As the National Drug and Alcohol Research Centre stated after Standen's testimony became public: 'People do die from cocaine.'

In the end, Tom handed over $1.1 million in cash to the Crime Commission – the proceeds of the sales he'd made around the city. And the operation did later result in major arrests of Sydney organised crime figures.

As for Neville Tween, he was becoming even more erratic as a result of his cocaine use. Kylie recalls an incident where he was found wandering naked in Wyong, the result of one of his binges, which could last for days.

'He was coming down off the coke,' Kylie recalls.

However, when police arrived, Tween faked a heart issue and they took him to hospital instead of a cell.

Given the crimes of which he'd been convicted and those of which he was suspected, running around naked in public wasn't a big deal. Still, Tween was never charged. Nor did his behaviour or demeanour apparently spark any suspicion. He got away with it again.

* * *

While Tween and Standen were engaged in their separate cocaine capers, the NSW Unsolved Homicide Unit had been quietly working away, once again, on the murder of Trudie Adams.

In November 2005, Strike Force Keldie was set up to re-investigate the circumstances surrounding her disappearance and the 14 sexual assaults, in particular the involvement of Tween.

One of the officers involved was Detective Senior Constable Ashley Bryant. After going through previous investigations and the statements of the 14 female rape victims, and that of Jimmy Holten, Detective Bryant and others came to the view that Tween could still be brought to justice.

In January 2006, he asked former Detective Inspector Bob Inkster, by then retired from the force, to take investigators to the area where Tween and Garry Batt had taken polaroid photos of Jimmy Holten as he was sexually assaulted in Ku-ring-gai Chase National Park. Inkster had little trouble finding the area, which was off a fire trail just 3.6 kilometres from where Tween used to live in Terrey Hills.

A check of Tween's drivers licence and the electoral roll revealed he'd given his 2006 address as 8 Lakeside Parade, The Entrance, and had three motor vehicles registered in his name.

In an affidavit Ashley Bryant prepared to gain a warrant to perform surveillance on Tween, he wrote that he believed Tween was guilty of the offences of rape, buggery, indecent assault of a female, carnal knowledge of a girl aged ten to 16, kidnapping, murder and manslaughter.

Bryant sought 'the authority to use three listening devices and two cameras by installing two such devices and one camera into premises situated at 8 Lakeside Parade, The

Entrance'. Bryant also wanted to put a listening device and a camera in the 1994 silver Mitsubishi Magna station wagon Tween had been seen driving. Bryant spelt out the intention of investigators to 'speak with friends, associates and relatives of [Tween] regarding the 1978 disappearance of Trudie Adams'.

Part of Bryant's plan involved using the media and it was expected there would be 'extensive coverage' of police searching Ku-ring-gai Chase National Park 'where it is suspected the body of Trudie Adams is buried'. And he said investigators would seek to formally interview Tween regarding the abduction and murder of Trudie Adams. He also noted that there had been 'no previous applications made or warrants granted under the Listening Devices Act 1984 in respect of the prescribed offences'.

Physical surveillance was carried out in Lakeside Parade on 27 and 28 February 2006. Police saw Tween's car in the driveway on the first day and then Tween leaving and returning in one of the vehicles he owned on the second day. There is no public record of any more surveillance until three days in August 2006. Once again, Tween was seen on the premises.

However, once again, nothing happened, although at least this time there was a likely explanation – for the first time in years, other law enforcement agencies were also taking a serious interest in Tween. It all started in New Zealand. On 7 June 2006, the cargo ship *Tampa* left Panama in South America bound for Auckland and then Australia.

After it arrived in Auckland on 25 June, divers working for the New Zealand Quarantine Service conducted what was later described as 'a routine inspection of the hull'.

They discovered a large, watertight aluminium container 'secured by chains below the waterline'. Upon removing and opening the container, customs officers found 25 'Décor'-brand plastic containers full of cocaine. All up, there was 18.3 kilograms with a street value of $8.2 million.

If the *Tampa* sounds familiar, that's because it was the same ship that a few years earlier had sparked one of Australia's biggest political controversies and was the catalyst for Australia's tough stance on border security, a legacy that still reverberates today.

In August 2001, the *Tampa*'s Norwegian commander had rescued 433 asylum-seekers from a dilapidated Indonesian fishing boat in the Indian Ocean. He tried to bring them to Australia, but then Prime Minister John Howard refused to take them. The ensuing tug of war ended with John Howard making his election-defining statement, 'We will decide who comes to this country and the circumstances in which they come.'

Now, five years later, New Zealand authorities decided not to reattach the container of cocaine to the *Tampa* and alerted their Australian counterparts as to what they'd found. The ship docked in Brisbane on 29 June.

By this time, it appears Mark Standen had either decided that Tween had outlived his usefulness or that, given the New Zealand authorities had alerted their Australian counterparts, matters were now out of his control.

He has since claimed he was responsible for bringing about the arrest of his informant and family friend. Standen says that when New Zealand Customs found the cocaine attached to the hull, he gave a very detailed 20-or-so-minute briefing to the Australian Federal Police 'about Tween's historic connections with such activity and the modus operandi of such types of importations'.

Standen said his team at the NSW Crime Commission provided telephone interception, staff and other support to the AFP-led investigation.

Which begs the question: If Standen knew about Tween's 'historic' connections and his 'modus operandi' from 1992, why hadn't he ever done anything about it until New Zealand authorities found the cocaine attached to the *Tampa*?

Was it because Tween had 'given' him Ian Saxon, and maybe other major crims?

An official document detailing Tween's suspected cocaine importations in 1992 states, '[These] inquiries are on hold so as not to jeopardise the security of the inquiry. Future inquiries into the financial affairs and possible money-laundering activities of [Tween] and associates have also been placed on hold.'

Fourteen years is a long time for inquiries into a suspected major drug importer to remain on hold, and the period coincides with the time Tween was Standen's informer.

Within days of the Auckland discovery, the AFP put Tween under physical and electronic surveillance. The day after the *Tampa* arrived in Brisbane, Michael Anderson (Tween's son from his first marriage to Dulcie) flew to Brisbane while his dad drove there towing a boat.

But the *Tampa* departed Brisbane on 30 June, perhaps not giving father and son enough time to dive for the drugs, and sailed for Fremantle in Western Australia where it was to stay until 11 July.

On 4 July 2006, Tween telephoned Michael and left a message regarding the *Tampa* and that he would be going to Perth. The AFP listened in as Tween told his son, 'The lady's birthday is on or about the 9th, so if, er, you could make, get her present and that by about Thursday or Friday, say

Friday the 7th or 8th. Make sure that we don't miss giving her presents. Okay, bye for now.'

Not long after that phone call, Neville Tween flew to Perth with flippers, a mask and a wetsuit in his luggage. From there he went to the port of Fremantle, where he hired two oxygen cylinders and weight belts from a dive hire shop. He also picked up a 2.7-metre inflatable dinghy, an outboard motor, anchor and rope.

After Michael joined him, they went in search of the *Tampa*. Surveillance police watched father and son on 9 and 10 July as they scouted areas close to where the *Tampa* was moored in Fremantle Harbour. Finally, on the evening of 10 July 2006, Neville and Michael took the dinghy out to North Quay wharf, where the *Tampa* had docked.

Police surveillance continued as they propelled themselves towards the *Tampa* by hanging onto pipes underneath the quay. A police sonar operator observed an object about 1.9 metres in length 'swimming purposefully' around the bow thruster of the *Tampa* for about 20 minutes. Police later said it was Michael Anderson diving on the hull, looking for the aluminium container carrying the 18.3 kilograms of cocaine.

It wasn't there. The next day Michael flew back to Sydney, but his father stayed in Perth for a few days.

***

Neville Tween didn't give up, but neither did the police.

Two months later, in September 2006, the *Taronga* arrived in Auckland Harbour. On 28 September, divers inspecting the hull found a metal container similar to that on the *Tampa* attached in the same way to the bow.

When customs officers opened it they found plastic containers containing 8.7 kilograms of cocaine with a purity of 76 per cent, the same as the previous shipment.

This time, New Zealand authorities substituted the cocaine and reattached the container to the hull. As the ship left New Zealand bound for Brisbane, Federal Police officers continued to tap Neville Tween's phone calls. He was in constant contact with a person called 'Jamie' in Panama, whom he rang more than 40 times in a single month. They discussed vessels, calling them 'senoritas'.

It became apparent during the course of the calls that Tween was not going to be able to remove the containers from the bow thruster of the *Taronga* without somebody's assistance. That assistance was never forthcoming and Tween didn't dive under the boat or recover any cocaine.

* * *

On 25 October 2006, Federal and NSW Police raided five homes, units and other premises known to be associated with Tween including his home at The Entrance.

Kylie had just dropped her son off at school when she got a phone call from one of her brothers. 'Kylie, the cops are here!' he said. 'They're searching the house … looking for drugs'.

Knowing it must be something to do with her stepfather, she jumped in the car and went straight to Tween's other residence, thinking he'd know what was going on. However, all she found was Bonnie the dog, alone in the front yard.

Kylie jumped back into the car and went straight to the house where her brothers were. The street was full of cop cars. Kylie bolted into the house.

Police told her that her stepfather had been arrested, and showed her their search warrant. It revealed they weren't just looking for drugs, but also for night vision equipment and various tools Tween would have used.

Officers then went out to the back of the house where there was a pool with several bags of pool cleaning chemicals lying around. One of the officers cut a big hessian bag open, thinking it contained cocaine, and put some of the powder into his mouth, all of which was videotaped.

Watching the tape later, Kylie could see the chemicals were burning his mouth, and she remembers saying to herself, 'You've been watching too many cop movies, mate.'

The search of Tween's home turned up a plastic re-sealable bag containing 11.5 grams of cocaine, later found to be 75 per cent pure. Meanwhile, police recovered a plastic re-sealable bag containing a quantity of cocaine at Michael's house in Mona Vale, which turned out to be 76 per cent pure.

At a unit in Wyong – not far from where Tween had been found naked in public a year or so earlier – police found numerous items including a large amount of Mannitol, which is a cutting agent for cocaine, as well as test tubes and plastic pipes that contained residues of cocaine. Crucially, they also discovered the same 'Décor'-brand containers as the ones New Zealand customs officers had taken from the *Tampa* and the *Taronga*.

They found internet searches done by Tween and his son in August, September and October looking for information about the movements of the *Tampa* and the *Taronga*. To top it all off, they located documents detailing how to pack small quantities of cocaine.

It was clear to investigating police that Tween had been in the cocaine business for some time. New Zealand customs had kept the Décor containers they'd retrieved from the *Tampa* and the ones on the *Taronga* had never been collected. Tween's previous importations had clearly been successful.

Indeed, father and son had travelled to Panama the previous year, Michael going there in October and November 2005, while his father was in Panama from 21 October to 10 December, travelling on a false passport in the name of Victor Patrick Harris.

Tween was arrested, as was Michael, who until then had never been in trouble with the law and had actually been studying law at the time of his arrest.

Police alleged the combined street value of the cocaine on the *Tampa* and the *Taronga* was $11.5 million.

Tween didn't speak to the arresting police at the time. However, four months after his arrest and after he was served with the police brief of evidence against him, he provided a handwritten statement and did a tape-recorded record of the interview in the presence of his lawyer.

He had an explanation for what had happened – it was all about emeralds, not cocaine. He claimed that in 2000 or 2001 he'd been in Hong Kong and met a bloke by the name of Jamie Hotta, who owned an emerald export company known as 'The Green Future'. Tween said he'd decided to team up with Mr Hotta to smuggle uncut emeralds into Australia to avoid paying customs duty. He claimed he'd become suspicious at a certain point, thinking it was possible the containers would contain cocaine instead of emeralds, but he'd been too afraid of repercussions to pull out of the enterprise.

The arrest of Tween didn't stop Strike Force Keldie, but it did cause Ashley Bryant to take stock. He was subsequently promoted to detective sergeant and posted to Bourke in the state's far west. This meant another officer would have to take over the cold case investigation into Trudie Adams' presumed murder and bring himself up to speed with the mass of material relating to Trudie, Tween and the rapes.

Once again, the investigation had been set back, but the arrest of Tween and his son also offered an opportunity. Tween was 66 when he was busted. He and 29-year-old Michael were in jail on remand while they awaited trial. If found guilty, both were facing long jail sentences. Police hoped they would be able to leverage the situation to their advantage and finally find the answer to what had happened to Trudie.

Chapter 21

The Yelavich Connection

As fate would have it, around the time Tween and his son were awaiting their cocaine importation, NSW Police officer Jayson Macleod was assigned to review the investigation into the 1985 disappearance and suspected murder of Tony Yelavich. The case had sat in the unsolved homicide pile for years. It wasn't easy work, with detectives having to juggle numerous inquiries with some matters that went back decades. And in the case of Tony Yelavich there was no body and no witnesses. Just as there was no trace of Trudie Adams, or any of her clothing.

Many cold cases are reviewed, but for an unsolved murder to be revived into a full-on investigation there needs to be some prospect of success. Maybe clothing seized decades earlier could be subjected to new DNA procedures. Perhaps the marriage of a suspect has broken up – relationships change and so do the prospects of a former partner or lover giving some new evidence they'd previously been too afraid to reveal. Or it might be that the suspected offender is in jail for other matters and witnesses are no longer as frightened to come forward.

Jayson Macleod was still relatively new at Manly Police Station, having arrived there in 2006, and he was eager to prove himself. He now had carriage of what was called Strike Force Bredin. He dived into the files of the original Yelavich inquiry in 1985 and 1986. 'I lived and breathed it,' he recalls. 'Despite all the dramas … it was fantastic … I loved it.'

It didn't take him long to work out that Neville Tween was the main suspect in Tony's disappearance. He put Tween's name into the police case management system known as Eagle Eye and was astonished by what he found. For a start, there were all the aliases, at least 12 of them, and the litany of offences – more than 100 – with which he'd been charged since the age of nine.

And there were the matters in which Tween was a suspect – the murders of Trudie Adams and Tony Yelavich. He was mentioned in connection with the disappearance of Andrea Wharton and the 14 rapes of young women on the Northern Beaches.

'Everywhere I looked the matter was just growing,' he recalls.

He wondered how many other bodies or how many other missing people were linked to Tween and his associates.

He was rattled by the complexity of the inquiry and what he was up against, describing the interconnected cases as like a 'hornet's nest'.

He also smelt a rat. It was a shocking list of apparently related crimes that had somehow never been brought under the one umbrella or received the intensive and cohesive investigation they deserved. The detective was troubled by the obvious question: 'Why not?' He felt something was 'really, really wrong, really wrong.'

He discovered that while he'd been looking into the Yelavich case, the Unsolved Homicide Team had been separately reviewing Trudie's case via Strike Force Keldie. Macleod wanted to join Yelavich's case, Trudie Adams' case and the 14 rapes into a single, high-powered investigation with Neville Tween as the main suspect.

He spoke to Detective Mitch Dubojski, who had taken over carriage of the Trudie Adams' case from Ashley Bryant. The two officers, working on separate cases, had both formed the view that Neville Tween was a very strong suspect for the murders and sexual assaults.

Macleod got in touch with Ashley Bryant and expressed his concern that there was evidence available that should have been acted on much earlier. He said that Ashley Bryant agreed.

Macleod then turned to the NSW Crime Commission, which had the power to interrogate suspects in secret and compel them to answer questions and produce documents, including financial and bank records, property transactions and purchases of things like boats and motor vehicles.

He contacted Mark Standen to ask for help. While Macleod didn't know Standen, he did know he was a senior and powerful investigator – a mover and a shaker, a law enforcement officer who could get things done.

Macleod said he was encouraged by Detective Dubojski, who said he'd already been in touch with Standen to see if he could help with Strike Force Keldie.

According to official police documents, Standen told Dubojski he was not aware of any holdings or information that could assist an investigation targeting Neville Tween. In 2007, Standen also informed Macleod that he was not aware of any holdings, or any informants who could assist in his inquiry. However, Macleod continued to liaise with Standen over the following months, while Neville Tween was on remand for the cocaine importation.

According to Macleod, Standen told him he'd had dealings with Tween 'over many years' and had a 'similar rapport with Raymond Johnson'. Standen encouraged Macleod to forward a proposed reference to the NSW Crime Commission on the disappearance of Tony Yelavich and not wait to see whether the NSW Homicide Squad wanted to merge the two strike forces.

In January 2008, Macleod sent a comprehensive overview of his investigation into both the Adams and Yelavich murders as well as the dates, times and places of the 14 sexual assaults between 1971 and 1978 and the assault in 1975 of Jimmy Holten. He also included the fact that Neville Tween and Ray Johnson had been identified as the attackers by some of the victims. The document further undermines Standen's claim that the first he ever heard of Neville Tween being a suspect in the rapes was in 2011.

As part of the strike force, Macleod had targeted Tween via the internal NSW Police administration system COPS. This meant he would get a notification when anyone else searched for Neville Tween or the name he'd by now been using for years, John Anderson. Macleod says he applied to get a bigger team on the case. 'It was pretty clear that this was something that needed a large task force to address it competently.'

Macleod emailed Mark Standen, saying he'd drafted a request for assistance from the Crime Commission regarding Neville Tween for the murder of Tony Yelavich on 2 September 1985. He added that the Homicide Squad had agreed to a meeting on 26 February 2008 to discuss a merging of their Strike Force into Trudie Adams' disappearance and possible future directions in the investigation. He added that Tween was presently sharing a cell at Parklea with his son Michael for drug importation and their trial was due to commence on 14 April 2008.

'I believe that it is a great opportunity for an L.D. [listening device] in their cell, in conjunction with perhaps some coercive hearings/media, etc.'

He then asked Standen if the commission was to take on an inquiry into the Yelavich/Adams cases 'do you have any idea how long it would take for the commission to list a hearing?

'I'm just considering time frames and I understand that the [April trial date] is looming very quickly.'

He closed his email by saying that 'any feedback would be greatly appreciated'.

Macleod recalled faxing the investigation plan to Standen and following it up with a number of phone calls and other emails clarifying what they were going to do.

According to Macleod, Mark Standen initially appeared keen to help, making it very clear that he wanted to be in on the investigation and was going to support it. Macleod also said Standen provided him with some intelligence about Tween, telling him Tween had 'lightened up' and 'softened up' over the years. This was despite Tween actually being in jail on major cocaine charges at the time.

'It made it very clear to me that he knew him. I thought okay he's … potentially got an informant here or he's got some exposure to him.'

Although Macleod didn't know it at the start of his dealings with the Crime Commission, his instincts were correct that Tween had been an informant to Mark Standen.

At first, Macleod was buoyed by the idea that Standen would use this connection to help him with his investigation. But his confidence started to waver when Standen began to stall.

'He was offering excuses as to why we couldn't come in and meet, competing jobs, the Crime Commissioner wasn't available, and so forth.'

An email from Standen to Macleod on 28 March 2008 starts: 'Sorry about being uncontactable last week, but we were flat out on that job re 28kgs heroin which was on the news last Friday.'

It goes on to say: 'Phillip [Bradley – the commission head] is still not back. Yesterday the Minister was at a funeral.'

He told Macleod he needed Phillip Bradley and the minister 'in the one place at the one time. Frustrating, I know. Will keep you posted.'

As the weeks stretched on, Macleod became more concerned because the help he thought he was going to get from the Crime Commission simply wasn't forthcoming. Something wasn't quite right – Standen was giving him the runaround.

Then a police computer system alert showed that someone in the force had searched for Neville Tween. Macleod's unease grew when he discovered that the search had been done by someone in the Recruitment Branch. Puzzled, he emailed the young constable.

'Hi … I have a current investigation where Neville Brian Tween … is listed as a target via case management. I noted that you accessed his CNI [Central Names Index] … could you please let me know why you conducted this access?'

The recruitment officer told Macleod that Standen's son Matthew had applied to join the NSW Police Force and that

Matthew had put down Neville Tween as a referee. Macleod says: 'The constable was good enough to read to me verbatim what was written on that job application, and it was making reference to the fact the Neville Tween was going away on family weekends with the Standen family, and they were diving trips, scuba diving trips.'

Macleod asked the constable to put Matthew Standen's job application in a safe and treat it as an exhibit. Then he was told that the recruitment branch officer had done another search and discovered that, at some point, Mark Standen and Neville Tween had both lived at the same address in Lakin Street, Bateau Bay, on the NSW Central Coast.

To Macleod this made no sense.

'I just recall being quite faint, to be honest with you. I was seated but I felt quite dizzy at that time.'

He thought his investigation, and his personal safety, had been compromised.

Macleod made a formal report to his superiors and then sat tight. He expected them to knock down doors and demand answers, given he thought he'd uncovered a potentially corrupt connection between a serious criminal and one of the most senior law enforcement officers in the country.

But nothing happened, and days turned into weeks with no phone calls and no interviews. For Macleod, it was perhaps the worst time he had ever endured. He was acutely aware that Neville Tween had form in violent crimes and it didn't matter that he was in jail. After all, he had plenty of associates.

The situation became unbearably tense and started to take its toll. Macleod felt completely isolated and stopped sleeping, concerned as he was for his personal safety. 'These guys were explosive experts,' he explained, 'and they had no qualms about taking somebody out if they needed to.'

It was heading towards winter at the time and Macleod said he was waking up at 5am for his drive to work in the pitch black and cold. He recalled being very nervous whenever he walked out to his car, which was normally parked on the road and accessible to anyone. 'There were occasions obviously going to work, starting the car … and waiting for a boom.'

This might sound like an exaggeration, paranoia, but it's not unheard of for criminals to target police.

In June 1984, NSW Police undercover officer Michael Drury was at home with his wife and children when he was shot twice as he stood at the kitchen window – most probably by gun-for-hire Christopher Dale Flannery. It was a miracle Drury survived.

Flannery, the suspected gunman, disappeared in 1985 and his body has never been found. Former NSW Police Detective Sergeant Roger Rogerson was subsequently charged with conspiring to murder Drury but was later acquitted.

In March 1986, a car bomb exploded outside the Russell Street Police building in Melbourne, killing 21-year-old police officer Angela Taylor and injuring 22 others. In January 1989, an assistant commissioner in the Australian Federal Police, Colin Winchester, was murdered with two bullets to the head from a rifle fitted with a silencer as he pulled into a driveway next to his home.

David Eastman, a disgruntled public servant, was later convicted of Winchester's murder but always maintained his innocence. Some senior police believed Eastman was incapable of committing such a sophisticated killing and instead blamed Winchester's death on the Italian Mafia – the 'Ndrangheta – which was active in growing large marijuana crops at the time.

After serving 19 years, Eastman's conviction was quashed and he was found not guilty at a re-trial that revealed some of the evidence against him had been fatally flawed. He was later awarded $7 million in compensation.

Macleod's car wasn't blown up but his belief in NSW Police, the organisation he loved and had worked in for 12 years, was utterly shattered and he quit.

* * *

Mark Standen says categorically that Neville Tween was never a referee for his son Matthew, describing the idea as 'absurd', pointing out that Tween was in jail when Matthew applied. He says that somehow Macleod must have been confused by the information he was given. He also asserted that someone from the AFP, knowing about the Tween connection, might have alerted the NSW Police recruiters in an effort to torpedo Matthew's job prospects.

Macleod is just as adamant that he wasn't confused and later gave evidence on oath to that effect.

Chapter 22

Downfall

Mark Standen didn't know it, but a countdown on his controversial career had started. Time was running out. Just over a year after the Crime Commission's 2005 cocaine capers – selling 7 kilograms onto the streets of Sydney – the Australian Federal Police had started an investigation into a drug trafficking syndicate based in the Netherlands.

The syndicate was thought to be sending hundreds of kilos of drugs – ecstasy and pseudoephedrine – into Australia.

In June 2006, the AFP teamed up with their colleagues in the Dutch National Crime Squad in what was called Operation Octans.

Quite coincidentally, it was around the same time the *Tampa* was sailing into Auckland Harbour with cocaine attached to its hull.

The joint investigation soon learnt that the syndicate's plan was to import pseudoephedrine – a precursor necessary to make the drug ice, cheaper and more lethal than cocaine.

It was to be brought in disguised in foodstuff.

Investigators received a tip-off that the syndicate was using a company called MDL Food and Services, which was based in India. However, the Federal Police had not been able to identify the company and came to the conclusion it didn't really exist – it was a front.

Then, on 15 May 2007, a fax was sent from the phoney company, but it wasn't sent from India – it came from an internet café in Amsterdam that was under surveillance by the Dutch Police who were cooperating with the AFP. It was addressed to a small company called BJ's Fine Quality Foods, located in Blacktown, in Sydney's western suburbs. The AFP identified the directors of BJ's Fine Quality Foods as Bakhos (Bill) Jalalaty, then 44 years old. His co-director was his wife, Dianne Jalalaty, previously Dianne James. Eyebrows were raised. Dianne James was a former police officer who had worked for the AFP and the National Crime Authority investigating drugs.

The fax was a crucial breakthrough – it revealed the Dutch syndicate wanted to send 'rice' from Pakistan to Bill Jalalaty in Australia. Telephone intercepts and listening devices were put in place in Australia and the Netherlands within days.

On 24 May 2007, investigators were stunned as they listened to a conversation Bill Jalalaty had with another man in Sydney. It was Mark Standen. After greeting each other, Jalalaty asked Standen if everything was alright.

'Yeah, yeah, okay,' Standen replied. 'Are you on target for your trip?'

As Commander Jan Boersma from the Dutch police later told the ABC's *Four Corners* television program, the revelation was 'shattering.' Standen was 'not just an ordinary police officer but an important police officer also in the collaboration with Europe.'

In other words, Standen had been involved in investigating international syndicates for years. Now it appeared he'd joined them.

The joint investigation also discovered that, in January 2007, Bill Jalalaty had met up with Standen in Dubai. Standen had taken a colleague he was having an affair with, a 20-something Crime Commission employee, Louise Baker. She'd been employed by the commission as a Listening Post Monitor since September 2005.

Her job was to listen to tapped telephone calls, sometimes in real time as they were happening, sometimes at a later stage.

While Standen and Bill Jalalaty were in Dubai, they met up with a third man, James Henry Kinch, an Irishman born in July 1958 and who, like Neville Tween, had been in trouble with the law since he was just a kid, in Kinch's case the age of 11.

In many ways, his record was not unlike his Australian counterpart. Like Tween, Kinch's childhood misdemeanours were followed by dozens of convictions for break and enter, stealing, fraud, firearms and drug offences. Like Tween, Kinch had spent years in and out of jail.

What does this have to do with Trudie Adams and the unsolved rapes?

Just this. There are parallels between Standen's relationship with Kinch and his relationship with Tween. Standen was close to both men, much closer than he should have been. Over the years, favours were done, money was paid, charges were dropped and investigations that should have been launched didn't get off the ground.

The story of what happened between Kinch and Standen can tell us a lot about Mark Standen, and what he did, and didn't do.

***

While Standen was in Dubai, rumours about his behaviour swept through the high-security offices of the NSW Crime Commission in Sydney's CBD. They caught the attention of the commission's head, Phillip Bradley, who mentioned it to John Giorgiutti, the commission's chief lawyer. After Bradley, Giorgiutti and Standen were the two most powerful and influential figures in the commission.

After returning from leave, Standen told John Giorgiutti that he had been to Dubai with Louise Baker. He apparently thought their affair was 'an open secret'. Subsequently, Standen told Giorgiutti that the relationship had started in August 2006. He also said that the Dubai trip had been paid for by Jalalaty. Giorgiutti said he reported this to Bradley but made no file notes.

Alarm bells should have been ringing, though they were perhaps muted because Bill Jalalaty's wife, Dianne, had known Standen since the 1980s. They had first met when she joined the Australian Federal Police, and again later while working for the National Crime Authority, where Standen had been a colleague. After leaving the NCA, she met her future husband, remained friends with Mark, and later introduced them.

While there is no suggestion that Louise Baker was in any way implicated in Standen's corrupt dealings, Crime Commission boss Phil Bradley was not impressed by the relationship between Standen and Baker and the circumstances by which Jalalaty had come to pay for Standen's trip to Dubai. Both matters had caused tensions within the management team.

Giorgiutti was present at one meeting between Bradley and Standen, though again he made no file notes. One outcome of the meeting was that Standen took further leave and Giorgiutti acted in his position.

In all of this, Louise Baker was a junior player while Standen was one of the most senior, powerful men in the commission. He lavished her with expensive gifts, including designer handbags and jewellery, and took her away for stays in five-star hotels.

In order to reduce the 'tensions' in the office, she left and took up a job with the NSW Independent Commission Against Corruption.

It appears that while on his return Standen mentioned his affair, he didn't bother to mention that he'd met with the career criminal Jimmy Kinch.

Perhaps for a very good reason. He and Kinch had a history, a rich history, a bit like the one Standen had with Tween.

In March 2003, Kinch had been arrested in Sydney as a result of a joint operation involving the Crime Commission, the AFP and NSW Police in which Standen was front and centre. Kinch faced two charges of supplying and possessing a commercial amount of a prohibited drug and a third charge of money laundering. Both Australian and overseas police regarded him as a major criminal and a key player in importing and selling massive quantities of drugs and moving millions of dollars in cash.

Yet within months, Kinch was doing secret deals with the Crime Commission – like Tween, he knew the system and how to play it. Kinch had rolled over and become an informant or, officially, a 'Commission Human Source'. He was ultimately registered later that year, assigned a number, 704, and given a code name – Hogan. His 'handler', that is the person he dealt with, was Mark Standen.

On 24 May 2003, Phil Bradley wrote to the NSW Director of Public Prosecutions (DPP) saying that Kinch 'had indicated a willingness to plead guilty to the drug charge in return for the NSW DPP not proceeding on the money-laundering charge'.

Bradley's letter was supported by one Standen had written a day earlier, which said that Kinch had consented to the forfeiture of cash and real estate valued at $1 million. The money-laundering charge was duly dropped but the drugs charges remained.

But then the prosecution hit an unexpected snag. Mark Standen had taken the original statement from a key female witness on the drugs charges against Kinch. But questioned further by the DPP, the woman claimed Standen had 'verballed her' and that her original statement was not entirely true. When she was asked about specific parts of her statement implicating Kinch she told the DPP, 'Mark put that in.'

As required by law, the DPP notified the legal team acting for Kinch of this, which for Kinch was gold. He made an application for a 'no-bill' – that is, for the drugs charges to be dropped.

On 28 November 2003, Standen wrote in response to that application that 'Mr Kinch has been providing frequent, high-quality information to the commission. His original information led directly to the seizure of 229 kilograms of ecstasy.' Standen acknowledged the money-laundering charge had been withdrawn, adding, 'It is fair to say the money-laundering case was far from strong.'

Kinch had agreed to forfeit assets to the value of about $1.3 million. And, yes, the Crime Commission had advised the DPP that Kinch would plead guilty to the two drug charges. But as Standen wrote: 'That did not eventuate.'

He added: 'Mr Kinch has stated that he did not give such an undertaking and that we [the Crime Commission] were mistaken.'

Standen attempted to explain this extraordinary chain of events by saying: '[Kinch] asserts that he did say he would plead guilty to the "right charge" ... it is unclear what this means.'

Between a key witness saying part of her statement had been fabricated by Standen, and Kinch digging in his heels, on 27 January 2004, the DPP dropped the drugs charges against James Kinch and returned his passport.

On 15 February, he left Australia less than a year after he'd been arrested.

At the centre of it all was Mark Standen, whose relationship with Kinch bore striking similarities to his relationship with Tween.

Kinch got off a major drugs charge and Tween got just 18 months for growing 1200 hydroponic plants in 1994. Standen had turned up in a small-town local court presumably to make sure that his 'gig' got bail. Not only that, Tween continued to import cocaine. Then in 2000, Tween received a good behaviour bond for fraud that, according to Kylie, involved at least $90,000. But by the time it got to court it only involved an amount of between just $5000 and $15,000 and the cops allegedly said Tween had receipts for the cash.

Kinch may have left the country but he continued his relationship with Standen. According to Crime Commission records, he remained a registered informer for Standen until around the end of 2005. But after leaving Australia, he also went back to what he did best – crime. Drugs, specifically international drug smuggling. Jimmy Kinch had played a blinder with a little help from his Crime Commission handler.

No doubt appreciative, in December 2005, Kinch sent Standen £20,000 (approximately AUD $47,000 back then), which was used, in part, to pay off some of Standen's credit cards.

As to the allegations Standen had made up parts of the female key witness's statement? Nothing happened. The DPP asked Standen for an explanation, but Standen never bothered to give one. After all, he worked for the NSW Crime Commission and there were secrecy provisions covering just about everything the commission did. Mark Standen did things his way and while the NSW Crime Commission continued to make arrests and bring in tens of millions of dollars in seized criminal assets – cash, luxury cars, property – the organisation 'paid' for itself.

Politicians didn't care or didn't want to know and a lot of others, including criminals, were happy doing deals to hand over assets like houses, boats, and/or cash (though in some cases not all of it), in the hope they'd be able to strike some sort of deal.

* * *

Throughout 2007 and into 2008, the AFP and their Dutch counterparts continued their inquiries into the syndicate planning a massive drug importation into Australia. They monitored communications between Bill Jalalaty, Standen and Kinch, the latter no longer a registered informant. Standen didn't tell anyone he was still in touch with Kinch, though he most certainly should have. Kinch was accessing Hotmail addresses from various countries, including the Netherlands, Portugal, Dubai and Germany.

As the AFP and Dutch police listened in they discovered that Kinch had given Jalalaty $1.7 million to set up the food importation business in order to give it a legitimate history. There would be some initial, legitimate importation of food, such as rice, to set things up.

Astonishingly, they also discovered that while Bill Jalalaty had invested some of the money to that end, he had also given more than $500,000 to a businessman named Bruce Way, who promised massive returns on investments. The money given to Way, who also claimed to be a clairvoyant, disappeared somewhere in a tax haven in the Bahamas.

In May 2007, Standen made inquiries about trying to find Bruce Way. A private investigator was called in to try to get the money back. Bruce Way met with Standen at the offices of the Crime Commission in June 2007, where he claimed that he too had been ripped off, something a clairvoyant presumably should have seen coming.

The $500,000 invested by Jalalaty with Bruce Way was never recovered.

Over the next few weeks, Jalalaty, Kinch and Standen remained in contact. During this time, Kinch met with members of the Dutch syndicate, who were known drug traffickers.

On 5 July, Jalalaty received a fax from 'MDL Food and Services' saying a sample shipment of rice would be sent in a container. The same day, law enforcement officers listened as the Dutch drug syndicate members spoke about sending the same fax from Amsterdam. The Dutch authorities also took photos of Kinch meeting with the syndicate members based in the Netherlands.

So far, the AFP had kept details of their operation secret. But with a shipment on the way their hand was forced.

Chapter 23

A Mountain of Rice

On the morning of 6 July 2007, Phil Bradley met with AFP Commissioner Mick Keelty and the Commissioner of the NSW Police, Ken Moroney.

It must have been an uncomfortable meeting. While Keelty had pulled the AFP out of the operation orchestrated by Standen to sell 7 kilograms of cocaine on the streets, Ken Moroney had backed it to the hilt. Keelty's news to his two counterparts that morning was almost unbelieveable. The AFP and their Dutch colleagues believed that Mark Standen was involved in a conspiracy to import pseudoephedrine into Australia along with Bill Jalalaty and James Kinch, as well as overseas syndicate members.

Not long after, Bradley called John Giorgiutti into his office at the Crime Commission and told him the news.

Both Bradley and Giorgiutti were gutted and didn't want to believe that Standen was involved. But there was only one course of action available.

As Giorgiutti later said: 'As a result of what Bradley was

told by Keelty, I was directed by Bradley to undertake a covert internal inquiry in relation to Standen.'

No one else in the Crime Commission was told but, thereafter, even more intensive monitoring of Standen's communications was put in place. Coincidentally, the commission was about to upgrade its phones. Standen's new mobile made a pit stop at the AFP before being handed over. Now it had an inbuilt listening device. As a result, even if Standen went for coffee, his conversations could be monitored.

An IT expert was brought in to enable the monitoring of Standen's computer and his emails.

Tim Morris, the AFP officer in charge of the inquiry, told Giorgiutti that Standen had approached the AFP out of the blue to ask if anyone was investigating a man by the name of Ray Spadina. At the time, the Crime Commission wasn't investigating Spadina, who was well known and well connected in the world of drug dealing and drug importation and also had connections in the Netherlands. Was Standen involved with another syndicate?

Morris also told Giorgiutti that according to what they had learnt so far, Standen was not going to be involved in the sale of any drugs but was to be the 'eyes and ears of the syndicate'.

From some of the intercepted conversations, the AFP believed that at the time of the arrival of the drugs, Standen was going to refer other matters to his federal counterparts in an effort to distract them.

With Bradley now acutely aware that the management of the commission's numerous informers was an issue, he instituted changes. As of November 2007, the commission had a total of 764 active and inactive 'human sources'. A list was made of all those still active – there were 61. James Kinch was not one of them.

That same month, Bradley circulated an email detailing a new Informer Management Policy, saying the management of informers was 'an area of real vulnerability for the commission for a number of reasons which should be obvious to all of you'. He went on to say that, in the past, the commission had been 'fortunate in that we have not had any major mishaps in relation to informers'.

But things had to change because 'adherence to previous plans … would not bear close scrutiny'.

While Bradley knew about Kinch, he might as well have been referring to Standen's handling of Neville Tween, a suspected murderer and serial rapist.

Standen had been to Tween's home for dinner, been scuba diving with Tween's wife and walked his dog with the old crook. He and his family had moved into rented premises on the recommendation of Tween's wife, and Standen's brother had gone into business with her.

Bradley was apparently unaware of all this. Mark Standen didn't much believe in paperwork or telling people what he was doing. It seems he wasn't alone.

* * *

On 5 September 2007, Jalalaty received a fax from a company called Elegant Hosiery in Pakistan claiming to be acting on behalf of MDL Food and Services. It said a container of 17,000 kilograms of rice in 5-kilogram bags was on its way and should arrive in Sydney within a few weeks. The fax provided a container number. Ten days later, Jalalaty and Standen met at the Café Laurella in the North Shore suburb of Wahroonga.

AFP officers listened to Standen telling Jalalaty it was silly to be getting an importation of rice from a hosiery company because it would only draw attention. The two men discussed the commercial viability of rice. According to the AFP officers recording their conversations, Standen said they didn't even know whether it was rice or not.

If it was rice, what were they going to do with it?

Jalalaty said he had no idea and that he didn't order the consignment but thought that Kinch was just 'testing the water'. Jalalaty was way out of his depth.

Indeed, Kinch expressed his frustration over Jalalaty, who in their communications had been codenamed 'Myrtle'.

In an email to Standen, who was codenamed 'Maurice', Kinch wrote: 'I have been waiting for positive news from Myrtle, honestly, I do not know where you found her?? She is a complete Walter Mitty … [the] Mr Bean of the business world.'

The consignment duly arrived in October. It was in fact rice, some of which contained bugs and had to be fumigated before being released. It was just a dummy run.

But investigators had no doubt the intention was to bring in drugs.

In the conversation at Café Laurella, police listened as Jalalaty asked Standen how much he thought 'it' was worth. Standen replied that it depended on how much the syndicate paid for it and how much they sold it for. 'Allowing to pay for all costs, they'd probably make from one hundred to one hundred and twenty a kilo,' Standen said.

Jalalaty replied: 'So if they bring in 100 kilos, it makes $12 million profit and he goes half with [inaudible] … biggest mule and we go, we go thirds.'

'Yeah,' Standen replied.

The two men discussed Standen's financial and family troubles, with Standen relating in detail how he'd come to be in debt and how he'd contacted James Kinch to ask for financial help. But of course, Kinch couldn't send money directly to Standen. Instead, he would pay Jalalaty who would in turn make out cheques payable to Standen as well as handing over large amounts in cash.

Standen's financial woes featured throughout the covert inquiries. He was constantly pleading for money from Jalalaty or Kinch. At one stage, he begged for some cash, saying he only had $22 to his name. This from a man on a salary of $285,000 a year. It appears bad property deals were one source of his woes, but others believed his gambling was also a factor, although Standen dismisses the stories of his gambling as baseless.

As all this was unfolding, with the Australian and Dutch police covertly piecing together their case, another event was taking place in the District Court in Sydney. It was the trial of John Anderson, aka Neville Tween, charged with conspiring to import a commercial quantity of cocaine into Australia on the *Tampa* and the *Taronga*.

Standen's informer was in deep trouble. On 7 May 2008, customs officer Fiona Wood gave evidence about raiding some of the properties associated with Tween back in 2006. She told the court she was equipped with a chemical detection system known as an Itemiser, which had been programmed to detect narcotics. She said a number of objects found in Tween's unit in Wyong, including Décor-brand containers, had tested positive to cocaine.

A fraud investigator, John Payne, gave evidence about a false passport obtained way back in 1997 in the name of Victor Patrick Harris, but which in fact contained a photograph of Tween. He had used it to travel to South America. A second false passport dating back to 1997 in the name of Samuel McCutcheon also contained Tween's photo.

Tween never gave evidence, never got into the witness box to defend himself, as is his right. His recorded interview with the police – the story about how he thought it was emeralds, not cocaine – was by this time even less convincing.

Whether Standen took much interest in what was happening to his old informant is not known. By this point he was far more interested in talking to another old informer – James Kinch.

At the same time the evidence against Tween was mounting in the District Court, Standen was meeting Jalalaty in his car, confiding he was in 'constant' contact with Kinch and talking about the 'food' having arrived but not being released because it needed to be checked by quarantine. Indeed, another consignment for BJ's Fine Quality Foods had arrived via a container ship in late April. It, too, had been under surveillance.

On 8 May 2008, Kinch sent Standen an email from his hotel in Dubai saying he'd heard a shipment of MDMA was on its way from China to Australia, hidden in a batch of bath salts. On 12 May, Standen called an Australian customs officer and relayed Kinch's tip-off. It was all rather vague, although Standen said the information had come from someone living in Europe who had a 'very good history' with the Crime Commission.

'All he knows is that it's crystal MDMA and it's in a consignment of bath salts from China.'

It may be that Standen was trying to create the diversion he'd alluded to in earlier intercepted conversations. There's another theory about his call that day – it was to see if his syndicate was under investigation. Put altogether, the conversations via Hotmail, SMS or mobile phone were entirely consistent with an international syndicate attempting to import drugs.

During the many months of Operation Octans, Standen was in contact with Kinch on numerous occasions. Often they spoke in code, with Standen still being called 'Maurice', Jalalaty 'Myrtle', Kinch 'B52' and one of the Dutch syndicate dubbed 'Rashid'. But at no time had Standen been authorised by anyone to get involved in such an operation.

As far as the Crime Commission was concerned, Kinch was an 'inactive' human source, so there was no reason for Standen to be dealing with him. He hadn't reported any contact with Kinch, including during the trip to Dubai.

John Giorgiutti, the commission's chief lawyer, who had by now been working alongside his colleague for almost a year, knowing he was under investigation, wrote: 'I can find no evidence that Kinch provided information to the commission in relation to a commission investigation after July 2006.'

In other words, Standen had gone rogue.

***

By the end of May 2008, John Anderson/Neville Tween's trial had concluded and he'd been found guilty on the cocaine charges and was in jail awaiting sentence. He was almost 68 years old and was facing the prospect of a sentence that would see him die in jail.

His son Michael who had no previous convictions, had already pleaded guilty.

Just days later, on Monday, 2 June 2008, John Giorgiutti spoke to his long-standing colleague and, on some pretext, took Standen down to the basement of the NSW Crime Commission building.

There, waiting, were officers from the Australian Federal Police.

It was 1.56pm.

'Mark,' one of the AFP officers said, 'I want you to listen to me very carefully, okay? We're here to arrest you for conspiracy to import into Australia a commercial quantity of border control precursors. Do you understand that?'

'I hope you're kidding me …' Standen replied.

'I'm not, mate. I am deadly serious. Do you understand that?'

'Is this a gee-up?'

'No, it's not. Do you understand that?'

'Yeah,' Standen said.

'You are now under arrest,' the AFP officer said. 'You are not obliged to say or do anything, as anything you say or do may be given in evidence. Do you understand that?'

'Yeah, it's got to be a gee-up,' Standen replied.

The AFP officers raided Standen's office, taking his computer and other items. The 51-year-old father of four was handcuffed and taken to AFP headquarters, a short distance away.

There they sat in a small room and conducted a recorded record of interview. Which is remarkable in itself. Lawyers will always tell their clients to say nothing until they get the advice of a legal representative.

Not Standen. He went on, and on, and on, for hours, giving his version of events. He could explain everything, it was all innocent, it was all a mistake. It wasn't true.

Yes, he had accepted large amounts of money from Jalalaty, but never from Kinch and he believed their business dealings were legitimate. Indeed, on a number of occasions, he had given Jalalaty information about importing rice. He had no knowledge of any drugs.

It was all the more extraordinary given Standen was studying law himself, and had been for some years. He had only two units to complete, and on the weekend before his arrest he'd been at the University of Sydney pursuing his degree.

Eventually, he contacted a solicitor to get some legal advice. At that point, he shut up.

Standen was accused of being involved in a conspiracy to import 600 kilograms of the chemical pseudoephedrine, which had the potential to make 430 kilograms of methamphetamine. The AFP alleged it had a potential wholesale value of $120 million.

Bill Jalalaty and Dutch members of the syndicate were also arrested and charged, as was James Kinch, who was in Thailand at the time.

There was a slight problem. The container supposedly bringing the drugs into Sydney had been exhaustively searched over three days between 23 and 25 May, just over a week before the arrests. Authorities had found 537 bags of rice, ranging from 15kg, 25kg to 40kg in weight. But that's all. No drugs, no pseudoephedrine to make ice, not even a trace.

Somewhere along the supply line, the syndicate had been ripped off by another bunch of crooks, most likely in Pakistan.

Criminals can be so unscrupulous. After all that time, all that planning, all that effort and angst, all that had arrived in Sydney was a mountain of rice.

PART THREE

Chapter 24

The Connection

On 8 June 2008, just six days after Mark Standen's arrest, Neville Tween, aka John Anderson, was publicly named for the very first time as a murder and rape suspect. Tween's intimate relationship with Mark Standen was also revealed.

That Sunday, *The Sun-Herald* ran an article by John Kidman and Matthew Benns with the headline 'Jailed cop linked to drug runner'. The first paragraph read: 'Accused corrupt cop Mark Standen is now facing a second investigation – this time into his long friendship with a jailed drug runner suspected of a rape and murder.' It went on to say that Homicide detectives wanted to quiz Standen over 'his close relationship with underworld identity John Anderson'.

The article said Manly detectives investigating a cold case had stumbled across the 'extraordinary connection' just weeks earlier, and that Standen had been a close friend of Tween's for years and a 'regular visitor to his Central Coast home'.

Former neighbours of Tween's who, by coincidence, had also known the Standen family in Sydney years before said they'd often seen Mark Standen at Tween's home.

The Sun-Herald said it was alleged Standen had 'massive gambling debts' and had set up the drug deal in Dubai.

The article didn't mention Trudie Adams or Tony Yelavich by name, nor did it say Tween was the suspect in at least 14 sexual assaults. But plenty of NSW Police and Crime Commission officers knew the background.

In law enforcement and legal circles around Australia, Standen's arrest caused a sensation. He was one of the most senior law enforcement officers to be charged with such major corruption in Australia's history. NSW Crime Commission boss Phil Bradley was devastated. At a press conference, he acknowledged that his chief investigator might have had a serious gambling problem.

Even some of Standen's fiercest critics, who thought his 'cowboy' tactics were highly questionable, were shocked. They weren't the only ones. Just after *The Sun-Herald* article appeared, Ashley Bryant, who'd headed up Strike Force Keldie, the cold case review of the Trudie Adams murder, spoke to Jayson Macleod, who'd taken over the investigation into the disappearance of Tony Yelavich. It was Macleod who'd discovered the link between Standen and Tween and the men's families.

Bryant was furious about the leak to *The Sun-Herald* and asked where it had come from and how had Tween's name made its way into the papers. That sort of release of information was usually planned, with a strategy in mind.

On 12 June, Standen prepared a bail application with his barrister, Paul King, providing information about his background. Standen had been educated at St Patrick's College, Strathfield, in Sydney's inner west, where he'd attained his Higher School Certificate. He had continued an association with the school in music for a further ten years.

His lawyer went through his career – the Narcotics Bureau, the AFP, the NCA and the Crime Commission, where he was the senior investigator.

Mr King said that despite Standen's intimate knowledge of international drug smuggling, he was hardly a man of the world, having travelled overseas only twice – once to Fiji with his family and once to Dubai in February 2007. This wasn't quite right. Standen had been to the United States to assist in the arrest of fugitive drug trafficker Ian Saxon, who was brought back to Australia.

King outlined Standen's financial woes – how his home was 'fully encumbered' because he had borrowed everything to buy it. It was now likely the home would have to be sold as the monthly mortgage was $5000.

His lawyer said Standen's family had already suffered distress in part due to the story in *The Sun-Herald*, which had included a mention of his girlfriend, Louise Baker.

He acknowledged the charges were serious – he was alleged to have been involved in a conspiracy to import 600 kilograms of pseudoephedrine potentially worth $120 million. On the other hand, no drugs had ever been found in the shipment of rice found in the container in late May. In fact, no drugs had been imported full stop.

Standen's lawyer said his client was clearly in need of protection from the rest of the prison population, was isolated in his cell for almost 24 hours a day and would be safer on the outside. While there was a presumption against bail, he had a wife and family, had never previously been charged with an offence, and the charges were not of a violent or sexual nature. In other words, he had strong family ties and was unlikely to flee Australia.

Not surprisingly, the application failed.

***

In the long history of the Trudie Adams case, the years 2008 and 2009 proved to be a watershed. By July 2008, Neville Tween and Mark Standen were both in prison, one awaiting sentencing, the other accused of being a corrupt cop.

Jayson Macleod, who'd been so frustrated during his dealings with Standen while investigating the disappearance of Tony Yelavich, had resigned from the police force, distressed and disillusioned. Although at least he now understood why nobody at the highest levels of the NSW Police had wanted to act on his alarm over the relationship between Standen and Tween.

In August 2008, NSW Police appointed 32-year-old Detective Senior Constable Gavin McKean, from the Unsolved Homicide Squad, to take over Strike Force Keldie. Established in 2005, Keldie had originally been led by Ashley Bryant, before he handed the reins to Mitch Dubojski.

Now, it was McKean's turn, along with his partner, Detective Nicole Jones. Together, they were charged with carrying out the most comprehensive and in-depth investigation into Trudie Adams' disappearance, re-examining all the theories regarding Neville Tween, Len Evans, Ray Johnson and the Roselands Lads.

In July, even before McKean took charge, NSW Police had put telephone intercepts in place as a result of the arrest of Mark Standen the month before and *The Sun-Herald* article naming Tween for the first time.

On 29 July 2008, in a bid to generate new information, NSW Police announced a reward of $250,000 for information leading to the arrest and conviction of any of the offenders involved in the disappearance of Trudie Adams. The then head of the Homicide Squad, Detective Superintendent Geoff Beresford, said: 'The disappearance and suspected murder of Trudie Adams impacted deeply on the Northern Beaches community. It is our belief she was kidnapped by two males and murdered.'

In other words, the Roselands Lads theory – launched in 1995 in a blaze of publicity – had been ditched and, once again, Tween was at the centre of police inquiries.

McKean and Jones started going back through thousands of pages of material, reviewing witness statements, re-interviewing some of the rape victims, Trudie's girlfriends and witnesses who had not previously been spoken to. They went back to Brian Walker, the park ranger who'd contacted Pymble Police and then Homicide detectives about seeing car lights and hearing gunshots across the valley three decades earlier. As it turned out, Walker had never been asked by police back in 1978 to make a formal statement. Detective Jones took one on 30 October 2008 in which Walker set out his recollections of what had happened all those years earlier.

The following day, McKean, Jones and a forensic expert set out with Walker to re-examine various locations in the park. It was all recorded on video and sound.

First, Brian Walker took them to the gravesite he'd come across decades earlier. It was still there, and Walker repeated what he'd originally told police, how, back then, the site was accessible by car via a bush track.

Then it was on to another location, another track, which led to a road that connected up with Terrey Hills. Brian Walker reckoned it would take maybe 20 to 25 minutes to walk from the bush to the nearby suburb, which was where Tween lived at the relevant times.

Next stop was the site where the mattress and oxy bottle had been found back in 1978. Walker told the police that he used to ride his trail bike through the area regularly.

On the walk-through with the detectives, he said: 'There was always a double bed-type mattress laying there … I found ladies' underwear and bras and things and it was obviously [sic] that there was some sort of sexual activity going on here on a regular basis.'

What was recorded next was telling.

'So you said you noticed an oxy bottle back in 1978,' Detective Nicole Jones said to Walker, 'and that's actually recorded in our police running sheets … could you take us to that area now?'

'Yeah, okay,' Walker said. 'There it is.'

'Does that look like … a similar oxy bottle that you located in 1978?' Jones asked.

'Yes, it does,' Walker said, 'and I'm still surprised to see it there.'

It appears Constable Jones was surprised as well to see an old oxy bottle in the bush. Her response was, well, you could call it understated. She replied to Walker with one word. 'Yeah.'

Jones asked him if he thought it could be the same bottle.

'I believe there's every possibility, yes.'

Indeed, the date imprinted on the bottle still sitting in the bush was '1st 72'.

Walker said that back in 1978, he'd brought investigators to the same area so it could be searched, but he hadn't stayed. Police had called him a couple of days later asking if he knew whether there was a gas bottle in the vicinity.

He told Detective Jones he'd replied: 'Well, you searched the area, you should know.' He said they replied, 'Well, we didn't find one.'

Walker took them back into the bush.

'I brought them back out here and led them to this area and showed them a gas bottle which I'd nearly be prepared to say that's probably the same one.'

'And to your knowledge did they take away that gas bottle?' Jones asked.

'No, I can't say yes or no,' Walker replied.

Jones then asked if he was aware whether they'd moved or taken away the mattress. 'No, they did not take the mattress away,' he replied. 'I'd seen the mattress here many years after that.'

Detectives Jones and McKean seized the oxy bottle for examination. With the camera still filming, Nicole Jones said: 'It is now 1.12pm. Detective McKean has just been searching in this general area [the co-ordinates had been taken] and we've come across what appears to be an old burnt-out rusty car wreck.'

She addressed Walker. 'Brian, you have just had a look at this and you made the comment that you believe that this wreck here is a VW Beetle?'

Walker, a self-described car buff, replied that it was definitely the remains of a VW Beetle.

After identifying parts of the vehicle, Detective Jones said the VW was pale blue in colour.

So an oxy bottle, a mattress and a blue VW had been left lying in the bush.

Two of the sexual assault victims, Kate Hamilton and Jessica Winch, had told investigators in July 1978 they'd been picked up in March that year by two men in a dark-blue Volkswagen. What's more, when they were shown a number of photos of suspects, they had identified Tween and Ray Johnson as very similar to their two attackers.

Ray Johnson had bought a 1961 Volkswagen two years earlier. Just 11 days after the assault on Kate and Jessica, he'd transferred the ownership of the vehicle. In the transfer documents, the vehicle was a different year, with different number plates but then the two men managed to change the description of cars – rego, colours, you name it – as often as other blokes would change their socks.

And of course, Tween and Johnson had been under surveillance from time to time in 1978 as a result of being arrested near Lismore the year before. On 24 May 1978, police had observed a blue, early 1960s Volkswagen in the driveway of Neville Tween's home at Terrey Hills.

In addition, Andrew Kingston had made a statement just days after Trudie's disappearance detailing how Len Evans had told him crooks never used the same car twice and how he and Tween used to dump vehicles in Ku-ring-gai Chase National Park.

Was the Volkswagen found by Detectives McKean and Jones 30 years later the same one used to abduct Kate and Jessica?

The detectives also found and photographed a small part of a safe that hadn't been recovered during the original searches. It had a 'Bulldog' brand plate such as would be attached to the front of a safe. The plate carried the words 'Fire, burglar and explosive resisting'. Perhaps not to Neville Tween.

Having recorded, photographed or seized every piece of evidence, McKean and Jones called in Senior Constable Andrew Daley from the Engineering Investigation Unit to examine the remains of the vehicle as well as a Yamaha motor cycle that had also been found partially buried in dirt and overgrowth to the east of Mona Vale Road near the Cooyong/Neverfail Trail in Terrey Hills.

On 7 November 2008, Senior Constable Daley confirmed what Brian Walker had thought – it was a Volkswagen Beetle, albeit the rusted remains of one. After carrying out a forensic examination of the car, Daley noted that, unfortunately, 'the section of metal which would have contained the factory chassis number was corroded to the extent that no numbers were visible or able to be restored'. However, he concluded that 'the rusted remains of the vehicle I examined were that of a light-blue Volkswagen Beetle produced from the early to mid-1960s'.

As to the Yamaha motorcycle, Constable Daley located the engine number – 352-300310 – despite the bike being a wreck. Checks with Yamaha Australia revealed it was a 1975 model, though enquiries to the Roads and Traffic Authority (RTA) proved fruitless. Because of the age of the motorcycle, Daley said, 'no record remained of its originality'.

One of the key figures in this saga did own a motorcycle.

In 1976, Garry James Batt had been the owner of a bike registered as a Honda. The following year he transferred the ownership to 'Mr John D. Anderson' of Booralie Road, Terrey Hills. Sure, it was a different make but then Tween had been observed driving a Holden panel van with the same number plates – HCA-634 – which was 'officially' registered as a 1972, 1962, 1965 and 1966 model. Same car. Different colours. Just as Tween had dealt with some corrupt police on the inside, it appeared he also had people in the RTA who would alter official records for a small fee.

The bush was giving up some of its secrets, which, the detectives knew, should have been discovered years before.

As Detectives McKean and Jones pressed on with their time-consuming but essential inquiries, Tween and his son Michael were about to share a cell.

Investigators thought that some leverage might be possible. After all, the sins of the father should not be visited upon the son, or at least not all of them. Police had picked up on the fact that Michael was not at all happy with his dad. Michael had never been in trouble before and now he was looking at a long stretch in jail. He was hardly blameless, of course – he was old enough to know what he was doing.

Perhaps Tween would give up some information about Trudie Adams, Len Evans, Ray Johnson, the sexual assaults, anything, in return for his son having his prison sentence cut.

Strategies were put in place, including a listening device in the cell occupied by Tween and his son. Meanwhile, McKean and Jones continued their inquiries. In March 2009, they re-interviewed Suzanne, the woman who'd had sexual relationships with Tween and Johnson during the 1980s. Her story was consistent – she'd had a heroin habit and had sex with both men in return for money and drugs. But this time there was a little added detail.

Suzanne told McKean she'd lived on the Northern Beaches all her life, and at the age of 17, in the early 1980s, she'd met and formed an intimate relationship with a bloke called Eric. He'd introduced her to heroin and she'd soon become addicted. Through Eric she'd met another heroin user by the name of Tony Yelavich.

But then Eric and Yelavich had both gone to jail and she had found herself on her own trying to support her drug habit. Like Yelavich, Eric had helped with introductions to Tween and Johnson. Suzanne reiterated how she'd started having sex with both men in return for drugs and money, an arrangement that continued on and off for about five years with Tween and about 12 years with Johnson.

She said that Johnson and Tween had repeatedly asked her to set them up with young girls they could have sex with in return for money or drugs. Her addiction had lasted around 13 years and had led her going to jail, but eventually 'I stopped using drugs and sorted myself out'.

Suzanne said she last saw Ray Johnson in 2006 when he was released from jail. And she told Gavin McKean something she hadn't previously mentioned. 'During the years I have known Ray and Neville I have never heard them discuss anything relating to the disappearance of Trudie Adams or the murder of Trudie Adams.'

McKean recorded her interview via handwritten notes in his notebook, which Suzanne signed. It was March 2009.

He would have re-interviewed Andrew Kingston, but he had died in 2002. Similarly, Peter Bombala, who told police Tony Yelavich was on his way to meet Tween to score an ounce of heroin on the night he disappeared, had also passed away. Other surviving witnesses were less forthcoming than Suzanne. McKean and Jones went to see Dulcie, Tween's first wife. Perhaps now that her former husband was in jail she might provide some information. Dulcie said she couldn't help them. She didn't know anything.

According to Dulcie, McKean had become a little agitated with what he perceived as her lack of cooperation. Shortly after his visit, Dulcie had telephoned Susan Anderson and relayed what had just happened.

The conversation was recorded by an intercept on Susan's phone. The two women had stayed in touch with each other for a number of years, not surprising really, given they each had children with Tween. Dulcie said words to the effect that a young police officer had been throwing a bit of a tantrum on her front veranda after she told him she didn't want to talk at all and they could contact her lawyer. She told Susan he hadn't taken too kindly to her attitude.

One of the prime suspects in the rapes and the disappearance of Trudie, Ray Johnson, by now living in Queensland, was approached in May 2009, but didn't want to cooperate.

In a phone call, he told police: 'Mate, I know about the matter and the only statement I'll make is this – I don't know anything about the matter and I'm not going to say anything further.'

Asked if he would speak with investigators if they came to Queensland, Johnson replied that he wouldn't, adding: 'You're lucky I'm talking to you now.'

A former cellmate of Len Evans' was spoken to on the off chance he might know something, but he had nothing of use.

McKean and Jones also went back to the sexual assault victims to see if there was anything they could add.

Some were still traumatised and some were suspicious about the inquiries being made.

The fact that investigations over the years had gone nowhere may also have played on their mind. In addition, police corruption had been featured in the media for a long time.

In the mid-1990s, it had all come to a head when the Royal Commission into the NSW Police Service exposed rampant bribery, verbals and a culture of drunkenness in places like Kings Cross and Manly. And now, after all these years, two police officers were back asking them more questions.

As Gavin McKean recounted, 'A lot of these women when we spoke to them years later were still cautious of us because … they actually believed that they were raped by police, which made our job more difficult to gain their trust.'

***

There were two people the police needed to interview, neither of whom had ever been spoken to before.

Mark Standen was sitting in a cell, proclaiming his innocence, waiting for his trial when Gavin McKean and another officer went to see if he could shed any light on the disappearance of Trudie Adams 30 years earlier. Had his informant Neville Tween ever told him anything, slipped up maybe, perhaps even hinted at something?

Had he ever mentioned Trudie's name?

Their interview with Standen was informal and wasn't recorded, but the policemen took notes.

Standen was affable and chatty. McKean recalled that he couldn't tell them much about the 1970s or '80s. 'He was telling us what Tween was up to in the '90s and it was mostly drug related. He was a significant drug player in the '90s.'

The officers asked if Standen could shed any light at all on Trudie's case as a result of his relationship with Tween. It was always a long shot. Standen said he had no information that could assist in their inquiries. Above all, he emphasised he was an innocent man.

Standen wasn't nearly as forthcoming as he could have been. He made no mention of Tween telling him about the handful of corrupt NSW Police officers he'd dubbed The Union, who sorted out disputes between criminals, such as the dispute between Tween and Ray Johnson. In the end, McKean and his colleague left not much the wiser than when they'd gone in.

***

One down, one to go. Gavin McKean and Nicole Jones prepared themselves for one last potentially crucial interview. They weren't optimistic, but it had to be done.

At midday on 25 March 2009, the Homicide officers sat down at Silverwater Prison with Neville Brian Tween, aka John David Anderson, aka Neville Brian Tiffen, the kid from Kalgoorlie.

The man who in over 30 years had never been approached, let alone asked a single question, about Trudie Adams or the rapes.

It didn't start well. Tween didn't like the cut of McKean's jib, but he didn't mind being interviewed by a woman. Nicole Jones made the running.

The formalities took a while, with Tween saying he was prepared to be electronically recorded because he wasn't going to answer any of the questions anyway. He agreed he'd been given the opportunity to speak to his solicitor but had been unable to get through. And while he wasn't going to give any answers, he was keen to hear the allegations.

Detective Jones went back to the beginning – 1971. Police had been unable to locate Jane Hampshire, the first known victim, because she'd returned to Europe in 1974. So Jones recounted how two young girls hitchhiking on Pittwater Road, Brookvale, on 6 March 1971 had been picked up by two men in a sedan. She repeated what Jackie Billings and Sarah Sharpe had told police, how the men had produced a gun before driving into bushland, where they'd been sexually assaulted.

'You were positively identified by both females as being one of the men responsible. Do you understand that?' Jones asked.

'Yes,' Tween replied.

When Jones asked Tween if there was anything he wanted to say about the attacks, he said that he wanted to discuss it with his solicitor, Gordon Elliot, who by this time had replaced Goldberg. 'This is the first time I've had any allegations like that ever made against me … the first I've heard of it,' Tween added.

On that point, the old crook was absolutely right. He'd been identified in 1978 and now, 31 years later, he was being asked about the rapes of 14-year-old Jackie Billings and 15-year-old Sarah Sharpe for the very first time.

Jones pressed on and asked Tween for an explanation as to why the girls had nominated him as one of the men responsible for the rape.

'No. Hang on, I shouldn't have answered any of these,' Tween replied.

Jones asked him if he wanted to respond to the accusation at all or make any comment.

'No,' Tween replied, 'it was not me, simple as that. Or anyone that I know.'

Jones then asked him about the sexual assaults of Kate Hamilton and Jessica Winch in bushland on 18 March 1978, after they were picked up by two men in a blue Volkswagen Beetle on Pittwater Road near the milk bar/hamburger shop in Narrabeen where they'd had dinner. 'We believe that you and Ray Johnson were the men responsible for these rapes,' she said. '… Do you understand that?'

'I do,' Tween replied, 'and I deny all these allegations, which I will possibly answer later with my solicitor.'

Jones told him that one of the women sexually assaulted on 18 March 1978 had identified him and Ray Johnson as being very similar to the men who had raped her. Was there anything he'd like to say about that?

'No. It wasn't me. Well, why wasn't I interviewed when this happened when the girls allegedly said it was me and Ray Johnson? Why didn't you … come and arrest me?' Tween said.

Jones replied: 'I can't answer that because I wasn't investigating it at the time … Do you have any explanation as to why you may not have been interviewed back then?'

'No,' Tween replied.

Did he have any comment about the girls identifying him?

'You should've interviewed me or come out … a way back,' he said. 'Why, why is this the first? It's just … it's just wrong. Something's wrong about it all.'

Detective Jones methodically went through all the attacks but Tween denied any involvement. He admitted he'd legally changed his name to John Anderson 'donkey's years ago' but said he'd never been known as 'Tweeny'.

'No, never … not Tweeny, no. I'll take a lie detector test on that.'

As would become apparent, he was quite keen on the idea of a lie detector.

He said he couldn't remember when he'd been in jail but he did know Ray Johnson and used to see him 'occasionally'. And yes, he knew Len Evans.

'He's a big fellow, a Kiwi you know … he got a job on the ships … just as a deckhand.' It had been 'donkey's years' since he'd seen him.

Detective Jones raised the 7 July 1978 statement of Andrew Kingston who'd been in jail with Len Evans and remembered Tween visiting.

'We have a signed statement,' she said, 'which states … you told Leonard Evans, while he was in custody, that you had done … a couple of Ku-ring-gai jobs in his honour.

'Can you tell me what you were referring to when you made this comment?' she asked.

Tween asked the detective if she could say that again, which she did. Tween stalled. 'Well, that is an absolute lie, 100 per cent,' he said. The whole thing stunk of a 'verbal'. He then suggested police should check the prison records to see whether he'd visited Evans at the time.

McKean chimed in: 'The records don't go back that far.'

To which Tween smugly responded: 'Just when you need 'em.'

Interestingly, at no stage did Tween ask Detective Jones what 'a Ku-ring-gai job' meant. It seems he knew what she was talking about. He denied involvement, apparently without any curiosity about what it was that he was denying.

She asked about the assault on Jimmy Holten in 1975 and the fact that police had found women's pink briefs, handcuffs, parts of a safe and a spent 9mm bullet cartridge along with alcohol, black electrical tape, marijuana and company finance books.

Tween didn't really answer any of the questions but he did ask one himself. Were there any fingerprints found on the tape?

He already knew the answer. No prints. After just over two hours, the interview came to its conclusion.

'A final question, John,' Detective Jones said. 'Did you kill Trudie Adams?'

'Absolutely not,' he replied. 'I've killed no one my whole life.'

Chapter 25

The Inquest

In early 2011, a final push to discover what happened to Trudie Adams got underway in the NSW Coroner's Court. Her family and friends were hopeful that finally someone, somehow, might shed some light on the events that had taken place so long ago and which had affected all their lives.

Trudie's father, Charles, and her brother John were there. So were some of her close-knit circle of girlfriends – Gillian Dollery, Debbie Jeffries, Leanne Weir – who had gathered a lifetime ago on the beach in Avalon and talked about boys, school and the future.

They wanted to hear all the evidence, no matter how sad, frustrating and painful it might be. And they wanted to see Neville Tween, aka John David Anderson, in the witness box.

Tween had once been a clever criminal – a safebreaker – respected decades earlier, if only by his peers. But by now he was reviled by the same men who had worked alongside him on the wrong side of the law because he'd been Standen's informer, a 'dog' and, as some of them knew, a sexual deviant. One major heroin trafficker told the authors he'd first heard about Tween being responsible for the Northern Beaches rapes in the late 1980s, in Parklea Prison in Sydney. He'd been told by John Sadler, the big time heroin supplier.

Meanwhile, across town, the trial of Mark Standen was taking place in the NSW Supreme Court. In the end, it would last for five months.

Once so powerful in law enforcement, Standen had become an acute embarrassment to honest cops everywhere.

***

In his opening address to the inquest, Counsel Assisting the Coroner, Peter Hamill SC, said the seven lever-arch folders comprising the brief of evidence contained 'a dense and sometimes dizzying amount of product' from the files of police investigators from over the years.

He told the NSW Deputy State Coroner, Scott Mitchell, there had been a huge amount of publicity about the case, which had resulted in the police being provided with 'vast amounts of information from members of the public, all of which had to be considered and, where appropriate, investigated'.

'As a result the investigation is a little like the Hydra in Greek mythology. Every time a head or line of inquiry was removed, others grew or sprang up.'

Some of the information received by police was good, some was bad. But all required some investigation. Peter Hamill said that, looking back, 'the investigation seemed somewhat disjointed.' This was not so much a criticism but the 'inevitable result of the fact that there was so much information coming to different police officers'. In addition, he said, there had been several investigations into Trudie's disappearance.

The first witness was former NSW Police Detective Senior Constable Gavin McKean, who was now an officer with the AFP.

Gavin McKean and Nicole Jones had put together a 133-page summary of the evidence – the various leads, statements, theories, investigations and suspects. It covered the 1995 investigation into the Roselands Lads by Detective Ian Lynch.

But as Peter Hamill pointed out, they were constrained to an extent, as was the coronial inquest, because the secrecy provisions of the NSW Crime Commission (NSWCC) stopped anyone working there from revealing information except under 'pretty confined circumstances'.

Commission investigators could divulge information necessary for a criminal prosecution, but there was no provision for them to hand over information to an inquest 'even where that inquest concerns, as this one does, a possible abduction and murder'.

Hamill added that he and others involved in the inquest had been to the NSWCC and 'a few documents have been provided to us'.

'The truth is we simply cannot know whether we have been made (aware) of everything the Crime Commission knows.'

The end result, Mr Hamill said, was that 'Your Honour may or probably won't know, except in the blandest possible terms, whether the NSWCC does have any information which might assist this inquest or assist Trudie's family to understand what happened to her'.

It wasn't exactly a promising start.

The inquest set about exploring the possible involvement of the Roselands Lads, dismissed decades earlier by Gary Matthews. Giving evidence to the Coroner, Detective Lynch recounted how the tip-off from fellow detective Gary Jubelin in 1992 had brought about his interest in the group. At the time, Lynch had been a detective senior constable attached to the Homicide Squad when the green Kombi and Witness A had first surfaced.

He said that his workload being what it was, it had taken several years to investigate the hypothesis that Jubelin had put to him about the involvement of those associated with the green Kombi.

While the evidence of Witness A was hearsay, others had confirmed that a number of men had been boasting about killing Trudie. And while they might have been 'big-noting', in Lynch's view it just couldn't be ignored. He said Jubelin had also mentioned a number of names associated with the vehicle, including Raymond, Emile and Sam Khoury, Garrian (Garry) Carr and Gary Ireland.

Reviewing the documentation from the original investigation by Gary Matthews, Lynch said he'd discovered that Ray Khoury, Ireland and Carr had all been 'mentioned in the index cards of the brief but none of them had ever been interviewed'.

He'd also found that at the time of Trudie's disappearance, Ray Khoury had been the owner of a green Kombi van, and that he and some of his associates had been charged with raping a woman in that vehicle two years after Trudie's disappearance. All of them had been found not guilty. He'd also discovered that three of the persons had panel vans at the time.

Lynch said Garry Carr had sold his panel van 'a few months after the disappearance'. By the time he'd interviewed him in the mid-1990s, it was clear Carr was mentally ill.

Lynch said he had followed a number of leads into the whereabouts of Trudie's body.

Information gathered in 1995 suggested that her remains might be near the wharf at Meadowbank, about 15 kilometres north-west of the Sydney CBD.

Lynch had divers search the area. He told the court there was mention of Menai, but there was a mention of Belrose, Cooks Bay and Huntley's Point Road below the Gladesville Bridge.

It turned out Ray Khoury had been employed as a landscape gardener at the time and Lynch had arranged for inquiries to be made with the local council about any works that might have been happening in 1978.

Hamill asked if it was his view that the Roselands Lads should have been investigated more thoroughly in 1978.

He replied: 'Yes, I believe they should have been interviewed at the time, and in relation to the Batt and Tween/Johnson inquiry, I saw that as being a big hole that had to be re-investigated.'

Lynch told the Coroner there were a lot of coincidences associated with the respective motor vehicles – the green Kombi and beige Holden panel van – and in the entirety of the running sheets, 'these were the only people who spoke of any personal involvement in the events.'

He said Gary Matthews' opinion that the Roselands Lads story could be discounted because Trudie did not have a handbag on the night was no reason 'to not interview three people who have in various forms made admissions about being involved in the offence'.

In addition, the men 'were associated with the two motor vehicles that were mentioned in the respective wireless messages and had a connection (through a girlfriend) with the Northern Beaches'.

Lynch agreed with Peter Hamill that the discrepancies

between the vehicles described in the first two wireless messages were 'a conundrum' that was unlikely to be solved.

As to the Tween and Johnson angle, Lynch's evidence was revealing.

'Seemed to be there,' he told the court, 'it was begging and nothing ever happened so I recognised that as a hole that would have to be the subject of a separate inquiry.'

It was a blunt assessment. In Ian Lynch's view, there was evidence there regarding Tween and Johnson 'begging' to be investigated – but nothing happened.

Witness A also gave evidence to the inquest. She said she had 'concerns for my safety' and her name was suppressed.

When asked who she feared, she nominated the Khoury brothers – 'Emile, Sam and Raymond'. 'I knew they were not very good people,' she told the court.

When Hamill asked Witness A what had made her form that opinion, she replied: 'Just that they did a lot of drugs and things like that.'

She described her relationship with Keith Hurney as not a happy one, despite them having lived together for a number of years, because they were both using drugs 'like marijuana'.

She repeated the information she'd previously given to the police. She'd first heard about Trudie when Keith had come home one afternoon and seen a photo of the missing girl in *The Daily Telegraph*.

Witness A said Keith had 'freaked out' and when she asked him what was wrong, he said, 'I was there.' When she asked 'where', he'd replied, 'I know what happened to that girl.'

He had named Sam Khoury, Ray Khoury, Garry Carr and others as being in a green Kombi that had picked up Trudie. She told the court she could not remember Emile's name being mentioned.

She said that Hurney had told her the men had raped Trudie in the back of the Kombi van, but she struggled, got away and jumped out of the Kombi, hitting a telegraph pole and splitting her head open.

She said he'd told her the men had buried Trudie somewhere 'between Palm Beach and Narrabeen'.

Witness A told the court that Hurney had also mentioned that two vehicles had pulled up after seeing Trudie hitchhiking – the Kombi and, directly behind it, a panel van.

She said she'd gone to the police in September 1983, because she had a child herself.

Witness A said when Hurney found out she had gone to the police he assaulted her and said words to the effect that the Khourys would kill him if they found out.

Witness A had told pretty much the same story to the NSW Police twice, in 1983, then to Ian Lynch in 1995 and now, finally, to the Coroner's Court.

When Keith Hurney, her former boyfriend, was called to the inquest, he gave a different version of events involving what he called 'The Ray report'.

He said that when the group of young men gathered at the Roselands Shopping Centre, Ray Khoury would tell stories about how he got into fights on his nights out and various other tales to impress those known in the loose group as 'HWs', which stood for hero worshippers.

Hurney told the inquest that was the first he had heard about any involvement in the Trudie Adams case.

'[Ray] just said that we picked her up and that they had sex with her and that was it. I can't remember anything more. It was very blasé details, they weren't much.'

Hurney categorically denied the evidence of Witness A. He'd never told her that he and Ray Khoury, Garry Carr and others had picked up Trudie, tried to rape her and that she'd jumped from the vehicle and hit her head on a telegraph pole.

But Hurney had been interviewed formally by police in 1984, something which it seems he'd forgotten because what he'd said then was at odds with what he was telling the court in 2011.

Counsel assisting, Peter Hamill, confronted Hurney with the contradiction between what he was telling the inquest and the statement he'd signed in 1984 in which he'd agreed he had in fact told Witness A what she had subsequently reported to police

Hurney told the inquest he couldn't read or write very well at the time.

'I can't remember making that statement, and I couldn't read the statement so I signed the statement without even knowing that that was in there.'

He agreed he'd told police he was not involved in Trudie's disappearance and that 'any information I have came from Ray [Khoury]' who also used to boast about things like being involved in fights with ten people at a time.

Hamill asked if it was true Ray Khoury was supposed to be the hero and if Hurney and others were supposed to be the hero worshippers. Hurney agreed but added that Ray 'exaggerated things' and 'thought he was great'.

In the end, he said any stories about Trudie had come from Ray Khoury and anything he'd said to Witness A had happened when he was smoking marijuana and was just big-noting himself. He told the inquest he had absolutely nothing to do with the disappearance of Trudie Adams.

* * *

Raymond Joseph Khoury, nominated as one of the leaders of the Roselands Lads, gave evidence that the first he'd heard about a green Kombi being involved in the disappearance of Trudie was in 1995 when police had launched their new investigation with a massive publicity campaign.

Khoury said he'd bought the Kombi on 4 April 1978 but that any suggestion he was involved in the abduction, rape and killing of Trudie Adams was 'total bullshit'. He told the court he'd never made any of the remarks Keith Hurney claimed he had about getting a girl into the van or her jumping out and hitting a pole. And he denied being a leader of the loose group of young men who gathered at the Roselands Shopping Centre, saying 'no one was a leader'. As for 'The Ray Report', he told the inquest someone had made it up.

He was adamant that he had never said anything to the effect that he and others had picked up 'some sheila from a dance' and tried to have sex with her. Similarly, he had never said to Keith Hurney, 'We took her to Palm Beach and buried her in the sand.' He added that he 'wouldn't know where Palm Beach is'.

Like Hurney, Ray Khoury seemed to have forgotten an interview he'd done with police. In a statement made in 1995, 16 years earlier, he told detectives that 'as a kid growing up' he used to go on family picnics to the Northern Beaches. He'd also said: 'We used to go down to Palm Beach, Newport Beach, Manly …'

Hamill asked him about the contradiction but Khoury continued to deny he'd been to Palm Beach.

He also distanced himself from Garry Carr, who he said had boasted about committing every major, high-profile crime that had happened, from the Truro murders in South Australia, to the bombing of the Hilton Hotel and the Wanda beach murders in Sydney.

As to when he knew Carr, Ray Khoury proved difficult to pin down. At first he said Carr was 'a friend of friends' and that around the time of Trudie's disappearance 'I didn't know him to talk to him'.

After lengthy questioning, Hamill asked whether at the time of the 1995 police investigation he'd rung Carr and said 'Garry, what's going on …'

Khoury said he had called but he hadn't been trying to warn Carr that the police were investigating them. There was no conversation about someone 'dobbing' on them and, he told the court, he did not try to suggest to Carr that he [Ray] didn't even know him at the time of Trudie's disappearance. Then came the crunch question.

Hamill asked: 'At the time of the 1995 police investigation you were concerned, weren't you, that your telephones might have been bugged.'

Khoury said yes.

Hamill then told him his suspicions had been well founded, that his phone had been tapped and that his call to Garry Carr had been recorded, including him saying, 'I didn't even know you at that time, Garry.'

Coroner Scott Mitchell weighed in on the two issues – never having been to Palm Beach and not knowing Garry Carr in 1978.

'If I take the view that you're lying … I'm going to have you charged with perjury,' he said, to which Khoury responded, 'Yeah, no, that's fine.'

When Mitchell asked Khoury why he'd denied knowing where Palm Beach was, he initially replied that it 'must have been a mistake, sir'.

Mitchell said: 'That was a lie, wasn't it?' to which Khoury ultimately agreed, saying: 'Probably was a lie, yeah.'

Counsel assisting, Peter Hamill, chimed in, saying he was concerned that in trying to distance himself from the Trudie Adams case, Ray Khoury was actually making it worse for himself.

Hamill asked if he was doing that because he had in fact buried Trudie at Palm Beach. Khoury told the court: 'I've never buried anyone in my life.'

His stint in the witness box ended on a rather tame note when he was asked about the relationship between Garry Carr and Gary Ireland.

'They lived across the road from each other … I figured they were friends,' he said.

***

There was nothing tame in what was to come. Gary Eric Ireland was clearly not pleased to be at the inquest.

When Hamill asked him if he was aware the Coroner was looking into the disappearance of Trudie, Ireland replied, 'Mm', then 'yeah'. Then, when Hamill asked him, 'Is that a yes?' Ireland replied, 'It is a no, idiot.'

After the Coroner chided him for calling Hamill an idiot, Ireland said, 'Get on with it.'

By the time he'd finished giving evidence, Ireland had called Hamill a 'prick', 'a cunt' and 'a fucking maggot'. As for the police, Ireland dubbed them 'leeching fucking copper cock-sucking mates' and said they were to blame for fucking up the investigation back in 1978.

When the Coroner pointed out that Hamill was not a police officer, Ireland replied, 'Really?'

The evidence of Alf Sergi, by now a chief inspector in the NSW Police Force, was put to him. Sergi had told the hearing that after Trudie disappeared in 1978 he'd heard both Gary Ireland and Garry Carr – though mostly Carr – bragging five or six times about raping and abducting Trudie Adams. Sergi told the inquest he hadn't believed it at the time and dismissed it as young men big-noting themselves.

Ireland didn't take kindly to the evidence of his one-time acquaintance from the Roselands shopping centre, describing Sergi as 'some sort of wanky sergeant'. Informed by Hamill that he was 'a bit better than a wanky sergeant', Ireland replied, 'Well, he's not because he's just as dirty as we are on this matter because he was part of it. We had nothing to do with the actual disappearance or anything. We just fluffed up our own importance.'

Ireland admitted he might have said something about Trudie to the 'LTs' who hung around the group, annoying them. When asked what LTs were, he replied it stood for 'little titter, sheila'. He thought that the story of their involvement in Trudie's disappearance might have stemmed from either him or Carr saying to the LTs, 'Look, you want to end up like Trudie Adams?'

It was on his second day in the witness box that Ireland got really upset. Rather than sitting, he was given permission to stand to give his evidence because he had a 'bit of a dicky back'.

It was only a few minutes into the day's proceedings when Hamill asked him about the car he'd had in 1978 and why he'd sold it.

'I'm fuming about this … do it right and don't fuck people around,' Ireland yelled.

When the Coroner called for the sheriff or police to escort Ireland outside, he screamed, 'You want me to go, I'll go. Lock me up, who cares. This prick's a cunt and he knows it. You're a fucking maggot.'

As a defence lawyer, Hamill had dealt with some difficult clients and witnesses so he wasn't particularly fazed. However, some in the court in close proximity to Ireland standing and shouting were scared and in tears.

Ireland was apologetic when he returned, revealing that his essential beef was that the police should have spoken to him, Carr and Ray Khoury back in 1978 or 1979 when their names first came to notice and cleared it up then. He insisted that he had nothing to do with Trudie's disappearance and he didn't believe that Carr or Ray Khoury did either. 'The police let us down bad in this state,' he said. If they'd investigated it properly at the time 'this could have all been squished in 1978'.

* * *

Now a NSW Supreme Court judge, Peter Hamill recalls that Ireland 'just started abusing me, screaming at me from the witness box'.

'It was quite frightening … particularly after he left the witness box he had to walk pretty close past where I was standing, and his venom was directed at me.'

'It didn't immediately affect me. But when I looked around I saw that my solicitor was actually in tears, that's how crazy it was.' He said Ireland looked like 'a really aggressive, dangerous man, capable of anything, including abducting poor Trudie and killing her'.

'But I don't think that's what happened, but that's how it presented. I think it was because he honestly thought he was being victimised by the process. I thought he was coming from a place of a genuine victim rather than a place of someone with something to hide.'

Courtrooms, he said, could be emotional places 'and people like [Ireland] aren't used to being there … it's an uncomfortable place. And we're essentially accusing him of murder. You know, if you're innocent of that, then I think you've got a right to be pretty angry.'

Neither Leanne Weir nor Steve Norris, who were in the court, thought the Roselands Lads were the likely culprits.

They and their friends discussed the day's proceedings on a regular basis and though they didn't like what they saw or heard about Garry Carr, Gary Ireland, Ray Khoury or any of their associates, they didn't believe they had anything to do with Trudie's disappearance.

Attempting to placate Ireland when he was angry, Scott Mitchell had said: 'I agree with you that the investigation in the past – well, I think was inadequate, let's put it that way.'

To which Gary Ireland had responded: 'Three times it was inadequate, mate, three times.'

On another occasion the Coroner said to Ireland that he was 'not the first person who has been concerned about the quality of the investigation … so you are not Robinson Crusoe'.

Gary Matthews was too ill to attend the inquest so he – and other police – never got a chance to rebut this off-handed criticism.

But Matthews could probably take comfort in the fact that Trudie's friends, counsel assisting and others essentially agreed with his initial judgement back in the late 1970s that the Roselands Lads had been young men bragging and boasting, however awful and distasteful that might be.

Chapter 26

I'm No Angel

On Wednesday, 2 February 2011, 70-year-old Neville Tween entered the witness box at the Coroner's Court in Glebe for questioning.

Peter Hamill knew better than most that cross-examining Tween was not going to be an easy job. Having been a defence lawyer for years, he knew Tween's type as well as his background: in the Children's Court at the age of nine before moving through the system firstly at Mount Penang and then graduating to more serious offences and higher courts and prison sentences. The old crook knew the criminal justice system backwards.

Still, others in the court the day he appeared were hoping something would be achieved by the questioning of the chief suspect in Trudie's disappearance 33 years earlier. But it was driven more by hope, wishful thinking that some new clue might emerge after all these years. They wondered if Tween would crack under cross-examination and reveal something he didn't mean to.

Trudie's father, Charles, watched as the man believed to have killed his daughter took an affirmation rather than swearing an oath on the bible. Her former girlfriends looked on from the public gallery.

Tween stared at them and they stared back, wanting to meet the old crim's gaze.

From the very first question, Tween wasn't very cooperative, saying his full name was John Anderson instead of John David Anderson.

'I think it's the case that you are serving a sentence of some 11 years for an offence that you were convicted of, importing cocaine,' Hamill said.

Tween replied: 'Alleged.' While acknowledging he was in prison, he refused to admit to the cocaine importation despite a jury having found him guilty and the NSW Court of Criminal Appeal upholding the verdict – describing the prosecution's case as 'compelling' and Tween's defence as 'threadbare'.

But say nothing, admit nothing, even when you've been caught, sentenced, done and dusted. It tallied with what Tween had advised his stepdaughter, Kylie, over the years: 'One of the things my dad told me was never volunteer information. Never.'

Hamill pressed on and Tween begrudgingly admitted he'd pleaded not guilty to the cocaine charges but had been found guilty. He described himself as being in poor health and currently staying in the Long Bay Jail hospital.

He said he knew why he was at the Coroner's Court – it was in relation to the disappearance of Trudie Adams. Hamill asked Tween if he understood that he was also a suspect in the rapes of 14 young women on the Northern Beaches between 1971 and 1978.

Yes, Tween said, he did because 'I read that in *The Sun-Herald*. No police told me that. No-one ever come out and interviewed me about that. No-one ever showed me a photograph, asked me to go in a line-up in 30 years. And they reckon they've got a red-hot case.'

It was an unsettling answer for many of those closest to Trudie, because it was true. Despite evidence back in 1978 pointing to Tween's involvement in the rapes, and strong suspicion he was also involved in Trudie's disappearance, police hadn't been near him for decades, until his prison interview with Nicole Jones and Gavin McKean in March 2009.

Then came the questioning about his criminal history, starting in Kalgoorlie, a lifetime ago, through to his recent conviction for cocaine importation. There were more than 100 charges and jail time in New South Wales, Victoria and South Australia and New Zealand.

Hamill: 'Do you agree that you've led a life of crime?'

Tween: 'No'.

'Seriously?'

'I'm serious.'

'You don't think you've led a life of crime?'

'No. Do you?'

'Let's talk about your criminal history then, shall we?'

'You're saying I'm making a living out of crime.'

'Well, that would be true as well, wouldn't it?'

'Well, that comes down to a monetary thing, making money.'

'Certainly a number of the offences that you have committed over the years were designed to make you money, weren't they? 'Hamill asked.

'I can't remember. I can't remember now.'

Some of the sexual assault victims had mentioned as far back as 1978 that one of the offenders had a stutter or slight speech impediment.

Listening to the tapes of Tween giving evidence, it's not so much a stutter as a mispronunciation of certain words, saying 'cwime' instead of crime and 'photogwaph' instead of photograph.

Tween couldn't pronounce his Rs, a bit like that old cartoon character Elmer Fudd, who was forever chasing Bugs Bunny – that 'wascally wabbit'. Except there was nothing funny about the performance Tween was giving.

He told the Coroner that many of the offences of break, enter and steal when he was a kid were for things like 'a couple of lollies out of Woolworths'. He claimed the police had set him up, although he agreed 'not every time'.

When Peter Hamill asked Tween whether he'd agree that by the age of 20 he had appeared in court charged with a great many crimes, Tween replied, 'I don't know about a great many.'

'Well, more than average?'

'Well, what's the average?'

'I don't know, you tell me.'

'I don't say I'm an angel, I'm not saying that.'

***

For Steve Norris, Charles and John Adams and a small group of Trudie's friends, including Leanne Weir, who turned up to the inquest almost every day, it was a difficult, frustrating experience.

Leanne recalls Tween being led in, handcuffed and made to sit in the witness box. She said he would lean forward and give them all 'the death stare, as if to say, I'm looking at you. He tried to make everybody feel intimidated. I think that was his power, that was his mind. His mind was that he could make everyone feel like they were next. And it was very intimidating.'

But Trudie's friends and family weren't easily stood over. 'We all leant forward and gave it to him back. In the eye, of course.'

* * *

In his questioning of Tween, Hamill turned to the events of 1 March 1971, the beginning of this story. He brought up the case of the woman we've called Jane Hampshire, who was abducted at gunpoint in Manly before being handcuffed and sexually assaulted.

'You are a person who had access to handcuffs, aren't you?' Hamill asked.

'Oh, anyone can get access [to handcuffs],' Tween replied.

Hamill said he wasn't talking about 'anyone'. 'I'm talking about you … you had access to handcuffs, right?'

'Anyone else in this community can get a set of handcuffs today.'

'Yeah, including you in 1971, right?' Hamill said.

Coroner Mitchell intervened and asked Tween if he'd had a set of handcuffs in 1971. When Tween said no, Mitchell asked, 'You can remember that?'

'Oh, I can't remember having had handcuffs. But they were certainly everywhere. They weren't a thing that people hid,' Tween responded.

After that, Hamill moved on to the sexual assaults of 14-year-old Jackie Billings and 15-year-old Sarah Sharpe on 6 March 1971 and their account of one of their attackers taking polaroid photos of them. 'Did you have a polaroid camera in 1971?'

'I don't know,' Tween said. 'I believe there was one in some of them years. There's a family one that kicked around, the cheap one. But I believe that yes there was.'

In the space of his very short answer Anderson had gone from 'don't know' to 'maybe' to 'yes'.

Tween was asked about being pinched by the Consorting Squad at the hotel in George Street on 10 March 1971 and whether he had been charged with two offences – goods in custody and offering a bribe to a police officer – then not turning up at court the next day.

'What you did was flee to South Australia, didn't you?' Hamill asked.

'That's right,' Tween said.

Hamill pointed out that he had hurriedly left the state 'just a short time' after the three women had been 'brutally abducted and raped'.

'Not brutally abducted,' Tween replied. 'They pinched on a handcuff key.'

Hamill said he didn't understand what Tween was saying.

'Well that's what I was pinched on and the next day they wanted to go home and sleep, and it was going to be on the next day, they were going to clean their books up,' Tween replied.

His answer was both illuminating and confusing. On the one hand, he was admitting he'd been arrested in the hotel for possessing a handcuff key, which clearly suggests that as of 10 March he had also had some handcuffs. But then he included the obfuscation that 'they wanted to go home and sleep', which just didn't make any sense.

Cleaning the books up was a constant thread in Tween's evidence. He claimed that police would charge him with one offence and add a few others in to boost their clean-up rate.

When Hamill asked Tween if he'd offered a bribe to a police officer to get out of the charges, he denied it.

When Hamill pointed out Tween hadn't fronted up to the Central Court, Tween agreed. 'I don't believe so at that time.'

Hamill suggested Tween had 'continued his life of crime' in South Australia to which he replied, 'No, no, no, no.'

Never mind that he'd had been jailed in South Australia later in 1971.

Having asked Tween about handcuffs and polaroid cameras, Hamill moved on to guns. 'You were a man that had access to guns in 1971, correct?'

'Who can't get a gun?' Tween replied.

'Well, don't worry about everyone else. I'm just asking about you.'

'I'm just stating the facts. I'm also stating the fact you're making me out as the only one who can get a gun. That's crap.'

Coroner Mitchell intervened once more, telling Tween that 'most people can't get a gun'.

'Oh.'

'You think they can, do you?'

'Yes.'

'Well, we must have spent our lives in different social circles, is all I can say.'

On this, at least, Tween appeared to agree. 'I didn't know judges in my earlier day, either. But guns are easy to get. It's as simple as that.'

Hamill moved on to the 1975 assault on Jimmy Holten in Ku-ring-gai Chase National Park, retribution for Holten supposedly ripping them off in a drug deal. Garry Batt had driven Holten there. Tween, dressed in overalls, wearing a motorcycle helmet and armed with a machine gun, had turned up a short time later.

In the witness box, Tween made out that there was really nothing in it – the women's clothing, the cabanossi sausages – it was all a bit of a lark. Nobody had got hurt and when the matter came to court later, even the presiding judge had had a bit of a laugh about the Cabanossi Kid.

Neither Hamill nor the Coroner were amused, with the latter describing what Holten had suffered as 'outrageous and horrible'.

When Tween said, 'I don't know …' Mitchell replied: 'Then there's something wrong with you. Do you think it was horrible?'

'Yes. Of course it was,' Tween conceded.

He admitted he had taken the polaroid photos after dressing Holten up 'in some women's clothes and things like that and it's sick'. He added that he 'took them photos which were to be held if he didn't get the money back. And that was basically it.'

'You made him dig a grave for himself?' Hamill asked.

'Where did the shovel come from? What, did he carry it himself?' Tween said.

'Where did the cabanossi come from?' Hamill countered.

'Well, I didn't bring it there. Don't look at me. He probably put it in his own pocket. He probably brought it with him, mate.

Hamill: 'Mate?'

'Yeah … the guy is a heroin addict,' Tween said. 'Let's get to the facts. Agree? You don't agree?'

Hamill replied that he didn't know anything about Holten.

'Well, neither do I. Never met him before. Ever. But Dinger had.'

Tween told the inquest Holten had promised them a pound of 'primo smoko' but it had turned out to be 'sawdust'. He agreed the assault had taken place not far from his home at the time in Terrey Hills.

Was it about a 20-minute walk? Hamill asked.

Tween wouldn't agree though he admitted it was 'not over an hour'.

Having previously said he'd ordered Holten to put on women's clothing, Tween then denied it. When Hamill pointed out he'd already admitted it, Tween replied, 'I said that?'

Hamill put it to Tween that he'd told Holten to get down on his knees 'and suck Dingers cock', to which Tween replied, 'I don't think I said that. I think he done it voluntarily.'

'What, after you'd fired the machine gun?' Hamill asked.

'No,' Tween replied.

'Well, before you fired the machine gun?'

'I don't know about that.'

Hamill pressed Tween, saying it must have been before or after Tween fired the machine gun or as he was firing it, and asked him which one it was.

'I just don't remember exactly which one, I mean you're going back a long time.'

Tween denied he had forced Holten to do anything at gunpoint.

Hamill: 'It was a power trip?'

Tween: 'Why would he bring all the stuff there.'

Hamill: 'Which stuff is that, the cabanossi?'

Tween: 'The women's dresses and things like that.'

Tween maintained that neither he nor Batt had taken the women's underwear or the cabanossi, so it must have been Holten.

Hamill reminded him of the conversation Holten had with Garry Batt as they drove out of the bush after the assault.

Holten had told police in 1975 Batt had said 'that cunt [Tween] is mad. He picked up two sheilas hitching, took them up there and we took a lot of good pictures of them.'

Hamill questioned Tween about 'the remarkable coincidence' of Holten repeating a story he'd been told by Batt that polaroid photos had been taken of some girls in the bush – as indeed they had been in 1971.

'Well, isn't that convenient,' Tween replied, suggesting it was another police frame-up.

Furthermore, he was prepared to take a lie detector test. Tween mentioned his readiness to do a lie detector a few times during his day in court, knowing full well that New South Wales courts don't accept them into evidence.

***

The frustration was evident all round, for counsel assisting, the Coroner, Trudie's friends and her family. But Tween didn't care. He knew there was nothing anyone could do. He was 70 years old, in poor health, in jail and likely to die there.

Still, Hamill persisted. What about Andrew Kingston's statement to police that Len Evans had confessed to raping girls in the bush with him? he asked.

Tween said it was another police fabrication. Evans would never speak like that to an inmate, particularly one he didn't know. Kingston had made the story up to get a reduction in his sentence.

But Tween did admit he'd visited Lenny in jail, saying it was to make sure he was alright and that he had money for food, clothes and 'a monthly buy-up'.

He had never said anything to Evans during the visit about having done 'a couple of Ku-ring-gai jobs' in his honour or about continuing to assault young women. He told the court he'd never assaulted anyone and never would.

When Tween was asked about possessing wigs and false beards, once again, he deflected the question. 'Anyone can have access to these things.'

'Have you ever had access to an oxy bottle?' Hamill asked.

'Yes, of course I have,' Tween replied.

Had he ever used an oxy bottle to get into safes?

'Well, so what? Ninety per cent of safes are done by oxy,' Tween replied.

After some more back and forth about whether he had used oxyacetylene to open safes, he said, 'Never used it, no. Absolutely.'

Towards the end of his questioning, Hamill asked the 70-year-old about his relationship with his first wife, Dulcie. Had he ever been violent towards her?

'No. She wouldn't say that if you brought her in here.'

Coroner Scott Mitchell interrupted to say that in fact Dulcie had been brought 'in here and she did say that'.

'Well, I have never really assaulted Dulcie or any other woman,' Tween replied.

Hamill then read out what Dulcie had told Detective Nicole Jones three years earlier about holding 'some fears for her safety' because she'd been assaulted by her then husband.

Tween categorically denied it. 'I've got a good memory on that. I would not hit her. I'll take a lie detector on that too. I'm hurt just hearing that.'

On the question of the panel van that Steve Norris had seen picking up Trudie, Tween claimed the description exonerated him from any involvement in her disappearance. Norris had described the vehicle as having no side windows.

Hamill: 'You say that in 1978 your panel van had side windows?'

Tween: 'Right … I've got these photos now that show they did have these windows in and the photos were taken one month before, before someone kidnapped Trudie.'

It was remarkable evidence. He couldn't remember much at all about having handcuffs, guns, wigs or using oxy bottles but he could clearly remember the photos were taken just before she disappeared.

Hamill then raised Garry Batt's evidence to the inquest the previous day that he had installed side windows in the panel van at around the time of Trudie's abduction.

'Well, actually I don't know who put them in,' Tween replied.

In any case, he was adamant: '[Norris] had a perfect view. When he said "no windows", well, he meant no windows. That means it was not my car.'

He was then asked about some more of Batt's evidence – that he was frightened of Tween who had gone 'a bit crazy' and was 'a sexual deviate'.

'He was frightened of me, you're joking.'

'You told him to disappear or you'd make him disappear?'

'That's crap,' Tween said.

In fact, that's exactly what Batt had told the court, and, what's more, it's exactly what he'd done. After serving his jail sentence for the 1975 assault on Holten, Batt had disappeared off the radar to such an extent that NSW Police believed he'd been murdered – probably by Tween. Indeed, Bob Inkster had expressed 'extreme amazement' when Batt turned up to the inquest. He and others were astonished that Batt had managed to 'keep his head down for 30 years' given he was well known in Sydney as a career criminal for whom jail was no deterrent whatsoever.

Apparently, Batt was far more frightened of Tween than he was of jail.

Hamill moved on to probing Tween about the telephone calls he'd had with his wife, Susan, after going to jail for the cocaine importation. He also asked about his conversations with Michael in the jail cell they shared, after it became apparent his calls were being recorded and the cell was bugged.

It was all about a possible alibi. Apparently, somewhere along the line Tween had given his wife and son the idea he wasn't in New South Wales in 1971 when the first three rapes had occurred.

Hamill reminded him of a telephone call in July 2008, in which Susan had said, 'If only we would look into the fact that you weren't even in New South Wales in 1971.' The idea being that if the family could prove he wasn't in the state that year he could be exonerated.

'What was my response to that?' Tween asked.

'Well, that was the interesting thing,' Hamill said. 'You didn't respond to that. You remained silent to that.'

Hamill put it to Tween that he'd remained silent because he knew full well he'd been charged on 10 March 1971 and had bolted to Adelaide.

'Listen, I would not have a clue,' Tween replied. 'I'll take a lie detector on it. I had no idea of dates and even now I don't.'

Hamill persisted: 'And what your family was trying to get you to do and what at least your son was trying to get us to do was to establish that you didn't come to New South Wales until '74, because that would rule you out as being the perpetrator of some nasty rapes in 1971?'

Tween obfuscated yet again. 'As you say, I was speaking to Susan on the telephone. How could my son be on the telephone too?'

Years later, Peter Hamill recalled that 'he would say anything until he was confronted with solid evidence that what he'd just said was a lie. He thought he was more in control than not. I think he thought he was pretty smart.'

There is a photograph of Neville Tween from this time, leaving court in the back of a police vehicle. One handcuffed hand is touching his face, and he's looking down. His iris is a bright light blue, which makes his pupil seem extra black. 'He just looks like an evil bastard,' recalled Hamill. 'And that's kind of how he presented in court. Like an old, evil man.'

The same photo also brings to mind the words of one of the victims from 1971: 'I remember that the driver had snaky type of eyes.'

In the end, Tween denied being involved in any of the sexual assaults or the disappearance and murder of Trudie Adams. Wherever he could, he denied pretty much anything.

Right at the very end, after Peter Hamill had indicated he had no further questions, the Coroner told Tween he could leave the witness box. Just before Tween did so, he repeated his defence that the police 'even now haven't told me exactly what's happened …' And then he offered this: 'And may I also say at this stage I have never ever known Trudie. I've never met her. I've never seen her from a distance. She was not a hitchhiker … that I got in the car as described by Mr Norris.'

Contained within this statement is one curious sentence: 'I've never seen her from a distance.' Because if Tween had abducted and killed Trudie, that's exactly how he would have seen her – from a distance – as his panel van glided along Barrenjoey Road, past the Newport Surf Club, to where Trudie was standing.

Chapter 27
The Evidence

As the inquest into the disappearance of Trudie Adams continued, a number of serving and former NSW Police were called to give evidence.

There was Detective Sergeant Ashley Bryant, who'd started looking at Trudie's case in 2005, Jayson Macleod, who had investigated the disappearance of Tony Yelavich. Gavin McKean and Nicole Jones, who had reviewed all the evidence, pulling together the many strands of the case as much as they possibly could.

Detective Sergeant Bryant told the court he'd joined the Unsolved Homicide Squad when it was formed in 2004 and that in his time there he'd been given 44 unsolved homicides to review or investigate. After reviewing Trudie's case, he'd decided there were leads that hadn't been followed up. Bryant described the mountain of information flowing into the initial homicide investigation in 1978 as 'extreme'. The fact that it all had to be typed and manually filed meant that 'information couldn't be properly addressed'.

He also identified problems in the 1978 inquiry that were not related to information overload. He told the Coroner: 'There were a number of identifications made by the women that had been sexually assaulted where persons Neville Tween and Ray Johnson had been identified. That had subsequently not been acted upon.'

It then emerged that there were problems with the way the women had been asked to identify the suspects. For reasons that are unclear, two photo boards of potential suspects had been used to show to the victims. One had 20 photos on it, the other 12. On the latter, Tween featured three times.

Bryant agreed with counsel assisting that this was 'plainly a problem … That wouldn't be admitted into evidence present day and I doubt if it would have been admitted in evidence back in 1978,' he said.

It wasn't said in court but the obvious point was that the more photos there were of Tween on the photo board, the more likely it was that a victim would pick him out. It was either quite deliberate or massively incompetent.

There was also some confusion over the 'crowd scene' identifications of men outside court.

The 1978 investigators had told Bryant the women who participated did not identify Tween or Johnson. However, he told the inquest that 'speaking with the victims in person it appeared clearly not to be the case. I can't remember the names of the victims but this document did specifically identify Neville Tween.'

It wasn't clarified any further but it appears that at least one, or some, of the victims had told Bryant they had identified Tween at court.

He told the court he'd left the Trudie Adams case after being promoted and sent to Bourke, in western New

South Wales. But, before leaving the Homicide Squad, he'd drawn up an action plan for the investigation into Trudie's disappearance and the multiple abductions and sexual assaults.

He agreed with Peter Hamill that at the time he left 'there was a vast amount of material still to digest and inquiries still to be made.'

Bryant also revealed his conversations with the original investigator in charge, Gary Matthews, by then retired.

The former detective had told him the reason Tween, Garry Batt, Ray Johnson and Len Evans were never interviewed was because 'he received a telephone call from then prominent solicitor Leon Goldberg, who informed him that his clients, Tween and Johnson, were not involved in the disappearance of Trudie Adams and would not participate in any interviews.'

Matthews had also expressed the view 'that there was a leak within the police' about the two men being suspects 'which had filtered through to Mr Goldberg'.

Matthews also told Ashley Bryant that Tween and Johnson 'were not worked upon to the fullest extent' due to 'other work commitments that he had'.

Counsel assisting, Peter Hamill, asked: 'On your review of the evidence, did you come to the same view?'

Bryant replied: 'Absolutely … I'm of the view that Tween and Johnson should have been prosecuted with respect to the sexual assaults. They at the very least should have been more thoroughly investigated …'

Not long after Ashley Bryant gave evidence, the dozens of cold cases and many other incidents he'd investigated or witnessed over his 24 years in the force finally took a tragic toll.

In 2012, Detective Sergeant Bryant was medically discharged due to chronic severe PTSD.

Just before Christmas 2013, he telephoned 000 and said, 'I understand that this call is being recorded. I'm about to take my life. I suffer post-traumatic stress disorder. I can no longer live with the trauma of it and I want this to go to the Coroner.' He wanted more support for people affected by PTSD and their partners. The operator tried to keep him talking, to no avail.

In 2017, Ashley Bryant's suicide became the subject of an inquest where he was described as a 'driven' and accomplished officer. At the time of his death he had been drinking heavily. He was 44.

His widow, Deborah, gave evidence that he had not been a drinker until he started working at Manly Police Station, where his night shift boss had told him to take the police wagon to the Steyne Hotel, where it was filled with cases of free beer. The beer would be drunk at the end of the shift.

The Coroner investigating Trudie Adams' death sought to get to the bottom of the 'leak' and the evidence that Leon Goldberg had phoned Gary Matthews to warn him against interviewing his clients. Matthews was too sick to attend the inquest. Mr Goldberg, who had started as solicitor in 1952, gave evidence on 21 March 2011 and said he remembered acting for Tween in the 1975 Jimmy Holten case. He recalled the charge being downgraded to a less serious offence. However, he said he had no memory at all of telephoning Matthews and saying Tween and Johnson would not be interviewed regarding the Trudie Adams matter.

Goldberg agreed with Peter Hamill that if a client instructed him to call the police he would have done so, especially given the police's use of 'verballing' in the 1970s, involving fabricated 'confessions' by suspects. He told the

Coroner there would be nothing improper in following a client's instructions.

Asked specifically whether Tween had given him instructions to call Detective Matthews, he replied that Tween 'could well have done', but he was 'fairly confident it didn't happen'.

Goldberg also said he had 'never' been made aware that Tween and Johnson were suspects in the rapes nor the disappearance of Trudie. He referred to Tween as 'Tweeny' twice in his evidence. But he made it clear that while he had represented him in court cases in the past he didn't like the man.

'I don't have any time for Tween,' he commented, saying, 'I have certain views about the man in relation to his general conduct.'

Goldberg agreed he'd acted for Tony Yelavich and that he'd visited him in jail to obtain instructions before his disappearance in 1985, though he had 'absolutely no memory of that man's face at all'.

He told the Coroner an allegation had been put to him that he'd tipped off Tween and Johnson about being suspects in the disappearance of Yelavich but was 'confident it never took place'. On the other hand, given the era, if he'd been told the police were going to do something improper, 'it is not beyond the bounds of conjecture that I could speak to the people involved. It is not a matter of tipping him off to something.'

But clearly Tween had been alerted by someone, meeting up with a detective in a car park twice in 1986 to make inquiries about the Yelavich matter and whether police were investigating his involvement.

There was no prospect of Ray Johnson possibly clearing things up either – by the time of the inquest he had died.

***

The day after Goldberg's appearance, Jayson Macleod, who had left NSW Police in 2008, gave evidence about taking over the Yelavich investigation and linking it to Trudie's disappearance and the abductions and rapes. Like Bryant, Macleod said he believed there was 'significant evidence or potential evidence' for those rapes that police should have considered a lot more seriously than they did.

Macleod referred to how some of the sexual victims had noticed one of the attackers had either a stutter or a slight speech impediment – which Tween had. He mentioned the detailed confession Lenny Evans had made to another inmate about sexually assaulting people in the Northern Beaches area.

Macleod believed that plenty of leads should have been followed, notwithstanding the contamination of the original photo identifications. To this day, Macleod is still troubled by the lack of action by NSW Police regarding the sexual assaults.

'The rape victims particularly, living with this on a daily basis, the trauma they went through, they deserved justice … they haven't had it,' he said in 2018.

The same applied to Trudie Adams and Tony Yelavich. 'They all deserved better than what I think they were afforded.'

Macleod said he'd resigned from NSW Police in 2008 because his investigation into the murders and his dealings with Standen had 'sucked the life out of me … It had taken its toll. I didn't sleep for two weeks … it was time to move on, refresh.'

***

Detective Senior Constable Nicole Jones from the Homicide Squad recounted parts of her videotaped 'walk through' Ku-ring-gai Chase National Park with Gavin McKean and Brian Walker, in particular their discovery of the oxy bottle. She confirmed that Brian Walker's immediate identification of the blue Volkswagen they'd found in the bush had been proved correct by later expert examination.

She was then asked about the mattress that had been found in the bushland and Walker's claim that it had not been seized by police and had in fact remained there for years.

Questioned by Peter Hamill, she confirmed she had not been able to find any record that suggested Walker was wrong.

'In other words, the police didn't take the mattress away?'

'Not that I'm aware of,' she replied.

Jones said that these days the mattress would 'absolutely' have been taken for DNA testing.

She told the court some DNA testing had been done on a set of handcuffs, three pieces of black plastic and eight pieces of electrical tape found in bushland in 1975. The testing had found a mixture of DNA but the sample wasn't strong enough to provide a proper profile, and an attempt to match DNA to some of the victims had been unsuccessful.

* * *

At one stage, on a Friday, the inquest took a sensational twist when, out of the blue, Carolyn Mary Drake told the Coroner that she was living close to the Adams house in Avalon at the time of Trudie's disappearance. She'd also gone to the same school as Trudie but hadn't known her well.

Drake said that between midnight and 12.30am on 25 June 1978, the time Trudie had last been sighted, she and her then boyfriend, John Milligan, had driven north on Barrenjoey Road, past the Newport Surf Club while the dance was still going.

Drake said she remembered the date and time because it was Milligan's birthday. When he'd turned left off Barrenjoey Road into Central Road to take her home she saw Trudie Adams hitchhiking.

She told the inquest: 'So I asked John to stop and we pulled over and she got in the car.'

During the short conversation, Trudie had said she'd hitched a lift from outside the surf club to Central Road. Drake said they'd dropped Trudie off outside her house.

Drake said she believed she'd spoken about this with a number of friends in the days after it happened. However, she had become seriously ill with glandular fever and been bedridden for about six weeks.

She'd not come forward previously because it was only that week that she'd read a report in *The Sydney Morning Herald* about the time Trudie had last been seen.

She said she'd never previously made the connection and never been to the police.

None of her friends had suggested she should.

Two of the newspaper headlines the next day were 'Startling new evidence in Trudie Adams case' and 'Twist to 30-year mystery of Trudie Adams'.

The officer then in charge of the case, Detective Senior Constable Angela De Ville, was called on to do some speedy investigation. When the inquest resumed on Monday, it heard that De Ville had spoken to the three friends named by Ms Drake, some of whom were in court.

All three said Drake had never told them about giving Trudie a lift home on the night she disappeared. And all of them said that if she had they would have told their parents or gone to the police.

One said it wasn't a matter of it all being a long time ago and that she couldn't remember. 'Never happened,' she told the court.

John Milligan, who was living in Tasmania, also said Drake was wrong and that they had never picked up Trudie. 'There is no way that happened,' he said, 'because I would have been straight to the police after I knew she was missing to tell them.'

Carolyn Drake's sensational claim just wasn't supported by any other evidence.

The inquest moved on.

* * *

The bulk of the police evidence provided to the Coroner came from Gavin McKean's time in the witness box and the 133-page statement he and Nicole Jones had put together.

He said they had re-examined thousands of pages of documents and re-interviewed witnesses, or tried to. Some key witnesses, such as Andrew Kingston, who'd been in jail with Len Evans, had died.

Asked for his view of the possible involvement of the Roselands Lads, he told the court he'd read through 'hours and hours' of documents and that at first glance, things like their 'confessions' and the mentions of the green Kombi had jumped out at him. But after delving into it further he'd formed the opinion 'it was just boys talking rubbish. Just big-noting themselves. I'm almost sure they were not involved,' he said.

Experienced detectives will tell you that, bizarre as it sounds, people will make up stories that they have murdered or raped, to big-note themselves.

As McKean told the authors long after the inquest, 'people do make up stories to gain attention … to be part of something they think is important. You might think it sounds insane for someone to do that, but it's not actually that uncommon for people … to want to be part of it all.'

McKean also said the circumstances described by some of the Roselands Lads were implausible. For a start, it wouldn't be that easy to jump out of a Kombi travelling at 30–40 kilometres per hour.

'There's [supposedly] five blokes in the car. You'd think they'd be restraining her.'

He also recalled the inquiries his team had made of some of the key suspects, including an interview with Garry Batt in Victoria on 17 July 2008.

McKean described how he and Nicole Jones had arrived unannounced at his home. 'Nicole and I knocked on the door and we heard through the door what sounded like the picking up of a metal pipe.' Then, he said, Batt called out, 'I've got a shotgun; I'm going to shoot you.'

Before the two detectives could work out what to do, Batt opened the door and said, 'I'm just joking.'

When Jones and McKean introduced themselves and explained why they were there, Batt said, 'Come on in, I'll put the kettle on.'

Batt told them he had no knowledge of the rapes or the murder of Trudie, but he was willing to talk about Neville Tween, whom he referred to as 'Tubby'.

He told them that Tween had been his best friend until the 1970s and that he'd also known Ray Johnson. He said he'd met Tween in juvenile detention back in the 1950s and they'd subsequently done numerous break and enters together. Batt described himself as the 'the mechanic' of the duo, by which he meant he was looked on as the expert safebreaker who could pick locks and knew how to use explosives.

He revealed that he and Tween had often visited Ku-ring-gai Chase National Park to bury firearms and cash. In fact, Batt said he'd once buried $3000 in the ground there, but then later couldn't find it as he didn't know the area very well.

Batt thought that if Tween had killed Trudie, her body would be in the national park. He told the detectives that Tween had gone 'a bit crazy' towards the end of their friendship, with the 1975 assault on Jimmy Holten being a prime example. Batt thought they were just going to scare the young bloke and give him a backhander. He said what Tween had done was 'excessive'.

Then there was a strange incident one day when Tween came to the garage where Batt was working as a mechanic. A young girl had approached them and said to Tween something like 'dirty old man'. Batt said he'd questioned Tween about what the girl meant, but he'd refused to answer and they'd had a blue.

At the inquest, Garry Batt basically confirmed what he'd told McKean and Jones about Tween being 'pretty crazy' and a 'sexual deviant' who was 'capable of murder'. If something had gone wrong when Tween was firing the submachine gun near Jimmy Holten, Tween 'wouldn't have left any witnesses'.

***

In his statement to the inquest, Detective McKean said that two weeks after visiting Batt, he went to New Zealand with Detective Chief Inspector Dennis Bray to ask Len Evans about the rapes and Trudie.

As he and Jones had done with Batt, he and Inspector Bray turned up on Evans' doorstep unannounced, although this time they were accompanied by New Zealand police.

McKean still vividly remembers Evans' reaction to their arrival.

'He thought he was done. [His] head dropped, his shoulders dropped forward to the point where I kind of looked at my offsider, Dennis Bray, and I thought this guy is going to make an admission right here.'

It was not to be, Evans 'just stayed quiet'.

They took him to the local police station, where he denied all the allegations in what McKean described as a 'very mousy, quiet manner'. He denied making any of the comments attributed to him by Andrew Kingston in jail in 1978.

However, he did admit to committing other crimes with Tween.

In his coronial statement, McKean said: 'Of interest, Evans was asked if he had ever been armed during these offences and had he ever fired shots at people.'

Evans had replied that he had been armed in the past 'and that he had never fired shots at people but had fired warning shots'.

McKean pointed out that this was consistent with what the sexual assault victims had said about the men firing warning shots into the ground or the air.

Living in New Zealand – and not charged with any crime – Evans could not be compelled to give evidence to the inquest.

In September 2020, 81-year-old Evans responded to questions put to him by the authors. In a short letter, he said he'd been in jail at the time of Trudie's disappearance (which was true), so could not have been involved in the matter.

He said that he had no knowledge of the rapes and had 'previously expressed my genuine view Tween is innocent in what has become a misguided investigation so be careful with assumptions and speculations'.

Evans ended the letter, 'Thanks kindly, L.E.'

***

When detectives went to see Dulcie Anderson, she told them she had no knowledge of anything to do with the rapes or Trudie. She did say she was fearful of her former husband. Susan Anderson wouldn't answer any questions and referred the police to her solicitor.

Called to the inquest to give evidence, Susan Anderson said she didn't believe her husband was involved in the disappearance of Trudie Adams in June 1978 because the two of them had met on Valentine's Day that year, more than four months before Trudie went missing. Susan said their relationship was at its 'peak' at the time Trudie disappeared.

When asked what she meant by the relationship being at its 'peak', she replied: 'Well he was very romantic, we did everything, went everywhere together, had dinners all the time, we spent a lot of time together in the evening … at my place at Villawood.'

She told the inquest she'd discussed the Trudie Adams case with her husband and had believed him when he said he wasn't involved.

***

Detective McKean's 133-page statement to the Coroner was an exhibit in the inquest. In it, he summed up all the evidence gathered over the years, by all the inquiries against the chief suspect, Neville Tween, aka John Anderson.

He said that Tween had lived 'in close proximity' to where the assaults on Jimmy Holten and the rape victims had taken place between 1971 and 1978 in Ku-ring-gai Chase National Park.

After the assault on Holten in 1975, police had found handcuffs, a spent 9mm cartridge, alcohol, marijuana and women's underwear. This was consistent with the attacks on the young women who had been handcuffed, offered marijuana and alcohol and shots had been fired.

Some of the victims had described one of their attackers as having a speech impediment, which Tween had. Also, Tween had admitted he knew Ku-ring-gai Chase National Park very well.

Then there was the 1978 statement of Andrew Kingston where he detailed admissions by Len Evans. Detective McKean said: 'These admissions contained details of the crimes that were never released to the public and could only have been known by the offender or someone who had spoken to the offender'.

Tween had been charged with possession of a handcuff key, guns, wigs and false beards and he had access to a blue VW similar to that described by some of the victims – it had been seen in his driveway by surveillance officers.

Tween had been described as a sexual deviant and the woman Suzanne had told police about Tween's requests for very young girls. Some of the sexual assault victims had identified Tween when they were shown photo boards of suspects. Some had also identified Ray Johnson.

At the time of Trudie's disappearance, Tween had owned a panel van similar to that described by Steve Norris.

Then there was the crucial matter of timing, with the sexual assaults on the Northern Beaches starting in March 1971 then stopping when Tween moved to South Australia where he was jailed. Not long after returning to Sydney, Tween and Garry Batt had assaulted Jimmy Holten. When they were jailed, the offences had stopped. They'd started again in 1977 after Tween's release from prison and stopped after Trudie Adams' disappearance. Gavin McKean believed the police investigation into her disappearance, along with the media coverage, was 'so large that both Tween and Johnson decided to lay low and move up to the Central Coast'.

'In my opinion as the officer in charge of the investigation I strongly believe that Trudie Adams was kidnapped off the street by Tween and Johnson for the purpose of sexual assault. I believe something went wrong as the two men went about sexually assaulting Adams and she has been killed.'

He said he believed Tween raped all the victims mentioned in his statement and that the sexual assaults culminated in the murder of Trudie Adams.

'It is [my] opinion ... Tween raped these girls with different accomplices, which were [Len] Evans and [Garry] Batt in the early 1970s and then [Ray] Johnson from '77.'

He also believed that Tween 'was the mastermind and perpetrator of all the sexual assaults committed against the females relevant to this investigation'.

McKean's investigation also revealed there were clearly more victims. In 2009, he'd taken a signed statement from a woman we'll call Cheryl. In January 1975, she'd been hitchhiking on Pittwater Road, Mona Vale, when she was picked up by two men in a Holden sedan. She'd been driven to bushland off McCarrs Creek Road, Terrey Hills, where she'd been raped. Cheryl was 17 at the time. She told McKean the men clearly knew the area well.

They'd let her go near her house and threatened to kill her if she told anyone. She never did – not her parents, no one – until Gavin McKean encouraged her to make a statement. The attack on Cheryl took place just weeks after Tween had returned to Sydney from Adelaide and six months before the assault on Jimmy Holten.

* * *

On 1 April 2011, the Coroner, Scott Mitchell, delivered his findings, beginning with the evidence that Trudie was a 'happy and feisty girl with lots of friends and her whole life to look forward to'. He said she was 'part of an extremely strong network of girlfriends'.

Friends and family had described her as 'very independent, confident, very warm and likeable and talented'.

He said: 'It is powerful evidence of how wonderful a girl Trudie was that, so many years after her disappearance, so many of her girlfriends turned up at court for so many days to pay tribute to their friend.'

He also commented favourably on Steven Norris's attendance at court 'almost every day'.

The Coroner dismissed the evidence of Carolyn Drake as 'untrue', although he said he could not say what had influenced her to give it.

Turning to the Roselands Lads, he said Gary Ireland had been 'extremely loud, abusive and threatening' in the witness box and he could not rely on his evidence. Notwithstanding, the green Kombi and the 'boastful, stupid and callous claims' of Ireland, Keith Hurney, Garry Carr and possibly Ray Khoury, he believed the evidence they'd been involved with Trudie's suspected murder 'really does not amount to much'.

He remarked that Dulcie Anderson 'had little to tell the inquest' and her marriage to Tween appeared to have been an unhappy one. Sometimes Tween had threatened her and sometimes he'd assaulted her, 'and she was frightened of him and, she told police, frightened of some of his criminal associates'.

The Coroner observed that Tween had 'played little part in the upbringing of his sons, leaving that all to his wife' and was scathing about him involving Michael in his drug importation activities, describing it as 'disgraceful'.

He took aim at Neville Tween's response in the witness box to questions about the assault of Jimmy Holten in the bush in 1975. 'He seemed to lack all empathy with his victim and to regard his behaviour towards [Holton] as a normal consequence of an unsatisfactory business [deal]. His was the sort of response to a gross outrage which one might have expected from a psychopath.'

And while Gavin McKean and other police believed Tween was definitely responsible for the rapes and most likely responsible for Trudie's death, the Coroner pointed to the case of a witness he identified as 'K. McK' who gave evidence to the inquest of being attacked by a man who hit her with a shortened broom handle and tried to assault her.

She'd escaped, but her story, he said, was a reminder that there was 'a lot of random predatory behaviour' on the Northern Beaches.

'Perhaps Trudie Adams fell victim to such a random attack by somebody of whom the police have never heard.'

At the end of the day, Scott Mitchell said there just wasn't enough evidence for him to say what had happened to Trudie, or who was responsible for her death. He found that on the balance of probabilities, Trudie had died shortly after 12.30am on Sunday, 25 June 1978, on the Northern Beaches or in the surrounding bushland 'as a result of a criminal act, or acts, or misadventure associated with a criminal act or acts by a person or persons unknown'.

He referred the case back to the NSW Police for further investigation.

And he paid special tribute to Trudie's father, saying:

> I feel certain that everybody involved in this inquest would wish to join me in expressing profound sympathy to Charles Adams. His loss need not be described and his presence and participation in these coronial proceedings is a mark of huge love and respect for his missing daughter.

Just over four months after the end of the inquest, on 11 August 2011, Mark Standen was found guilty by a jury of conspiring with Bill Jalalaty and James Kinch to import and supply 300 kilograms of pseudoephedrine, the amount having been reduced from the initial charge of 600 kilograms.

At a wholesale price of about $40,000 a kilogram, the 300 kilograms was worth $12 million and could have yielded up to 228 kilograms of methyl amphetamine with a wholesale value of $41 million.

He was also found guilty of conspiracy to pervert the course of justice.

Standen was jailed for 22 years with a non-parole period of 16 years from the date of his arrest in 2008. His earliest date of release will be June 2024.

In his judgment, Justice Bruce James found that the payment of £20,000 (AUD $47,000) by Kinch to Jalalaty in December 2005 amounted to 'a gift' to Standen. Jalalaty had in turn written four $10,000 cheques for his friend at the Crime Commission with the $7000 balance being paid in several cash transactions. Some of the money was used to pay off credit card debts.

Justice James said: 'The gift was not made directly, because Mr Standen did not want the Crime Commission to know that he was receiving money from Kinch.'

Standen, who was in the witness box for 25 days, claimed in his evidence that Kinch had offered to send him some money for laser eye surgery, but Justice James noted the cost of the operation would have been only $5000 or $10,000.

The judge said that by accepting 'this substantial sum of money Mr Standen was irretrievably corruptly compromised'.

There were other payments to Standen as well, including $20,000 in cash hidden in a box containing a Christmas ham, which was delivered by Jalalaty. The NSW Crime Commission itself estimated Standen had access to $98,000 from overseas sources around 2004 to 2005.

It later revised the amount down to about $87,000 but added: 'The commission cannot say that Standen does not at present have further moneys overseas.'

Bill Jalalaty pleaded guilty and was sentenced to ten years, the lesser sentence explained by his guilty plea, the fact he was judged to be more junior in the conspiracy than Standen and Kinch, and also the fact he offered to help law enforcement authorities. Jalalaty is now a free man.

James Kinch, who had been arrested in Thailand in 2008 and only extradited to Australia in 2012, also pleaded guilty. In 2016, he was finally sentenced to 22 years and will be eligible for release in February 2024, a few months before Standen, the man he once described as 'my eyes and ears'.

Standen has spent almost his entire time in jail in solitary confinement because of fears he is at high risk of harm from inmates in the general prison population, some of whom he helped put there.

He continues to insist on his innocence.

During his lengthy trial, his true relationship with Kinch was finally exposed as being corrupt. While Jalalaty did not give evidence at the trial, he told the NSW Crime Commission that, on instructions from Kinch, he had paid Standen about $300,000. And that was organised when Kinch was living on the other side of the world.

How much money did the financially stricken Standen get from Neville Tween, his informer and another successful drug trafficker, with whom he socialised and who lived 1 kilometre down the road?

One thing the trial did not resolve was Standen's alleged gambling habit.

Standen has denied he ever had a gambling problem and there is no hard evidence to suggest that he did. There are some unusual withdrawals from the Bateau Bay Hotel near where Standen lived. His bank accounts reveal he was making three to four withdrawals on both Saturday and Sunday, just hours apart, totalling $1000 a day. It looks like a bloke who's on the punt at the pub but even some of Standen's former colleagues say there is no evidence he frittered away the money on the horses or the dogs. No one ever saw any betting slips lying around.

What did he do with all the money from Kinch? It's difficult to say. At the time of his arrest, his home, as his first bail hearing had heard, was almost fully mortgaged. He had credit card debts of over $100,000. As Jalalaty was heard to say on one of the intercepted conversations, Standen was living beyond his means, but apart from lavishing gifts on Louise Baker, what he was spending the money on remains a mystery.

Chapter 28

Dozens of Predators

In late 2018, the ABC aired a three-part TV documentary series and a seven-part podcast by the authors into the disappearance of Trudie Adams. As the episodes aired, emails began to roll in. Many were from people who had lived on the Northern Beaches in the 1970s and 1980s who knew Trudie and her family. People who had a story to tell or a memory they thought might help. The show had reminded them of things that had happened, including close encounters and near escapes.

Several former journalists who'd looked into the story in the past wrote in as well, offering to help, saying the series had brought back memories of their time covering crime and corruption on the Northern Beaches.

Some of the messages consisted of just one line. Others were longer, a devastating sequence of events that ended in an attack or escape. People called the ABC switchboard too and left messages. One message recorded by ABC TV's *7.30* team read, 'Woman [phone number] asking for Ruby Jones, has a lot of information about the Trudie Adams' story.' Other people got in touch on Instagram, or commented on Facebook.

What became painfully clear as more and more people got in touch was that there weren't just one or two predators operating on the Northern Beaches in the 1970s and '80s. There were dozens, ranging from 20-year-olds to men in their 50s. They included men with long hair and men with short hair; men in groups and men alone; men with scuba gear and men with acid-laced joints. Some of them were flashers, opportunists and weirdos. And some were rapists.

Women who had never before told anyone about being attacked recounted their stories down the phone line, bursting into tears as, decades later, they relived the sexual assaults. Many of the women had never reported to police what had happened to them. One woman, Karen Lagalla, recalled being assaulted while hitchhiking just a few kilometres from the spot Trudie was last seen. At the time, she was a young woman with a tan and thick dark hair, on her way to a wine bar when she accepted a lift. She remembers the sheer terror she felt when the driver took her to an isolated patch of bushland. 'He grabbed me around the throat and pulled me back down on his knee and put his hand over my mouth,' she recalled. 'I just thought … he was going to overpower me and then I would be raped.'

Karen was lucky, managing to escape when her attacker was distracted by a passer-by. Like many other women, she didn't report what had happened to the police.

'I didn't want to tell the police because I thought I would be in trouble … because I was hitchhiking and in those days, well, you were asking for it.'

The message was clear – if you were out alone at night you deserved whatever happened to you. You'd been warned by the newspapers, your parents, by everyone who knew about what could happen to young women alone. Even if you did report a sexual assault to the police, they weren't always likely to take you seriously, Jane Hampshire being a case in point.

That's what one of the women who called the ABC said she discovered when a pack of men ran her off the road just two weeks after Trudie's disappearance. The woman, Beth, was 23 years old and driving home down Mona Vale road in July 1978 when she realised a group of men driving in three separate cars were trapping her. First, one car overtook her and then slowed down its pace to a crawl. Another car behind her moved up close, sandwiching her in. The men driving switched their high beams on, tightly cocooning her car so she couldn't see their number plates. There was no one else around on the quiet stretch of Mona Vale Road she was on. Then a third car drove up on her right-hand side, forcing her off the road.

About six or seven men piled out of the cars and walked towards her. As they approached Beth she put her car into reverse and took off, fast. She remembers reaching 160 kilometres an hour as she sped through the next intersection, desperate to get home. 'If they had managed to get me I don't like to think what would have happened. I was truly terrified and knew I was fighting for my life.'

When Beth got home she woke her dad, who rang Pymble Police Station. He tried to get police to do something about it, but they refused, saying the men would be long gone, so there was no point in trying to find them.

'They were not interested in talking to me, nor did they offer to send a car out to have a look,' she said. 'When I look back, I think I was extremely lucky to have had a good car and I'm horrified to think what might have happened.'

Beth was especially enraged because this happened just two weeks after Trudie had disappeared. If police weren't going to take attacks like this seriously then, when would they?

Beth's father became so concerned for her safety that he went to a knife shop in the city where he told the manager he wanted his daughter to be able to protect herself. The owner of the shop knew exactly what he was after, pulling out a 'Survival Mark One' and telling him 'this is what you want, this is what all the young girls have'. Beth kept that knife in the glove box of her car for years, years in which she avoided Mona Vale Road when she was alone at night.

While many of these attacks were historical, happening decades ago, they had a common thread. Women attacked, brazenly, without fear of repercussions. And police doing little to help. It's interesting to note how much – or how little – has changed since then.

In January 2020, the ABC published an investigation into the way police handle sexual assault reports. It revealed just how egregiously survivors were still being failed by the system. More than 140,000 sexual assaults were reported to Australian police in the ten years leading up to 2017. Just 30 per cent of those sexual assault reports led to an arrest, summons, formal caution or other legal action. Of the remainder, many were withdrawn by the survivor, or 'cleared' without an arrest or legal action. A portion were rejected by police, on the basis that they did not believe a sexual assault had occurred. More than 35 per cent of those reported sexual assaults remain unsolved to this day. So how far have we really come? Has the way our community views sexual assaults really shifted? And what will it take for policing to catch up?

* * *

As the final episodes of the ABC TV and podcast series aired, the emails multiplied. Among them was a message from a woman called Kylie. 'Hi, Ruby, I have been listening to your podcast *Unravel: Barrenjoey Road*. I may have information regarding your documentary; I knew Neville Tween. I would prefer contact by phone if that is okay please.'

Kylie turned out to be Tween's stepdaughter.

In her early 40s now, Kylie has bright blue eyes and often pulls her hair back into a tight ponytail. She talks fast, like she might run out of time to get it all out. She's also funny and sweet, even if the things she's talking about are neither. She'd never spoken publicly to anyone about Neville Tween, though she'd thought about Trudie's friends and family, and all the sexual assault victims and whether or not her information could help them.

When Kylie's mum, Susan, met Neville Tween on 14 February 1978, Susan was only 19. Kylie's biological father was out of the picture by then.

Susan knew Tween was married to Dulcie and it wasn't long after meeting him she found out he had a criminal record, although just what he told her isn't clear. The early part of Susan's relationship with Tween was intense, but then Tween went to jail around 1981 for the 1977 Lismore offences and the 1978 attempted robbery of the munitions factory.

When Kylie was about eight years old, she and her mum moved up the coast to live permanently with Tween.

Eventually, Kylie was encouraged to refer to Tween as 'Dad'. And he could act paternal, like when he would warn Kylie not to hitchhike.

The warning was stark. Her stepfather was blunt.

'I was [too] petrified to ever hitchhike,' Kylie said.

Kylie also remembered Neville Tween's friends. According to her, they would gather in the so-called Den of Iniquity. That was a little self-contained granny flat where Tween and his mates could talk and or smoke dope, indulge themselves. And she remembered Mark Standen as 'very much a friend of the family'.

And there was something else, something else she'd lived with but only now felt free to speak about publicly.

***

The first time Neville Tween molested her, Kylie was about six or seven years old and was going to Villawood Public School. This was during the period when he would come to stay with her and her mother, Susan, before they moved to the Central Coast.

On this particular day, Susan had gone up to the shops so there was a window of opportunity. Tween thought he wouldn't get caught.

'I remember mostly my school uniform and my stockings, you know, those ribbed stockings, navy blue ones. I remember he pulled my stockings down and laid me on my mum's bed ... I remember the bedspread, I remember the walls being green.'

Tween told her not to tell her mother. 'It's our secret, it's just kisses cos I love you,' he said.

Kylie didn't know what to think. Tween was telling her he loved her and cared about her and wouldn't do anything to hurt her, but, Kylie said, 'I don't think I really knew.'

But she knew, even then, that when he said, 'Don't tell Mum,' well, something wasn't right.

Kylie can't recall it happening again at Villawood. But it happened again after she and her mum moved to the Central Coast. 'I honestly think it was when he was off his head … on drugs' and 'his sexual deviate side needed its fix', she said.

It only took place when he knew Kylie's mother was going to be away, or when 'he knew I was going to be home alone for a day'.

The abuse continued for years until one night Kylie was at her biological father's house and refused to go home. She can't recall if she said anything specifically to her father. 'I think I just refused to go home … I was petrified. Just scared knowing what was going to happen …'

Kylie thought it was at that point that somebody said, 'I think we really need to call the police.'

***

Kylie ended up telling authorities what had happened. The police and the Children's Court got involved and she was moved from Susan and Neville's house to live with relatives. But although she was safe from Tween, Kylie was also lonely and homesick. She wanted her mum.

The only way Kylie could go back to live with her mother was if she told the police she'd made it all up. Eventually, the pressure got to her and she did. Court proceedings were dropped and she was allowed home.

Before long, the abuse started right back up again. Kylie believed that Tween 'kind of felt safe', given 'I'd already tried once and that didn't work out well for me … so the chance of me speaking up again … it wasn't going to happen.'

Kylie said that as she got older the pattern continued. Then, one day, after he'd molested her, Tween started doing something he was suspected of doing to other young girls. He gave her cash. 'Here's a hundred dollars,' he said.

'To a 12-, 13-year-old girl, a hundred dollars is a lot of money to go shopping,' Kylie recalled. 'So in a way, it was another kick in the guts that he was treating me like these women he didn't want me to turn out [to be], such as prostitutes, paying for your needs.'

Kylie said she used the money to jump on a bus and go to a local shopping centre. She'd buy makeup, pens and pencils and food, like chicken and chips with gravy at Charcoal Chicken.

***

Tween's drug use became heavier and he became more erratic as Kylie grew up. She remembers the incident where her stepfather thought Ray Johnson was under the couch, trying to kill him and the time Tween hog-tied the teenage boy he'd caught in the backyard.

As the years went on, Kylie grew old enough to know that she could outsmart her stepfather. When he offered her money for sex, she'd pretend she'd recorded him and threaten to show it to her mother.

***

It wasn't until Tween was arrested in 2006 and went to jail that Kylie began to feel free of him.

Asked whether she thought Neville Tween could be responsible for Trudie Adams' disappearance, Kylie said: 'I think everything points towards him doing it. I think there may have been something like ... the gun went off while aimed at her ... I don't think the intention was to kill her.'

But after Trudie was killed, Tween and his associates would have 'had to cover up everything'.

One thing that has always bothered her is that the date Trudie disappeared was just a few days before Tween's birthday. 'I can see him and someone else going out and partying for his birthday,' she says. 'Back then, even his mates were always looking for a good time, like an excuse to have a good time …'

'So that's something that's always got to me, that his birthday is in June.' Trudie disappeared in the early hours of 25 June 1978. Tween turned 38 the following Thursday.

* * *

Despite what she'd been through, Kylie survived. She now has a son, a loving partner and is working on setting up her own business, although things aren't always easy. She's also talked about become a counsellor one day, talking to women who've been through a terrible time themselves. She thought that maybe, just maybe, she could help them.

* * *

Neville Brian Tween died in jail in Sydney in 2013. Few mourned his passing. Even among the criminal fraternity, he went unlamented. About 20 people, including his family and their relatives, turned up to his funeral.

Chapter 29

Trudie's Whale Stone

Trudie Adams grew up with her family in Avalon, went to school there, made her friends and met her first loves there. She was part of a close-knit group of a dozen or so teenage girls from loving families and homes.

Trudie and her girlfriends sometimes wagged school from Barrenjoey High to sunbake and swim at Avalon Beach. At other times, they would gather nearby on the grass to talk, gossip, catch up and make plans for the night.

On weekends, Trudie's dad, Charles, used to take them out on his boat, up the Hawkesbury River, stopping off at little beaches where they'd go swimming under the waterfalls.

'There were really private little spots we used to go to. It was just fun,' Trudie's friend Anita Starkey recalled. 'We were together all the time.'

When they were in their early teens, the girls would go to the milk bar together. As they got older they went to the Newport Arms where they'd hang out in the beer garden.

They didn't go much further than Newport – no reason to, really.

Then there were the parties at friends' houses and the dances, particularly if the Bilgola Bop Band was playing. They'd invariably end the night with Fleetwood Mac's 'Albatross'. Anita remembers that was the signal it was time to go home. They'd turn the lights off.

Trudie's disappearance affected them all in different ways. They were sad, devastated, angry and disbelieving that Trudie, who'd been the glue that had held them together, could be there one day but not the next. Or the next.

One of the worst things was not knowing. Not knowing what had happened to her or who had done it.

As Anita said, 'We lost other friends, car accidents or that. But you bury them, or you went to their funeral and said goodbye to them, and you know it's over. You miss them and it's sad, but you know what happened to them and you can put it behind you.'

With Trudie there was no ending. She and her friends had never been able to say 'this is her funeral or her service'. No grave, no headstone, no memorial garden. Nowhere to put flowers.

* * *

For many years, some of Trudie's closest friends battled petty bureaucracy to organise a memorial for her on Avalon Beach.

In 2019, 41 years after she disappeared, it finally happened with the erection of a beautiful sculpture – Trudie's Whale Stone. The sandstone and blue crystal granite whale looks towards the headland, but unless you're a local you wouldn't know it's for Trudie, because there's no plaque.

However, some Avalon locals will tell you that at a certain time of day, at a certain time of year and in a certain light, you can see her name, 'Trudie', on some corrugations on one side of the sculpture.

Perhaps it's a myth but, regardless, those who knew Trudie, or know her story, can perhaps feel her spirit when they visit or pass by. There she is, never forgotten, looking over Avalon Beach, her gaze forever fixed on the blue horizon.

Notes on Sources

A significant amount of the material for this book is drawn from the seven-volume Brief of Evidence from the NSW Crown Solicitor's Office, comprising thousands of pages, which was presented to the 2011 Coronial Inquest regarding the death of Trudie Adams. The transcript of the Coronial Inquest and the Coroner's Findings also provided important detail.

Statements given by Trudie's friends and family and Northern Beaches locals in the days and weeks after her disappearance are included in the Brief of Evidence, providing a contemporaneous record of what happened. In addition, there are the statements from the sexual assault victims (with their names redacted) and also a number of the Roselands Lads.

Details of the various police searches conducted are included in the Brief of Evidence, and the 700 pages of police running sheets in volumes six and seven provide insight into the day-to-day operation and progress of the 1978 police investigation.

Several photographs and mugshots shown in the book were either tendered as evidence and included in the Brief of Evidence, or were publicly released during the course of various investigations.

Other material is drawn from interviews with former NSW Police officers who were involved in the case over the years or had knowledge of Neville Tween and his associates. Some former Police and law enforcement officers and some former prisoners spoke on the ground on anonymity.

Content is also drawn from hundreds of pages of other documents, some not publicly released.

BOOKS

The Dark Side: The Explosive Story of Corruption, Greed and Murder in the Australian Drug Trade, by Clive Small and Tom Gilling

Narc! Inside the Australian Bureau of Narcotics, by Bernard Delaney

Drug Traffic: Narcotics and Organized Crime in Australia, by Alfred W. McCoy

The Prince and the Premier: The Story of Perce Galea, Bob Askin and the Others who Gave Organised Crime Its Start in Australia, by David Hickie

Acknowledgements

The authors wish to thank the family of Trudie Adams, and her friends, particularly Steve Norris, Anita Starkey, Leanne Weir and Steve Otton, who generously shared their memories of Trudie and the impact her disappearance had on themselves and on the communities in Sydney's Northern Beaches.

Many former NSW Police officers gave interviews to the authors, or provided valuable insights, including Gary Matthews, Alan Herrmann, Gavin McKean, Michael Kennedy, Clive Small, Jayson Macleod, Ian Lynch, Brian McVicar and Bob Inkster.

We are also grateful for the cooperation of Peter Hamill SC, counsel assisting at the inquest (now Justice Hamill of the NSW Supreme Court), and Nicholas Cowdery QC, the former NSW Director of Public Prosecutions.

A number of journalists and colleagues, including Doug Ryan, John Kidman, Stephen Gibbs and Gary Russell, provided background about the Northern Beaches in the 1970s, introduced sources and helped check accuracy, although any errors belong to the authors.

Brian Walker, former park ranger, displayed an amazing ability to navigate his way through Ku-ring-gai Chase National Park and take us to crucial locations.

John Macritchie, history librarian for the Manly Library, shared his unique knowledge of events on the Northern Beaches over many years.

Former barrister Peter Livesey assisted with his knowledge of Neville Tween and the criminal milieu in the late 1970s and 1980s.

Mark Merriman generously shared his painful memories of Mount Penang.

Mark Standen responded to our written questions in considerable and unexpected detail.

We are especially grateful to Kylie, who contacted us at the end of 2018 and courageously agreed to tell her story publicly for the very first time.

A number of people from both sides of the tracks – former police and former prisoners – provided invaluable information and perspective on the grounds they remain anonymous.

This book would not have been written without the initiative of WildBear Entertainment, which took the Trudie Adams case to the ABC. Many people helped make the three-part television documentary *Barrenjoey Road,* which aired in late 2018 – we thank them all, in particular Alan Erson.

To all those at the ABC who put their heart and soul into the television show, podcast and online long-read, thank you.

The authors would like to thank Jude McGee and Barbara McClenahan at ABC Books, for their unfailing encouragement and support.

Finally, Neil Mercer could not have completed this book without the unwavering support of his wife, Rebecca Le Tourneau, his son, Spike, and his daughter, Melody, who in the year this project started turned 18, the same age as Trudie when she disappeared.

To contact the authors:
Email – bjoeyroad@gmail.com
Post – P.O. Box 56, Rozelle NSW 2039